A DICTIONARY OF
Human Rights

A DICTIONARY OF
Human Rights

DAVID ROBERTSON

EUROPA PUBLICATIONS LIMITED

First published 1997

Europa Publications Limited
18 Bedford Square, London, WC1B 3JN

British Library Cataloguing in Publication Data
   A catalogue record for this book is
   available from the British Library

   ISBN 1-85743-023-9

Printed in England by
MPG Rochester Ltd
Rochester, Kent

Bound by MPG Books Limited
Bodmin, Cornwall

(Members of the Martins Printing Group)

293546

CONTENTS

ACKNOWLEDGEMENTS

The author and publisher wish to give thanks and due acknowledgement to the following for their permission to reproduce texts of and from various of the documents which appear in the Appendix section of *A Dictionary of Human Rights*:

The Press, Information and Communication Department of the Ministry of Foreign Affairs, Paris, France, for: the Declaration of the Rights of Man and of the Citizen, 1789; and the Preamble to the Constitution of the French Fourth Republic, 1946.

The Press and Information Office of the Federal Government, Bonn, Federal Republic of Germany, for: the Basic Law for the Federal Republic of Germany, 1949.

The Treaty Section of the United Nations Office of Legal Affairs, New York, USA, for: the Universal Declaration of Human Rights, 1948; the International Covenant on Civil and Political Rights, 1966; the International Covenant on Economic, Social and Cultural Rights, 1966; the Convention against Torture and Other Cruel, Inhuman or Degrading Treatment or Punishment, 1975; and the Convention on the Rights of the Child, 1989.

The Publishing and Documentation Service of the Council of Europe, Strasbourg, France, for: the European Convention for the Protection of Human Rights, 1950; and the European Social Charter, 1965.

PREFACE

Legal and political concern for human rights was a hallmark of the immediate post-Second World War period, both within many political systems and, even more so, at the international level. In part this was because bodies like the United Nations, along with constitution-makers in countries such as the Federal Republic of Germany, able to start afresh, took human rights very seriously. Their concern for rights was not purely an expression of the sentiment that decent treatment and maximum freedom for individuals is clearly a good in itself; their analysis of the causes of war suggested that disrespect for human rights had major international repercussions. Much the same attitudes resurfaced with the ending of the Cold War, particularly among those who believe that liberal democracies are inherently un-warlike. The roots of this theory are very old, going back at least to Kant, if not to Rousseau. Political and cultural changes in the liberal democracies over the last half century have all helped to focus awareness of discrimination, intolerance and all assaults on human dignity.

These general changes have coincided, over the last 10 to 20 years, with an increasing activism by courts in many countries. Political systems, and that of the United Kingdom is an example, in which the courts had a rather shameful record of subservience to the executive, are now increasingly proud of their public law. The change is international in the true sense, as it stems from an internationalization of legal culture, rather than a simple change that has occurred by happenstance and coincidentally in several countries. In large part this has come about from the growing importance of supranational legal entities such as the European Court of Justice and the European Court of Human Rights. It has occurred also because international concern for the human rights records of many countries became a significant factor in international relations during the 1970s and 1980s. Finally, the development has been accelerated by the collapse of the USSR and the end of its hegemony over Eastern Europe.

In practice, observance of human rights always falls short of the ideal, and the successful attainment of rights itself promotes demands for further rights. No text book or survey on human rights or civil liberties published in any country is likely to be satisfied totally with the record of that country, and it is probably a subject where criticism is healthier than contentment. This reference book, a form of annotated dictionary, is for all those who are not legal experts and who want to get a quick grasp of basic issues in human

1

rights discourse without being either blinded by the endless legal technicalities or forced to ignore them. One cannot dismiss legal technicalities and cut through legal language entirely, because rights basically *are* legal technicalities. What cannot be expressed with some clarity in a legal document will not be preserved and protected. Nevertheless, it should be possible to grasp the essence of the legal and constitutional debates without actually having a thorough legal education.

There are a few necessary points of explanation. First, I have used the phrase 'human rights' as though it were interchangeable with 'civil liberties' and 'civil rights', purely to give some stylistic ease from endless repetition. There are those who think there is a 20ucial theoretical difference between the concepts, but I am not one of them, and I hope that in the rare case where something important might follow from the distinction, the context of my usage will make the difference clear. Similarly, I have used some analytic concepts in slightly idiosyncratic ways as expository tools; the most important is the use I make repeatedly of the distinction between positive and negative rights. My usage does not accord with that of some other writers, but I have explained what I mean by the concepts in separate entries, and have found it a labour-saving device for me in writing, as I hope it will be in reading. Where I have elsewhere used concepts or labels other than in the normal sense, to the extent that there is a 'normal' sense, I have tried to make this clear. This is not a creative or original work, and I have not sought to establish some particular substantive position of my own in my choice of terms. There are inevitable choices, of selection and emphasis, that have to be made in any book such as this, and the choices cannot be entirely neutral. The bias, if that is the right word, I am most aware of is my own preference for taking rights to mean largely political and constitutional entitlements and freedoms, rather than economic- and social-need satisfactions. I am entirely aware of the school of thought that holds these latter to be more important, perhaps causally prior to human rights of the sort on which I concentrate. For various reasons I disagree, chiefly because however crucial economic-need satisfaction may be, I do not believe its analysis and discussion is helped by using the very different language of rights discourse. Nevertheless, I have attempted to give basic coverage of such 'rights', especially as they are set out in international covenants. There may also appear to be bias in the sources I have chosen to quote and take my examples from. Certainly there has been a deliberate selection, but I hope it is not a bias in the pejorative sense. My examples disproportionately come from the USA, from the European human rights documents and institutions, and from the German Constitution. The reasons are twofold, very simple, and related. I have not attempted, no one could, to give an exhaustive account of the presence or absence and the meaning of every putative right in every major legal system. I have, instead, tried to take examples of all the major rights claims and arguments. For this one needs a small set of selected main sources.

I have concentrated on the ones I have because one can only fully understand the meaning and application of legal concepts where there is a considerable amount of litigation, so that we know what judges have made of the terms in which rights are expressed.

The US Supreme Court, the European Court of Human Rights and the German Constitutional Court simply have produced far more and, in my view, far more thoughtful and complex, interpretations of rights language than other potential sources. I could have chosen others; the Canadian Supreme Court, for example, has been very active over the last 15 years, but the Canadian Charter of Rights and Freedoms is too new to serve as effectively as the documents and courts on which I have chosen to concentrate. Ultimately, the human rights tradition as we know it simply is the product of liberal-democracy, and would be unthinkably different without the American experience of the last 200 years. The advantage of the other two sources is that the European Convention on Human Rights is the only thoroughly-enforced UN-derived post-war rights code, and is, at the same time, in the business of making sense out of different national cultures. The German Constitution is a brilliant and recent attempt to take a historic political culture and to graft on to it rights initially worked out elsewhere without losing what is best in the indigenous legal orientation.

Some advice may be useful on using this book. Cross references are to be found in most entries, indicated in bold type. These are of two main sorts. The more obvious is where I use, in one entry, a word or concept which has an entry of its own elsewhere, and where a full understanding of the subject of the main entry requires an understanding of the highlighted entry. For example, the entry on Torture refers to **cruel and unusual punishments**, and the bold type thus indicates that there is a separate entry dealing with this subject. Other cross references are based on the idea that a reader interested in X is likely, independently, to be interested in Y, which has just been mentioned in passing, and should be informed that there is an entry on Y. Despite this, each entry is designed to be as self-contained as possible. The wording of the title of an entry may not be exactly the same as that highlighted elsewhere, but will be close enough to avoid confusion. It would not have been possible, without rendering the text unreadable, to highlight every route by which a particular right, declaration or organization might be accessed, so some latitude must be allowed and the reader should not necessarily take the absence of highlighting to mean that there is no separate entry on a subject—this may necessitate a little searching around, but the related cross references should ensure that the hunt is not too difficult.

The final section of the volume consists of an Appendix, in which the reader will find reproduced texts, and extracts from texts, of the constitutional and human rights documents which are most pertinent to the entries in the remainder of the book.

I have no new particular thanks to make: I have more or less thanked everyone important in my life often enough for their unceasing help in my work, and nothing has changed. I would, however, like to draw the attention of my publishers to Article 27 (Clause 2) of the Universal Declaration of Human Rights.

David Robertson
Oxford
October 1997

A

Abortion

Abortion rights have been the most hotly-contested of all the new civil rights in the post-war era. Abortion, though regarded with horror by a majority of religious faiths and denominations, was not generally made a criminal offence in most jurisdictions until the 19th century, in part because it was so dangerous to the health of a woman that, before the advent of modern medicine, it hardly presented a serious threat to the prevailing moralities. Given that recourse to abortion has not been something lightly undertaken, except in those countries which, like the USSR from 1920, both made it legal on demand and provided free facilities, the actual effect of criminalizing it was largely to drive women into the great risks of illegal abortion by medically-unqualified 'back-street' abortionists. Partly to alleviate these risks, and partly because the increasing secularization of modern society removed the religious objection for many people, most Western societies began to liberalize their abortion laws from the 1960s onward. Nowhere has this move been uncontroversial, and in some countries, especially the USA, major and continuing political conflict has followed the initial and usually very restrictive decriminalization of abortion. Some countries, most notably the Republic of Ireland and Germany, have not followed the trend to legalize abortion. The Irish ban on abortion is almost complete as a result of the continuing enormous political influence of the Roman Catholic Church in that country, though the same church has not been able to prevent the legalization of abortion in Italy. The **German Constitutional Court's** repeated striking down of legislative attempts to legalize abortion is the only example, to date, of a country where such action has been taken on the grounds that abortion is forbidden by its equivalent of a bill of rights (see **Bills of Rights**). This has produced serious problems in the 1990s because, following the Soviet precedent, abortion on demand had been legal in the German Democratic Republic (East Germany) between the end of the Second World War and German re-unification in 1990.

In countries where a justiciable bill of rights exists, abortion has inevitably become a matter for intense legal conflict, because such lists of rights almost inevitably contain, explicitly or by implication, two core values which conflict in the case of abortion; there is, at the same time, a form of a **right to life** applicable to the foetus, and also some version of a right to **privacy**, to self-determination or to the inviolability of the person on the part of the mother. Thus courts have been forced into choosing between irreconcilable values, often because legislatures, inheriting 19th-century legislation, have shirked the electorally hazardous business of deciding whether or not to repeal them. Where courts have had to make rulings, as, for example, in the USA in the famous case of *Roe v. Wade* (1973) or in Canada in *Morgentaler v. The Queen* (1988), the resulting legal entitlements to abortion have usually rested insecurely on confused and inadequate rulings. There is probably no country where abortion is effectively absolutely forbidden on any ground at all, including that of saving a woman's life, and the actual debate over abortion rights is really about the extent to which, and the reasons for which, abortions may be controlled by the state. While countries vary widely in their legislation, there are common fundamental issues. These questions concern the stage of pregnancy at which the state may impose controls in the interests of the woman's health, the stage at which a foetus becomes viable, most intensely focusing on the issue of the right to life, and also whether or not the doctor has a duty to counsel against abortion on the grounds either of morality or of the woman's psychological health. The *Roe v. Wade* rules, while not particularly typical, stand as a good example of the sorts of compromises made between competing moral and medical arguments. Under *Roe v. Wade* a state may not prohibit abortion at all during the first three months of pregnancy, while during the second three months some restrictions may be placed in the interest of the woman's health. In the final three months, however, the state may prohibit abortions on the grounds of the right to life of the foetus, although some restrictions remain to allow for the protection of the mother's life.

Administrative law

Many countries provide separate legal systems for handling non-criminal conflicts between citizens and the state, which are usually called systems of administrative law. Even where, as in the United Kingdom, there is no formally separate system, a functional division is likely to exist, with judges specializing in such conflicts, and with the development of special procedures and legal doctrines. At one time the dominant thinking in the UK was that administrative law should not be a separate system, because there would actually be less control over the executive if public bodies were not subjected to the same controls as all other citizens through the common law. This view, associated with A. V. Dicey (1835–1922), held that European societies were executive-dominated because the administrative law system allowed public servants to hide from the scrutiny of truly independent courts. It has largely been discredited, at least in part because the UK found it necessary to develop *de facto*, if not *de jure*, administrative law courts of its own. Administrative law is characterized by a very strong insistence that all acts of public officials be clearly *intra vires*, fully authorized by a legitimate rule or statute. Administrative law seldom goes beyond that, because the courts in question are expressly not authorized to challenge the legitimacy of the authorizing legislation itself. Thus in countries such as Germany and Italy, and, in a different way, France, which have both administrative law and constitutional law, questions of the validity of the authorizing laws are strictly reserved to the constitutional courts. There are other doctrines, sometimes very powerful ones, used in European administrative law which, unlike the basic *intra vires* test, have no clear counterpart in common law jurisdictions. Two of the more important doctrines are those governing misuse of power, best known by its French label of *détournement de pouvoir*, and the concept of **proportionality** in administrative action. Misuse of power here means using an acknowledged legitimate power for ends that were not intended by the legislature, while proportionality means that no more far-reaching administrative action is justified than is minimally necessary to achieve the legitimate aims of the legislation authorizing the actions. This latter doctrine is beginning to be accepted into common law jurisdictions, especially in Canada and, to a lesser extent, in the UK. As the **European Court of Justice (ECJ)** develops increasing power, and hears more and more appeals from citizens of member states under the **Article 177** proceedings, something like a European administrative or **public law** system is developing, helped by the fact that the ECJ has incorporated the **European Convention on Human Rights** directly into European Union law.

Affirmative action

Once the need to provide legal recourse against discrimination became widely accepted in Western societies, from about the mid-1950s onwards, a new problem occurred. How far, and in what ways, could a state take positive action to remedy the consequence of past discrimination and inequalities? Policies intended to make up for a history of discrimination, for example, the setting aside of places in educational institutions for people of particular backgrounds, came to be known as positive discrimination, or affirmative action. There are, inevitably, philosophical, and therefore legal, problems associated with affirmative action. For example, a state might want to remedy past discrimination against racial minorities in access to higher education by having a minimum quota of places which must be filled by members of such a minority. The result might be that some members of this minority were accepted instead of more qualified members of the dominant racial group, which could itself constitute racial discrimination; in a classic case on these lines in 1978 (*Bakke v. Regents of the University of California*) the US Supreme Court ruled that such direct quotas were discriminatory. So complicated is the issue, however, that *Bakke* has long been seen as one of the least satisfactory and least clear of all pronouncements in civil rights law. In general, affirmative action has come to take the form of making special efforts to recruit the disadvantaged, or to train them to increase their chances of succeeding in direct competition with others, rather than directly giving them easier access to jobs or educational places. (See also **quotas**.)

African Charter on Human and People's Rights

The Charter was issued by the Organization of African Unity (OAU) in 1981, and entered into force on 21 October 1986. It takes its emphases from the OAU's own Charter, the United Nations Charter and the UN **Universal Declaration of Human Rights**. The African charter is one of a series of regional human rights documents encouraged by the UN as part of a general strategy for enforcing human rights world-wide, the most effective of which is the **European Convention on Human Rights**. Although the very universality of the original UN Charter implies that human rights are generally valid, there is an acceptance that regional world cultures may evaluate, and even partially define, such rights in different ways. The specific thrust of the Charter of the OAU is to bring its commitment to 'eradicate all forms of colonialism from Africa' to bear on the definition and support for human rights. Thus the enumeration of rights, though not very different in detail from what one would find in any classic listing, is set against a background which recognizes two points missing in, for example, the European Convention. First, some tension seems to be recognized, though it is posited to be a fruitful tension, between people's rights and individual human rights. The Preamble recognizes that: 'fundamental human rights stem from the attributes of human beings, which justifies their international protection and on the other hand, that the reality and respect of people's rights should necessarily guarantee human rights . . .', and: '. . . that it is henceforth essential to pay particular attention to the right to development and that civil and political rights cannot be dissociated from economic, social and cultural rights in their conception as well as universality and that the satisfaction of economic, social and cultural rights is a guarantee for the enjoyment of civil and political rights . . .'

The problem at the heart of drafting a document on human rights in a context like that of the OAU is the paradox of whether the 'niceties' of liberal democracy can be afforded where there is a massive political and economic problem of nation-building and an urgent socio-economic struggle for development. The language used is an attempt to bring together two very different traditions: the individualistic European-style promotion of

8

traditional human rights as the very basis for a successful political system, and a radical perspective which sees such rights as the consequence of a functioning, just economic substructure. There is the additional problem that the individualistic European approach stems from the European context, whereas the whole emphasis of a body like the OAU is anti-colonialist and committed, as the Preamble declares, to the 'historical tradition and values of African civilization which should inspire and characterize their reflection on the concept of human and people's rights'.

Outside the Preamble there is less mention of specifically African issues, except for the unusually emphatic statements on matters like the universal ban on **slavery** (Article 5), but there are still distinctive features. Chapter 1, entitled Human and People's Rights, outlines a general statement of rights, amounting to a denunciation of oppression, apartheid and colonialism, but contains wording which would sit uneasily with the judges of the **European Court of Human Rights**. Traditional rights to **freedom of assembly** (Article 11) and **freedom of movement** (Article 12) allow rather greater scope for state interference, because protection of 'ethics' and 'morality' constitute allowable reasons for such intervention. These may be more significant than the similar expression of a group right in Article 12 which forbids 'mass expulsion', defined as an expulsion 'aimed at national, racial, ethnic or religious groups'. This protection represents simply recognition of events in recent African history, and does not prohibit something which would be allowed under some other regional code. The real indication that the African Charter enshrines a principle which diverges from traditional human rights theory is the recognition, in Article 10, which otherwise protects the traditional freedom to associate or not, of something called 'the obligation of solidarity', which is then further detailed in a later article. There are also suggestions that the document may be radically different from its traditional precursors throughout Chapter 1, perhaps none more significant than the communitarianism accepted as a duty of government in Article 17, on educational rights, which declares, in Clause 3, 'The promotion and protection of morals and traditional values recognised by the community shall be the duty of the state'. The theme occurs over and again; family life is valued, as in other rights codes, but here especially because the family is 'the custodian of morals and traditional values *recognized by the community*' (author's italics).

The most distinctive feature of the Charter is its second chapter in the main substantive part, headed 'Duties'. Although there is a necessary theoretical acceptance that rights always entail correlated duties, it is rare for the duty aspect of human rights to be so clearly emphasized, in part because the bearer of the duties is normally the state, and the rights recognized are **negative rights**, so that the duties amount to forbearance on the part of the state from doing something against freedom. Here the duties, though probably not justiciable, are duties as much on the part of the individual as the state, because they are communitarian in nature: the duty 'to maintain relations aimed at promoting . . . mutual respect and tolerance'; 'to work for the cohesion and respect of the family; to respect his parents at all times, to maintain them in case of need'; 'to preserve and strengthen positive African cultural values . . . to contribute to the . . . moral well-being of society'. These aspirations are reinforced in Article 29, and by the specific inclusion in earlier articles of, *inter alia*, compulsion to join associations for the promotion of Article 29 values. The values protected in the Charter are a blend of individualistic freedoms and positive evaluations of a communitarian ethic, and they are put together in such a way as to allow considerable invasion of traditional autonomy towards the integration of a particular communal self-image.

The single biggest difference between the African Charter and the European Convention is that the former has no effective enforcement mechanism. Provision was made for an African Commission on Human and People's Rights, which was established in 1987; and states may refer the actions of other states to the Commission, as may, with less favourable terms, other bodies, and possibly individuals. However, the most that the Commission may do is to make a report after attempting to get the parties to 'the communication' to reconcile. It is hardly surprising that an individual-based enforcement machinery like the **European Court of Human Rights** does not exist, given that it does not exist for the Universal Declaration of Human Rights itself. Moreover, it seems probable that the force of African public opinion will always make a member state try to avoid the publicity of a damning report. In the final analysis the rights protected by the Charter are not justiciable, so deeply are they tied to the Charter's communitarian ideals.

Age discrimination

Although it has only recently come to be perceived as possibly unacceptable, decision-making concerning employment and pension matters, both by the state and by private institutions, based on grounds of age is one of the more deeply-entrenched and widely-experienced forms of discrimination. This form of discrimination, in an institutional sense, probably dates from the earliest days of state provided old-age pensions, since when retirement ages and associated ages for pension entitlements have been built into both state and private employment policy. Furthermore, such distinctions based on age have often been coupled with **sex discrimination** because, originally for entirely admirable reasons, women were thought of as either deserving or needing to retire, or to be eligible for pensions, earlier than men. So, for example, concessionary free entry to swimming baths in the United Kingdom for the retired has been held to be illegal because the age of retirement differs according to sex. As often happens with policies originally benevolent in intent, changing social conditions as well as changing attitudes to discrimination *per se* have led to increasing resentment that, at a particular age, retirement should be enforced. The country which has developed legal barriers to age discrimination most effectively is Canada, because Section 15 of the **Canadian Charter of Rights and Freedoms** expressly lists age as one of the factors on which it is impermissible to discriminate, and consequently there is now no legally-enforceable age of retirement in many Canadian institutions. Most thinking on age as a discriminatory characteristic treats it as being an asymmetric problem; it is usually thought acceptable to prevent people doing or getting things below a certain age (for example, the ages of heterosexual and homosexual consent are fixed at levels, often differing, according to the potential harm of sexual activity considered likely by the legislators of a country), but not to enforce restrictions at any age above legal maturity.

American Civil Liberties Union (ACLU)

The American Civil Liberties Union (ACLU) was founded in 1920 by a variegated group of US citizens. Some were eminent and orthodox liberals, like the distinguished judge Felix Frankfurter (1882–1965), others far more to the left, including socialist leaders like Eugene V. Debs (1855–1926) and Norman Thomas (1884–1968). The ACLU is organized into chapters located throughout the country. The ACLU has its own staff but does much of its work through co-operating attorneys. It tends to press for a liberal interpretation of constitutional law, focusing on **freedom of speech** and **religious freedom**; in the latter case it is seen by many as pursuing a deliberately secular line, being more concerned with ensuring the **separation of church and state** rather than protecting religious activity. Though it lobbies state and federal legislatures and executives, it is mainly known for its role in the courts. Relying heavily on the US system for allowing amicus briefs (where counsel is allowed to represent a person or organization who does not have a direct interest in the outcome of the case), it has been a party in many cases involving **civil liberties** of all kinds. It played a major role, along with the **National Association for the Advancement of Colored People (NAACP)**, in anti-segregation cases. It has very much taken a purist line in protecting civil liberties for all, with the result that liberals are sometimes horrified to find it acting on behalf of right-wing groups where their **freedom of expression** is hindered, although it is more often seen as naturally left-inclined because of its necessary opposition to state power.

American Convention on Human Rights

This Convention, also known as the Pact of San José, was signed in 1969 and entered into force in 1978. As with other regional human rights covenants

11

inspired by the UN **Universal Declaration of Human Rights**, such as the **European Convention on Human Rights**, based on membership of the Council of Europe, and the 1981 **African Charter on Human and People's Rights**, which is based on the Organization of African Unity, the American Convention is open to members of the Organization of American States (OAS). By 1992 it had been ratified by 23 states. It is more similar in content to the European Convention than to the African document, though like the African Charter it largely lacks enforcement machinery. It has a judicial body, the Inter-American Court of Human Rights, formally established in 1979, but only members of the Inter-American Commission on Human Rights can refer matters to the Court, and only then after the failure of a lengthy process of negotiation and **arbitration** by the Commission. Furthermore, each signatory to the Convention can determine the extent to which the Court may apply the Convention to that country's own domestic law. By the early 1990s only 12 of the states which ratified the Convention had taken the further step of accepting the Court's jurisdiction; in contrast all signatories to the European Convention accept the jurisdiction of the **European Court of Human Rights**. Consequently the jurisdiction of the Court resembles the essentially voluntary nature of the jurisdiction of the International Court of Justice (ICJ), the major international law tribunal of the UN.

The terms of the Convention are unusually specific. For example, in Article 4 the **right to life** is stated to extend 'from the moment of conception', and while this is not in itself surprising in a document drawn up inside a predominantly Roman Catholic culture, its specific nature is unique among human rights codes. Similarly, although Article 4 does not in itself outlaw the death penalty, it severely restricts it by banning the reintroduction of capital punishment where it has been abolished, forbidding its extension to any crimes for which it had not been the penalty when the member state signed the Convention, and setting minimum and maximum age limits for its use. (See also **restrictions on death sentence**.) Article 5 has several very precise rulings on **pre-trial detention**, including the demand for separate housing for remand prisoners and convicted prisoners, and even declares that the aim of imprisonment shall be 'reform and social readaptation'. Article 7, while banning imprisonment for debt, nevertheless allows family courts to imprison for 'non-fulfilment of duties of support'. Much of the precision, with the exception of those passages dealing with the right to life, is clearly affected by US constitutional practice. So, for example, 'freedom of thought and expression' (Article 13) echoes the US constitutional ban on 'prior restraint' (called here prior censorship) and its preference for *post facto* penalties in the case of **libel** and national security. Much of the document is almost utopian in its logical comprehensiveness, and anyone defamed by a 'legally-regulated medium of communication' has a right to have their reply published by the same medium. Usury is banned under Article 21's right to **property** (again possibly showing a US influence, as several US states have anti-usury statutes).

The general tone, though not economically conservative to a great degree, is noticeably less egalitarian than either the African Convention or much of the material in the UN's various covenants and protocols. Several issues echo the US Constitution (and the French **Declaration of the Rights of Man and of the Citizen**), notably the right to property: 'No one shall be deprived of his property except on payment of just compensation, for reasons of public utility or social interest'. The overall result is a mixture of broad constitutional principles akin to the great 18th-century human rights codes and a degree of precision similar to the **Canadian Charter of Rights and Freedoms**, along with local concerns such as **abortion** and excessive reliance on capital punishment. At the same time very broad statements are made in support of the principle of socio-economic progress, without beginning to make the sort of **positive rights** claims found elsewhere.

American Declaration of Independence (see **Declaration of Independence (American)**)

American Declaration of the Rights and Duties of Man

This Declaration came out of the ninth International Conference of American States, held in Bogotá, Colombia, in 1948, at the same time as the foundation of the Organization of American States (OAS). It was never intended to have legal effect, but instead to function as a statement of common values; not until the signing of the **American Convention on Human Rights** in 1969 was there a potentially binding human rights code covering the whole of the Americas. The Declaration has many of the hallmarks of its US intellectual ancestors, and the very language is redolent of the 18th-century rationalism of the US founding fathers in the **Declaration of Independence**. The Preamble opens with the words: 'All men are born free and equal in dignity and in rights, and being endowed by nature with reason and conscience they should conduct themselves as brothers one to another.' The document is also influenced by the European, and especially Roman Catholic, cultural inheritance of the region, with a much greater concern for moral and spiritual growth than is typical in traditional rights codes. The Preamble further declares: 'while rights exalt individual **liberty**, duties express the dignity of that liberty'; 'duties of a juridical nature presuppose others of a moral nature'; 'spiritual development is the supreme end of human existence'; and 'since moral conduct constitutes the noblest flowering of culture, it is the duty of every man always to hold it in high respect'.

Thus the Preamble, which runs to only 200 words in total, has a very distinctive intellectual and political flavour, which is echoed in the more technically-juridical, as well as legally-binding, Convention of over 20 years later.

Because it was never intended to be more than a set of principles, the authors were not constrained by the policy problems of including **positive rights** as well as **negative rights**, and Chapter 1, on Rights, includes both the usual listing of **freedom of expression**, **religious freedom**, **liberty of the person**, rights to **property** and so on, and an impressive list of basic entitlements to education, health care and social security. In addition it includes several articles supporting motherhood and the family, which were typical of all the international conventions of the time (see also **parental rights** and **right to family life**). Chapter 2, on Duties, is particularly remarkable, because it draws a picture of the ideal citizen. Education is included not only as a right in Chapter 1, but also as a duty in Chapter 2, where it is stated that it is the obligation of every individual to secure himself an education. Similarly, while Chapter 1 lists democratic rights to political involvement, Chapter 2 makes it a duty to vote and to serve in public office if elected. Above all, there is a duty to work, pay taxes, and co-operate in the process of everyone's personal development (see **development of personality**).

Amnesty International

Amnesty International, the London-based voluntary human rights organization, was founded in 1961 by a British barrister, Peter Benenson, as a result of his experiences as a civil rights advocate. It campaigns for the release of 'prisoners of conscience', effectively those imprisoned solely for their beliefs, colour, sex, ethnic origin, language or religion, but only where the victims have neither used nor advocated violence. It works for fair and prompt trials for all political prisoners, and opposes the use of **torture**, the death penalty and the **degrading punishment** of prisoners, and seeks an end to extrajudicial executions and 'disappearances'. Although most of its cases involve human rights violations carried out directly or indirectly by the authorities, it also tries to help and support the families of victims. It claims to be the largest completely non-partisan such body on the international scene, and has grown hugely. By 1996 it claimed over one million members in over 150 countries, with locally organized chapters conducting letter-writing campaigns. Its importance was recognized in 1977 by the award of the Nobel Peace Prize.

Animal rights

For a century or more there have been statutes forbidding and punishing cruelty to animals, and pressure groups, sometimes with royal patrons, for the protection of animals. Only in the last two decades, however, has there been talk of animals having rights. Belief in animal rights is a matter of private moral choice, linked to no general political ideology or theoretical position, but the concept touches on some basic points about 'rights language'. According to the most inclusive of all rights codes, the UN **Universal Declaration of Human Rights**, human beings are held to have rights because they are reasoning creatures and are endowed with conscience, and a similar reasoning is common to most theories of rights. Another strand of thinking comes from the social-contract tradition, in which men and women are imagined to live a perfectly free life in a stateless society which, for reasons of convenience, they transform by free choice into a governed state. In such a system the state could have only those powers which the original citizens had granted it, and could act only for purposes legitimated by their reason for creating it. Thus human rights come from an initial condition of freedom to do anything. Those opposed to the idea of animal rights might wish to argue that the language is purely evocative, as neither of these models can apply directly to animals.

One argument for asserting animal rights is to attribute relevant duties of consideration to humans. The thesis that rights and duties are correlative is only partially true; there are occasions when citizens can clearly have a duty to do something without having any corresponding right, even if it makes little sense to talk of rights without duties. This difficulty occurs when dealing with what are described in this book as **positive rights**, such as, for example, the right to work to be found in documents like the **International Covenant on Social, Economic and Cultural Rights**. It may be argued that the state should to try to ensure that everyone who wants to can get a good job, but there is no duty to provide such opportunities because there cannot be a duty to perform the impossible, and economic conditions may make full employment impossible to attain. The concept of animal rights can also be extended further to the attribution of legal entitlements to other non-human living things. American environmentalists have posed the question 'Do trees have standing?', debating whether or not they are entitled to have law cases brought on their behalf. In all such usage rights language is being used simply to heighten the sense of moral obligation, but while such rhetorical devices may have their uses, they obscure what is crucial about human rights. Human rights are predicated on some general theory about human nature, and on the idea of reciprocity; a right exists where an individual is not only entitled to some freedom or opportunity, but where someone else can avoid trampling on that freedom or can be sure to provide that opportunity.

Anisminic

The British case of *Anisminic Ltd v. Foreign Compensation Commission* (FCC) in 1968 is a classic example of how determined and successful courts can be in guarding their supervisory role of the judicial process from intrusion by the executive government. The Foreign Compensations Act of 1950 had set up the FCC to pay compensation to British companies who suffered from actions such as uncompensated nationalization by foreign governments. The Labour Government of the time, exhibiting a suspicion of the courts long traditional among the British left, had set up special machinery to hear requests for such compensation, and the legislation specifically excluded the courts by barring them from hearing appeals against any 'determinations' of the Commission. After an unsuccessful attempt to claim compensation, Anisminic Ltd then asked the courts to rule that the FCC had misinterpreted the Act and, despite the legislation, the courts agreed. The Lords of Appeal, led by one of the most prominent British legal figures of the 20th century, Lord Reid of Drem (1890–1975), held that although a 'determination' could not be appealed, if the Commission had 'misdirected itself in law' then it had not, in fact, made a determination at all, but only a 'purported determination', and therefore the courts could put it right. The 1950 Act was probably the last effort made by a British Parliament at **judge-proofing** a statute, and it has now effectively become a rule of the constitution that the courts may always supervise the doings of any body, whether or not it is technically a court, which exercises **quasi-judicial** functions.

Arbitrary

One of the commonest reasons for complaint against administrative or disciplinary action by the state or some public official is that their decision is arbitrary. It is improbable that any decision is ever actually arbitrary in the strictest sense of the word, because this would mean it was taken for absolutely no reason at all, and possibly that when deciding whether to grant a permit or impose a fine the official in question metaphorically, or even literally, tossed a coin. Complaints of arbitrary action in reality usually refer to one or both of two common problems with such decisions: either that they are not based on adequate or appropriate consideration of all the relevant factors, or that the reasoning behind the decision is not given fully enough or, indeed, at all. In order to counter this criticism the requirement to give a **reasoned decision** by a public body is often an important element in the rules of **administrative law**. If a decision is arbitrary in the sense that the relevant factors have not all been taken into account it will usually be found to be illegal for this reason. The stress of the need for a reasoned opinion is precisely to enforce this full consideration of all, and only of relevant, factors.

Arbitration

Arbitration is a form of alternative dispute resolution (ADR); when two parties go to arbitration, they are usually making use of a private legal system rather than of a state institution. Typical examples of arbitration are agreements that form part of contracts that if the two parties disagree they will take the disagreement to an arbiter mutually satisfactory to them. Arbitration is normally carried out by a panel in which each side appoints one or more arbitrators of his own choice; the panel then appoints a neutral chairman they can mutually trust and respect. This arbiter, often a lawyer, and in some jurisdictions frequently a retired judge, will listen to all the arguments and evidence, and hand down a judgment just as would happen in a real court. However, most of the procedure is decided by the arbiter himself, and proceedings are usually less formal, cheaper, and very much faster than in a state court. Arbitration only works to the extent that the parties are willing voluntarily to accept the decision of the arbiter, because he cannot have any enforcement powers. Usually such a decision will be accepted, though the alternative of rejecting it and re-trying the entire matter in a real court always exists.

Arbitration is used extensively in international law, both between individuals (usually 'legal individuals', that is, corporations) or between states precisely because of the absence of a positive law court. As a form of ADR however, arbitration is becoming increasingly popular in civil law. Because civil liberty law nearly always involves the state, and states are unwilling to submit themselves to private justice within their own boundaries, it has made little progress as a dispute-resolution mechanism in the field of human rights.

Arrest

An arrest is the formal deprivation of **liberty** of a suspect in a criminal investigation, as a result of which he may be detained, prior to a trial and possible conviction and sentence. It is the point in the criminal justice process at which the presence or absence of legal protection of rights first begins to be seriously important, and where provision of such protection varies most. The general position in Western societies is to guarantee, once someone has been arrested, that he be warned of his rights as an arrested person; failure to ensure that he has understood these rights may make his subsequent conviction difficult or impossible, however strong the evidence may be. Typically these rights will include some version of the **right to silence**, and some provision for a **right to counsel**, either of the arrestee's own choice or provided free by the state.

It is a common mistake to assume that a **warrant** issued by a court is required before an arrest can be made; although arrest warrants can be issued, authorizing any police officer to arrest a specified person on sight, their justification would be the usual grounds for an arrest. In general the power to arrest someone depends on the arresting officer having a good reason, in the USA called **probable cause**, to believe the person arrested either has committed, or is imminently about to commit, a crime. Mere suspicion of such a matter is not enough. An arrest warrant allows a police officer who knows nothing whatsoever about the person or what he may have done to make what would otherwise be an illegal arrest. Consequently it is usually held necessary to inform the suspect of the reasons for his arrest, and this reason along with the suspect's rights are usually contained in a specified list of things that must be said to him at the moment of his arrest. In the USA this list is known as the **Miranda warning**, established in the constitutionally important case of *Miranda v. Arizona* in 1966. Similar requirements are imposed on British police forces in the **caution on arrest**, as specified in the Criminal Justice Act 1994. Once an arrest has been legally made, police forces usually have a short maximum time during which they can hold a person in custody before either releasing him or formally charging him with an offence and bringing him before a court of some kind. Once the stage of formal charging or arraignment has been reached, further restrictions may be placed on police action, as well as further restrictions on the individual. (See also **interrogation**.)

Arrestable offence

An arrestable offence in British law is an offence sufficiently serious that a police officer is entitled to **arrest** anyone whom he thinks has committed, or is imminently likely to commit such an act. The distinction between arrestable and non-arrestable offences was introduced in 1967 to replace the old, and still familiar, language of felonies and misdemeanours, though there is no precise connection between exactly what used to be a **misdemeanour** and what is now a non-arrestable offence. The old misdemeanour, though popularly supposed to be a trivial offence was not necessarily so; for example, offences listed as misdemeanours included riot and assault, which are certainly arrestable. The arrestable/non-arrestable distinction is based on the likely conclusion if convicted as a way of making an objective test of seriousness. An arrestable offence is one for which a statute gives a fixed sentence, or where common law may impose a sentence of five years' imprisonment or more. The **felony**/misdemeanour distinction continues to be used in some other common law jurisdictions, for example, in certain US states.

Article 177

Article 177 of the **Treaty of Rome** governs the main way an ordinary citizen can bring a case before the **European Court of Justice (ECJ)**. In general access to the Court is restricted to member states, or to legal individuals to whom a directive is addressed by the Commission; these legal individuals will usually be corporations rather than particular people. It was a matter of political compromise in the original negotiations setting up the Court to allow such a special procedure, because states, not surprisingly, were unwilling to allow their citizens directly to challenge their own actions before a supranational Court. In cases where direct access to the **European Court of Human Rights** had been allowed, individual states had the choice of whether or not to accede fully to the jurisdiction of the court. In general, however, the European Union, the European Economic Community (EEC) as it then was, did not seek to allow its members only a voluntary duty to obey the Court, and consequently Article 177 allows a somewhat indirect approach to the ECJ by an individual. An individual cannot directly petition the ECJ, but, if during proceedings before a national court either party believes his case depends on the exact interpretation of European law, or on the compatibility between a government action and a right he may have under such law, he can request the court to halt proceedings and remit the question to the ECJ for a ruling. The ECJ must give an answer, and the original national court must follow that ruling when it resumes hearing the original case. It is a matter for the **discretion** of the domestic court whether to accede to this request, and a court at any level, even the lowest level of magistrates court, may grant the request to make an Article 177 referral, and may also do so of its own accord. If, however, a case reaches any domestic court from which there is no further appeal, and the request for an Article 177 referral is made, it must be granted.

For some time during the early years of the ECJ various national courts, especially the French, tried to get round what they perceived as a loss of independence by the doctrine of *acte claire*. This meant that when, in the opinion of the domestic court, the relevant EEC legislation was perfectly clear, there was no obligation to make a referral. The doctrine was so obviously incompatible with the ultimate supremacy of the ECJ in interpreting community law that it has ceased to be acceptable in any member state. Article 177 proceedings vary considerably in their frequency from country to country, but as the ECJ comes more and more to be seen as a general guarantor of civil rights, as well as the guardian of community interests, the attractiveness of the procedure increases. In the United Kingdom some important constitutional changes have come about by the use on appeal of requests for Article 177 referrals, the most notable being in the Factortame case in 1990, where the House of Lords was forced to rule that a Minister could be required by **injunction** to hold up the imposition of parliamentary legislation pending the ECJ's decision about its compatibility with Community legislation (further details of this case are given in the entry for European Court of Justice).

Asylum

The concept of asylum, usually called political asylum, allows an individual to leave his own country on the grounds of fear of persecution for his political acts and beliefs, or for membership of a particular religious, ethnic or other specific group, and to claim shelter in another country. Strictly speaking there is no right to asylum, but during the later part of the 19th century there developed a pattern in which liberal democracies would accept, and often give considerable honour to, political refugees from various tyrannies, especially when they were fighting for democracy in their home country. This developed into a vague understanding that international law protected such people, which was crystallized in the aftermath of the Second World War as part of the world-wide tide of approval for the protection of basic human rights. The Convention relating to the Status of Refugees, signed in Geneva in 1951, which has been incorporated into national law in various ways and to varying degrees by most members of the UN, specifically requires that no country deport a refugee to his own country or any other where he is liable to be persecuted. Even then there are considerable restrictions on the way individual domestic legal systems define and operate this right. Most countries apply a rule by which a refugee may be deported, though not to a persecuting country, from any safe country the refugee enters, other than from the first in which he could have a request for asylum.

There are two main problems associated with the legal status of political refugees, which were either not experienced in the earlier days of the recognition of this 'semi-right', or were present only in a far lesser degree. Firstly, the number of claimants for asylum status has risen quite enormously, especially since the early 1980s, and has done so in a world climate in which **immigration** in general has become a political problem and been severely restricted in most of the traditional host countries. In the United Kingdom, for example, there were over 40,000 claims for asylum made in 1994, compared with a only a few hundred each year in the 1950s. Thus countries like the UK and the USA, which have traditionally been popular destinations for immigrants of all types, and especially for the politically-oppressed, have come to entertain serious doubts about the genuineness of many claims for asylum. Secondly, fear of international anarchy, and in particular fear of importing or encouraging terrorists, have made host countries much less eager to believe that those who oppose the government of a country are necessarily less culpable than the government forces themselves. The problem arose as early as 1937, when the League of Nations regulations were drafted to deal with those escaping the jurisdiction of their home country, thus reviving a doctrine of **Grotius**, *aut dedere aut punire*, that countries which felt they could not deport someone guilty of certain crimes had the duty to punish them themselves.

The main way that modern international law has sought to deal with the need to distinguish between terrorists and those deserving asylum has been through the distinction between a 'political crime' and a 'serious non-political crime'. Those guilty of the latter may be expelled, even if that means they must return to a country where it is accepted they face danger and even death. In some specific contexts the limitations on what may count as a political crime are very closely demarcated: the 1977 European Convention on the Suppression of Terrorism, which forbids, *inter alia*, any case of murder to be counted as a political crime, would deny asylum to many of those granted it from non-European countries had they carried out their acts in Europe. Presented with a huge volume of asylum seekers from Latin America, successive US administrations have distinguished between 'political refugees' and 'economic refugees', the latter being deported on the grounds that they face economic hardship rather than any personal danger. In practice the distinction appears to be motivated as much by political considerations, as refugees from countries where there are documented human rights violations, but with the governments of which the US administration has close links, have been deported, while those from other countries, notably Cuba and Nicaragua while under Sandinista rule, have been accepted.

Aude alteram partem

Aude alteram partem, Latin for 'hear the other side', is one of two traditional components of the conception of **natural justice in English law**, which has a more restricted and technical meaning in English common-law jurisdictions than in political theory generally. Along with a rule forbidding anyone to act as judge in any case where he has any personal interest, *aude alteram partem* has been the basis for judicial development of a quite complex set of rules. It demands that the judge listen not only to the complainant but also to the defendant's arguments, and the judicial development has focused upon the precise process of giving a full hearing to a case. The actual level of protection will vary according to the context, but it is fairly uniform that both sides must have access to help in formulating their case (see **legal aid** and **right to counsel**). At the very least a defendant must be allowed someone to assist him in presenting his case, though professional legal counsel may not be permitted: for example, a police officer may not have a lawyer to assist him in the earlier stages of internal disciplinary proceedings. Furthermore, because a full defence requires information, some rights to see documentation may be granted, and invariably a full and clear statement of the charge against him must be provided. In a proper judicial court anyone facing a criminal charge will have the implications of *aude alteram partem* developed in his favour. In other contexts which are only **quasi-judicial**, for example a university disciplinary hearing, or a hearing to decide suspension from a trade union or professional body, the full entitlements may be relaxed. As the idea of natural justice developed, particularly in the 1950s and 1960s, these lower standards of provision to ensure that the defendant's case is fully and properly heard have converged more and more nearly to the standard of the state criminal trial. Even the minimal version, by which the one who may suffer from the decision of the official or tribunal must be allowed to speak in his own defence, at least removes the chance of entirely accidental injustice, though it may not go far by itself to protect against **arbitrary**, malicious or biased decision-making.

B

Basic Law (see **German Constitution**)

Bear arms

The right to bear arms is found in only one important statement of human rights, the US Constitution, and even in this case the implication of the relevant passage is open to interpretation. The Second Amendment, one of the original ten Amendments to the US Constitution (see **Bill of Rights (USA)**), stated: 'A well-regulated militia being necessary to the security of a free State, the right of the people to keep and bear arms, shall not be infringed.' This has become the keystone of the campaigns by bodies like the National Rifle Association, one of the richest and most powerful pressure groups in the world, against gun-control legislation in the USA. Although it is interpreted by those who believe in private citizens being entitled to own, and perhaps to carry, firearms as being supportive of that position, it is by no means clear that this was the intended meaning. Firstly, as the Bill of Rights was not intended originally to apply to the separate states, it would have been possible for any state government to ban the private possession of firearms. Moreover, even if the process of **incorporation** after the Civil War brought the Bill of Rights to apply to the states, it is by no means clear that the Supreme Court would ever give an interpretation that this Amendment had the power to restrict legislation. Although it is capable of interpretation as a personal right, a more plausible interpretation refers to a different sort of right, which is the collective right of political sub-units in a state, here the states within a federation, to be able to raise a military force. For much of its history the USA has not had more than a tiny standing army, and when engaged in armed conflict it has done so either by persuading the states to call up their state militias, or by raising temporary units. The Second Amendment covers precisely the need of a state to be able to keep a part-time militia, and in the primitive war-making conditions of the late 18th century such units were often dependent on the privately-owned weapons of citizen soldiers. A notable constitutional effect of any development whereby the federal government imposed a ban on private arms would be to weaken the separate states against the central power.

Bentham

Jeremy Bentham (1748–1832) was, along with James Mill (1773–1836), the founder of the philosophical school of utilitarianism, the philosophy under which traditional moral and legal arguments were to be replaced in justification of rules and laws by the principle of utility. This concept of utility holds that human happiness is the only legitimate aim of legislation, and that all laws should serve to maximize the sum of happiness over unhappiness, or pleasure over pain. Thus the greatest good of the greatest number, with good defined as happiness or pleasure, was the main test of validity. He wrote extensively on legal philosophy and was the founder, along with his disciple John Austen (1790–1859), of the school of legal philosophy known as legal positivism, which came to dominate legal thinking in the common law world, until it was challenged by **rights jurisprudence** late in the 20th century. In the Benthamite tradition the only form of human rights would be **statutory rights** because natural law would be illusory. The legal positivism of this school recognizes all law simply as the command of someone or something, basically the state, which can achieve its enforcement, and therefore recognized rights as valid only when desired and enforced by a sovereign power. By implication, this philosophy would negate the validity of any form of international law, because it lacked any sovereign power. Bentham was deeply concerned also with the penal system, and was the author of various plans, some of which had real policy influence, for prison design and reform, again based upon the principle of utilitarianism. His main works were *A Fragment on Government* (1776) which, among other things, amounted to a powerful attack on William Blackstone (1723–80), until then unchallenged as England's leading legal philosopher, and *The Introduction to the Principles of Morals and Legislation* (1789).

Bill of Rights (UK)

The full name for the British Bill of Rights is 'An Act Declaring the Rights and Liberties of the Subject and Settling the Succession of the Crown', which was passed by Parliament in 1689. It was the formal basis by which legitimate authority was passed to William and Mary after the peaceful revolution which unseated James II, and its prime political significance was in establishing a permanent Protestant succession to the English crown. Despite its common name it did not delineate any new civil rights (see **bills of rights**), and still less did it attempt to impose revolutionary ideas. Its purpose was to protect the rights of Parliament, by preventing the monarch from exercising 'the pretended power of suspending of laws' or 'the pretended power of dispensing with laws . . .' The language of the Act is retrospective, attempting to re-establish the relationship between monarch and Parliament held to have existed before James's accession. (The relevant section of the Bill of Rights is given in the Appendix.) In specific terms the monarch was obliged to call parliaments frequently, and to abide by parliamentary control over powers of taxation, and was prohibited from keeping a standing army without parliamentary approval, from interfering with the election of members of parliament, and from restricting parliamentary freedom of speech. Within the Act demands for individual freedoms were largely restricted to protecting the fairness of the judicial system, including, for example, a ban on **cruel and unusual punishments** which was to be echoed in the Eighth Amendment of the US Bill of Rights (see **Bill of Rights (USA)**). In the accompanying **Toleration Act** the penalties levied on dissenters for failure to attend church were lifted, but the bans on dissenters and Catholics from holding public office were reaffirmed. The Bill of Rights is seldom referred to in British legal and political debate over **civil liberties**, because most of what it covers is the subject of later and more detailed legislation. Nor can it have the sort of crucial role that the US Bill of Rights has played constitutionally, because it is not an entrenched code of rights; providing the necessary will and majority existed, there would be nothing to prevent Parliament from repealing it.

Bill of Rights (USA)

For US citizens the Bill of Rights means the first ten Amendments to the US Constitution. As originally planned the Constitution did not contain a list of citizens' rights against the state, largely because the framers of the Constitution judged that they had already sufficiently limited the powers of the central government. Before the Constitution could come into effect, however, it had to be ratified by the several states, and there was considerable opposition to ratifying the document without any overt limitation on government power. Several states refused outright to ratify without the firm promise of a bill of rights. Consequently James Madison (1751–1836), one of the original theorists of the Constitution, drew up a draft bill of rights on his first election to Congress in 1789, which, in amended form, was passed by Congress. Two years later, in 1791, the Amendments had been ratified by all member states.

Originally the Bill of Rights applied only to the federal government. Not only did the states have versions of their own, but several had institutions, for example, established churches, which were actually prohibited by the Bill of Rights. Not until after the passing of the **Fourteenth Amendment** in 1868 did a slow process of **incorporation** begin to apply the contents of the Bill of Rights to the separate states, a process which was not completed until the 1960s. The ten Amendments (listed in the Bill as Articles, but normally referred to as Amendments) cover a wide range of the most important **civil liberties** as understood at the end of the 18th century. While all of the Articles of the Bill of Rights have had some role to play in the development of US law and thinking about civil liberties, several stand out as vital. The **First Amendment**, protecting **freedom of speech**, is probably the best known; it is also a source of controversy because the implication of its **religious freedom** clause continues to be hotly debated. The other famous Articles are the **Fourth Amendment**, protecting against illegal search and **arrest**, and the **Fifth Amendment**, guaranteeing the **right to silence** in criminal trials, giving rise to the catchphrase 'I take the Fifth', where a person who has been detained for questioning refuses to answer a question for fear of **self-incrimination**. One Article that has sometimes been important in legal development is the Ninth, which simply says that because some rights are specifically mentioned, it does not mean that other rights 'retained by the people' no longer exist. This has allowed arguments for essentially adding to the Bill of Rights when the Supreme Court has wished to take a stand for which there was no obvious textual basis. (The full text of the Bill of Rights is given in the Appendix.)

Bills of attainder

A bill of attainder is a bill passed by the British Parliament, at the instigation of the monarch, which has the effect of convicting someone of a crime without his being tried and sentenced through the ordinary judicial process. Bills of attainder, which were initially presented to the House of Lords, were regularly passed by Parliament in England between the 15th and 18th centuries, notably under Henry VIII, as a way for the executive power to punish or control political opponents they could not convict through ordinary legal mechanisms. An act of attainder strips the named person of all civil, legal and property rights, giving him no chance to defend himself and making him, in effect, an outlaw. Though nominally passed for acts of treason, most of the victims could not be said to be guilty of treason, even under its most elastic common law definition, nor of any other clear-cut criminal offence. The last use of an act of attainder by a British Parliament was that passed in 1798 on Lord Edward Fitzgerald (1763–98), an Irish rebel leader, although the bills were not formally abolished until 1870. Though clearly antiquated, the fear of such executive and parliamentary persecution was serious enough for the US Constitution to include a specific ban on the passage of bills of attainder. As late as 1964 the US Supreme Court overturned a congressional act which sought to stop the payment of salaries to some named 'subversives' on the grounds that it amounted to a bill of attainder, and was therefore unconstitutional. The more important general constitutional restraint implied by abolishing bills of attainder is that acts cannot punish specific people for *ad hoc* reasons, and consequently the rule against retroactive criminal law would protect any likely victims of attainder-like legislation.

Bills of rights

A bill of rights is a document which is usually, but not necessarily, annexed to a **written constitution**, guaranteeing a country's citizens certain protection against action by their government. In addition to those documents directly called bills of right, there are also many declarations in the world's legal systems which have the equivalent function. The underlying doctrine is that of late 18th-century liberalism, based on the idea of limited government, and often derives from John **Locke** or one of the other social contract thinkers. The most famous is the **Declaration of the Rights of Man and of the Citizen** passed by the French Revolutionary Assembly in 1789, which still has considerable force as a primary document often relied on by the French *Conseil constitutionel*. The first ten Amendments to the US Constitution, ratified in 1791, are also described as a bill of rights (see **Bill of Rights (USA)**). Many modern constitutions include such a listing of basic restrictions on the government, either as part of a main formal constitution, or with some other legal status. Thus even before Canada incorporated the **Canadian Charter of Rights and Freedoms** in its 1982 Constitution Act, it had a type of bill of rights existing simply as an act of the Federal Parliament.

Any bill of rights sets up limits to what a state may legitimately do to its citizens, either as an intentional end, or as the means to attain an end which in itself would not be banned. The bills may not only forbid, for example, **torture** or censorship, but may also restrict police powers of **detention**, even when the latter are aimed at preventing ordinary crime. Some such constitutional restraints go further and limit forms of action between one citizen and another which might otherwise be illegal. So while **property** laws usually allow a landowner freedom to sell or refuse to sell as he wishes, there may be restrictions on discrimination such that someone wanting to sell a house cannot refuse to sell it to a legitimate would-be-purchaser because of, for example, the colour of his or her skin.

One of the most effective of modern bills of rights is contained in Articles 1 to 19 of the **German Constitution**. This is more far-reaching than the older model of a bill of rights in that it enjoins some positive duties on the government, rather than just forbidding it to carry out certain actions. For example, Article 7, on education, not only forbids the German government from discriminating in the provision of its educational resources, but is also seen as imposing a duty on the government in the provision of those resources. Such **positive rights**, more commonly found in supranational

27

rights documents like the UN **Universal Declaration of Human Rights** of 1948, raise major theoretical problems, and seem to make those parts of such a bill non-justiciable. A constitutional court cannot rule that a government has failed in its duty to provide employment, for example, if the government maintains that such provision is economically unviable.

Even where a legal system has no apparent equivalent to a bill of rights in terms of a particular document, the courts in liberal democracies increasingly use techniques of legal **interpretation** to grant the sorts of protections that a typical bill of rights would have. Many European countries rely more heavily on the fact that the **European Convention on Human Rights** is incorporated into their domestic law than on any formal protections within that constitutional domestic law. Courts have sometimes managed to produce powerful rights-protection from within the logic of their constitution or law without an explicit document. The Australian High Court, for example, has held that the very structure of the Australian Constitution guarantees some of the traditional content of a bill of rights, like **freedom of speech** and broadcasting, even though there is no explicit statement to that effect in the Constitution. Conversely the presence of a document called a bill of rights may guarantee none of what is usually contained in one. Thus in the United Kingdom the courts have developed common-law powers to protect human rights fairly adequately, but these are not, on the whole, derived from the British Bill of Rights (see **Bill of Rights (UK)**). Judges in the UK have often argued that traditional English common law provides better protection for basic rights, via judicial interpretation, than any formal document could. The problem arising from the form of rights-protection relying on judicial interpretation is that if the rights are contained in a document of lower legal status than a written constitution, then a subsequently-elected parliament may constitutionally repeal them.

Blasphemy

The offence of blasphemy, defaming God or sacred things, is a concept which comes from monotheistic religions, predominantly Judaic, Christian and Islamic. Strictly speaking the offence is against God or the faith itself, but from a human rights perspective blasphemy is treated as an offence against a religion's adherents. Legal controls against blasphemy, which still exist in some jurisdictions, can present problems for the doctrine of human rights. Inevitably, a law which places limits on **freedom of expression** on religious topics is a restriction on **freedom of speech**, leading to the problematical conclusion that the latter is not an absolute freedom. Even if it is accepted that there can be legitimate restrictions on the freedom of expression, through, for example, **libel** laws, some argument is still required to show that religious beliefs deserve protection in the same way that a person's good name is protected against false allegations amounting to defamation. Nevertheless, several jurisdictions do have laws forbidding blasphemy, and these have often survived legal challenges. Such laws fall into two main types. Most usual is a law making attacks against specific religious beliefs illegal. Thus the English criminal law crime of blasphemous libel, developed mainly during the 18th century, protects the Anglican version of Christianity, but no other religion or belief. Despite both its age, and this very specific protection of only one creed, the law still exists. As late as 1979 a private prosecution for blasphemy was upheld by the House of Lords in the case of *Lemon v. Whitehouse*, which centred on the publication of an erotic homosexual poem about Christ published in *Gay Weekly*. The Lords upheld this conviction, even though the law had not been used since 1922, and, though it was a majority opinion, upheld it with a very strong version of liability. The decision was challenged before the **European Court of Human Rights** on the grounds that such a crime breached the freedom of expression protections in Article 10 of the **European Convention on Human Rights**. The European Court ruled that the protection for **religious freedom** in Article 9 of the Convention was superior in this case to the Article 10 protections. The Court has given similar rulings in other cases, and, for example, upheld the seizure by the Austrian government in 1994 of a film deemed likely to offend Catholics.

What was more surprising about the protection against blasphemy in the *Lemon v. Whitehouse* case was that the Court did not seem to find it objectionable that British law protects only Christianity. In a later case the British courts refused to allow a private prosecution against a work claimed to be blasphemous against the Islamic religion. When this refusal was challenged before the Court on the grounds that it was discriminatory to protect one but not all religions, the British courts were still found to have acted legally.

Some national laws, for example the Italian law, with its definition of blasphemy as an attack on any conception of a Divine Being, attempt to give a broader protection against blasphemy. However, problems of definition clearly abound in such an area. The whole idea of forbidding blasphemy appears to depend on the right to freedom of religion being defined very powerfully as a **positive right** to peaceful enjoyment, rather than the more usual **negative right** not to be persecuted for religious beliefs. The British justification for criminalizing blasphemy has itself always been a very secular one of protecting public peace against publications likely to be either seditious when aimed against an established religion, or otherwise likely to provoke a breach of the peace. Because of the US constitutional emphasis on freedom of speech the concept of blasphemy is absent from US law.

Brown v. Board

Brown v. Board of Education of Topeka (1954) is one of the half dozen most important legal cases ever argued before the US Supreme Court, and arguably one of the most important legal analyses in the history of **civil liberties**. The case heralded the beginning of the civil rights revolution in the USA, because it ruled that racial segregation in education must cease. Until *Brown v. Board*, school districts in most of the Southern states operated parallel systems of schools for blacks and whites, and many of the institutions of higher education, both privately- and publicly-funded, were segregated on racial lines. Despite the general provisions in the US Constitution, and especially the post-civil-war **Fourteenth Amendment**, there was no clearly understood prohibition of segregation *per se*. Instead the hitherto ruling case, *Plessey v. Ferguson* (1896), had established that the **equal protection** of the laws clause in the Constitution was satisfied if provision of any service was *de facto* equal in quality. *Brown v. Board* held that, at least as far as education went, separate provision was inherently unequal. The arguments the Court relied on were partly sociological and empirical, to the effect that most of the educational provisions in black schools were simply not equal to those in white schools, or could not be relied on continually to be of equal quality. The more important part of the argument was the logical one that the mere fact that to deny someone entrance to a particular school for which he was otherwise qualified, and which he wished to attend, because of his race, was to treat him as an inferior. There were actually two cases, usually referred to as *Brown I* and *Brown II*. The latter, argued in 1955, dealt only with what legal orders should be handed down to remedy the situation that *Brown I* had deemed to be illegal. The problem was that the issue had been around for some time, and the Court had never been able to muster a strong enough majority agreed on all points to issue a powerful ruling. When Earl **Warren** became Chief Justice in 1954 he persuaded his Supreme Court colleagues to treat the issue in these two parts, because the more conservative members could be more easily persuaded to support a far-reaching general statement about the unconstitutionality of educational segregation if they were not simultaneously required to take immediately forceful action. The consequence was that *Brown II* was very disappointing for the anti-segregation lobby; instead of ordering an immediate ending of segregation, or even setting a definite timetable, the Court merely ordered that school systems should be desegregated 'with all deliberate speed' which, given the opposition to the general ruling felt in much of the South, could mean the continuance of segregation for some considerable time.

Brown v. Board was only the beginning of a lengthy process of desegregation, because it dealt only with overt legal, or *de jure*, segregation, and, as such, touched only the Southern states. The problem of *de facto* segregation arising from the geographical structure of school districts was not handled until somewhat later with the school **busing** cases, which, in their own way, were politically even more controversial.

Bundesverfassungsgericht see **German Constitutional Court**

Burden of proof

The burden of proof required by law in a trial or administrative hearing can be crucial for the protection of human rights, and it can be argued that it is a definable human right to have a specific doctrine on this matter enshrined in law. In its most familiar guise this matter is enshrined in the doctrine that a man is innocent until found guilty, a belief so widespread that a version of it even appears in Article 9 of the French **Declaration of the Rights of Man and of the Citizen**, despite Anglo-Saxon misperceptions of French legal procedures. There are two separate questions involved in the law on the burden of proof; firstly whether the state must prove misbehaviour by the citizen, or the citizen prove his innocence; and secondly the nature and amount of proof required. It is generally assumed that the state has to prove that a person did something that is pre-defined as illegal (see **retroactivity**), and, usually, that he did this knowingly and intentionally, although both of these latter questions are complex, and legal definitions of intent, in particular, are often very different from those of ordinary discourse. It is, however, by no means always the case that the law imposes the burden of proof entirely on the prosecution. There are several situations where all the prosecution has to do is to prove a specific fact, and where this fact will be held to be conclusive proof of a crime unless a convincing explanation can be given. Often drugs offences work this way, so that merely being in possession of a certain quantity of an illegal drug is in itself evidence of intent to supply that drug, always a more serious crime than mere possession, unless the court can be convinced, by the accused, that he had no such intent. Similarly some countries have anti-corruption laws by which a public servant shown to have money in his bank account that he could not just have saved from his salary will be held guilty of corruption unless he can produce convincing proof that he came by the money innocently.

On the question of the amount of proof there are two basic standards. In criminal law, at least in the common law world, it is usually held that the prosecution must prove its case 'beyond reasonable doubt'. Thus the fact that all the evidence seems to point towards guilt will not suffice for a conviction if there is any doubt, beyond the merely fanciful, that there is an innocent explanation. Civil law cases instead depend on the 'balance of probabilities' test, whereby it is suggested that given all the evidence the defendant should be held liable. The margin of balance can be varied; in some cases a simple 51 to 49 per cent probability may be acceptable, whereas if the consequences are at all severe, a tribunal is likely to insist on a much greater probability, but one that could still not be 'beyond reasonable doubt', before finding for the plaintiff.

Busing

Busing has been the most controversial, as well as virtually the only effective, way of handling *de facto*, as opposed to *de jure*, **racial discrimination** in education in the USA. Although the classic desegregation case of **Brown v. Board** had outlawed educational discrimination on racial grounds in 1954, this had referred only to formal, legally-based discrimination. In the Southern states effective discrimination continued because of the nature of school catchment areas, but this pattern was even more important in northern states where there had never been legal racial restrictions on entrance to individual schools. Furthermore, the pattern of residential segregation became more intense as blacks moved to the urban centres of northern states and whites moved out into the suburbs. By the late 1960s, when federal action to remove segregation became effective with the implementation of the 1964 **Civil Rights Act**, the *Brown* decision was clearly not having the desired effect. Consequently efforts were made to ensure that children were directed to schools to create racial balances, and in 1968 it was made possible to reject pure freedom of choice plans with the Supreme Court's decision in *Green v. County School Board*. Finally an order was made by federal judges imposing plans which required children to be bussed to schools outside their neighbourhood to achieve such a balance. This ruling was upheld by the Supreme Court in the most significant decision after *Brown, Swann v. Charlotte-Mecklenburg Board of Education* in 1971. The policy was enormously unpopular, particularly in the north which had been able to accept *de jure* desegregation mainly because their racial imbalances were not threatened. It was unpopular with some blacks as well, because the plans tended to involve more black children having to travel than was the case with whites. At one stage opposition to the policy of busing by the Republican administration of President Richard Nixon made the issue even more intensely political, but little change has been made to the policy until very recently, when there have been some signs of the Supreme Court being ready to relax the rules on enforced desegregation.

C

Canadian Charter of Rights and Freedoms

The Canadian Charter of Rights and Freedoms was added to the Canadian Constitution by the 1982 Constitution Act, which 'repatriated' a constitution, which had until then technically been simply a piece of British colonial legislation, the British North America Act of 1867. Modelled more closely on the US Bill of Rights (see **Bill of Rights (USA)**) than on the **European Convention on Human Rights**, it includes the classic 'political' **civil liberties** such as the rights to vote, and to **freedom of speech** and **freedom of assembly**, and an extensive version of the US **equal protection** clause. Inevitably it reflects specifically Canadian concerns for equality between language groups, but can be seen generally as a modernized, and more carefully drafted, version of the US document. Furthermore, the first generation of interpreting judges, both on the Canadian Supreme Court and the lower federal courts, have been almost unanimous in giving the Charter a more liberal rather than restrictive interpretation when problems have arisen. It is difficult to assess how effective the Charter will be in the future because the federal and provincial governments have themselves been very accommodating; if an attack on a statute on the grounds that it conflicts with the Charter is won by the plaintiff at trial, it is very common for the government not to appeal. Thus, for example, extensive interpretations of homosexual rights have been accepted under non-discrimination clauses that do not specifically mention sexual orientation, without the matter reaching the higher appeal courts. The Charter has a fairly complicated internal check mechanism, by which a government action can be said to be in breach of a detailed provision without being outlawed, if it is still shown to be necessary overall. Similarly the Charter contains what has come to be known as the 'notwithstanding clause'. This allows a legislature to insist that the Charter not be applied to the act in question. An earlier attempt at human rights protection in Canada had contained a similar provision which was almost never used, and neither the notwithstanding clause nor the internal two-track test have prevented the Charter being applied very extensively.

Implementation of the Charter has resulted in substantial legal business, and some have complained that courts are overwhelmed with Charter cases, often on trivial matters. More generally it has been argued that the Charter works well almost because it was not necessary, Canada already having a consensual and accommodating political culture. Critics nevertheless fear that the Charter will produce an over-litigious political system, moving away from reliance on community accord and the consensus-building role of politicians towards an over-disputatious and more Americanized society. The Charter has great significance outside Canada, as an experiment in grafting a codified **bill of rights** on to a developed common-law regime, an idea that is increasingly gaining popularity in other common law countries like the United Kingdom and Australia. It needs to be remembered that the Canadian Supreme Court already had, to some degree, the power of judicial review, through which it had helped shape the federal structure of the previous constitution. Thus the New Zealand Bill of Rights Act, much newer than the Charter, may be a more applicable model for the UK, while the Canadian example is likely to prove of continued interest in Australia. (The full text of the Canadian Charter of Rights and Freedoms is given in the Appendix.)

Cardozo

Benjamin Nathan Cardozo (1870–1938) is not only one of the half-dozen most famous judicial thinkers in American history, he is arguably the single most-quoted foreign judge in English law. He was, in fact, only on the US Supreme Court for the last six years of his life, and much of his fame rests on his achievements while a member of the New York State Court of Appeals, the most consistently distinguished of all the major state courts. Though the civil law areas in which he first rose to prominence, the laws of liability for negligence and contract law, are not normally seen as having much to do with human rights, his judicial approach in developing these areas was in itself both liberal and egalitarian, and was also based on a judicial methodology of great importance. He became famous as the leading exponent of a whole school of judicial decision-making when his book *The Nature of the Judicial Process* was published in 1921. The book advocates what has often been called 'sociological jurisprudence', an insistence on making law work in the real world, and allowing factual material, including sociological research, to influence judicial decisions. He was opposed to formalism and strict interpretations (see **strict construction**); in contract law, for example, he urged judges to interpret contracts to the real benefit of both parties, rather than strictly interpreting clauses leaving one winner and one loser. Similarly he took an expansionist approach in civil liability, widening the range of those who could claim for damages. In his constitutional work on the US Supreme Court he was the leader in the process of **incorporation** by which the Bill of Rights (see **Bill of Rights (USA)**) was brought to bear on the states rather than merely the federal government, thus enormously expanding the range of cases in which courts could enforce basic human rights. At the same time he was a leader in developing a more realistic interpretation of the Constitution which allowed Congress far more power in areas like economic regulation than had been experienced previously in strict constructionist courts. His jurisprudence was guided by his own commitment to what he described as anything which was part of the 'essence of any scheme or ordered liberty'.

Caution on arrest

As part of the general attempt to secure a **fair trial** process most jurisdictions in the common law world insist that a police suspect be warned of his civil rights at various points in the investigative process, because the **right to counsel** and protection against **self-incrimination** require, if they are to be truly effective, that their protection starts as soon as possible. If a suspect does not get to see a lawyer until some time after he has been in police custody, or if he is not clearly warned that he is under no obligation to answer police questions from the very beginning of the process, he may seriously injure his own defence. The details of cautions, some of which are contained in statutes, while others are compiled from constitutions by judicial inference, vary considerably, in part to fit the exact shape of the **right to silence** guaranteed by the particular legal culture. In general they contain: a statement of why the person is being arrested; a statement that there is no duty to answer questions nor to give the police any information; a statement about the possible use in court of anything which is said; and a statement of whatever rights there may be to the provision of legal counsel. Exactly how many of these rights, even when generally available in the system, must be in the caution varies. For example, under the **European Convention on Human Rights** an arrested person must be told more or less immediately why he is being arrested, but although the Convention does guarantee a right to silence, by judicial **interpretation** of Article 6 rather than the strict language, it is not clear when the suspect must have this fact drawn to his attention. Much depends on the general admissibility of statements made to the police, and of the role of investigatory magistrates in the criminal process. Where, as is common in Europe, something like the examining magistrate system applies, and the trial system is less accusatorial, it is less important that the suspect is warned against speaking in such a way which might harm his defence. The traditional caution in the United Kingdom, based on the protections in the judge's rules has been modified since the Criminal Justice Act 1994 in line with the limited incursions made by that Act into the right to silence. After the warning that there is no need to say anything, a second warning is given to the effect that it may damage a suspect's case if he relies in court on something he does not say to the police beforehand. Most systems require the caution to be repeated at various stages in the interrogatory process. What is often less clear is how much a police officer may ask a person he suspects of a crime before he is formally arrested, and how such material may be used by the prosecution. (See also **arrest**, **interrogation** and **legal aid**.)

Certiorari

Certiorari, the Latin word meaning be certified, is one of the traditional common-law prerogative writs, dating from before the 15th century. Like the writs of **mandamus** and prohibition, it was one of the techniques used by higher courts to control and discipline courts and persons with judicial responsibilities lower in the hierarchy. *Certiorari* is an instruction to a lower court to transmit the record of proceedings up to the court which orders it, so that they can do justice in the case. Such a transference was not, originally, technically an appeal. This is because *certiorari* lay only where, on the face of the matter, the inferior court had acted without jurisdiction, or had decided an issue wrongly in law. It could not, however, be used to re-try a matter of fact, nor in cases where the lower court, having legitimate jurisdiction, had misunderstood a legal point. This second refined distinction has largely evaporated, especially in the United Kingdom since the decision in ***Anisminic*** which effectively ended attempts at **judge-proofing** legislation. In the USA the granting of the writ of *certiorari* is the usual way in which appeals reach higher courts where no absolute right of appeal exists. When the US Supreme Court is said to be 'granting cert', it is exercising complete control of which cases it will accept, granting the *certiorari* writ to hear a matter that would otherwise terminate in a lower court.

Charter 77

Charter 77 is a dramatic example of how the sometimes apparently hopelessly utopian human rights movement can have real and lasting political consequences. Charter 77 was the banner behind which a group of dissident Czechoslovak intellectuals, among them Václav Havel (1936–), rallied to attack the Communist regime's human rights record. They based their claim largely on the fact that Czechoslovakia had signed the 1975 Helsinki Final Accord (see **Organization on Security and Co-operation in Europe**) which, for the first time, had obliged Eastern European regimes to pay at least lip service to a largely Western conception of human rights. Although the original membership of 242 was persecuted by the authorities, the movement expanded, with almost 2,000 public signatories prepared to face the state's oppression by the late 1980s. The international publicity the group gained was influential in keeping the civil rights emphasis alive in the country, and indeed elsewhere in Eastern Europe, because it was very difficult for the authorities to justify going against their own international actions. The group provided a focus for opposition to the Communist regime, which eventually bore fruit in the 'velvet revolution' of November 1989. Havel himself later became the President of both Czechoslovakia, and, in due course, the Czech Republic. Perhaps ironically, the issue on which Charter 77 was founded was outrage at the harsh sentences passed on a Czech rock band, 'The Plastic People of the Universe', rather than more classic entrenched repression of political activists.

Chilling effects

The idea of a law or practice having a 'chilling effect', the fear that certain legal action in pursuit of rights may place curbs on the freedoms of others, has developed from a narrow and precise doctrine in US civil rights law to have a more general usage both inside and beyond the US legal system. Originally the idea of a chilling effect covered the giving up of **First Amendment** rights by those frightened that challenging a possibly unconstitutional restriction on them would bring prosecution which it would be preferable to avoid, even if the prosecution ultimately failed. The First Amendment rights are the highly political rights to **freedom of speech**, **freedom of assembly**, press, petition and the various **religious freedom** rights. If people are deterred from claiming their political rights to protest against governments for fear that a court may deem their actions unprotected, the value of the rights themselves is much discounted. Aware of the danger of such concerns, US courts have been generous in allowing standing to such plaintiffs to maximize their own ability to cut down on unacceptable infringements of freedoms. The idea has spread to involve almost any actions taken, or avoided, for fear of what a court may interpret some legislation to mean, even when the person suffering from the 'chill' in question genuinely does not believe his behaviour should legitimately be interpreted as a breach of the rule. The idea has been applied, for example, to the tendency of the German Parliament to craft its legislation with an eye to possible contradictory interpretations by the **German Constitutional Court**. It has similarly recently been argued in the United Kingdom that the new doctrine allowing the courts to examine the parliamentary record to interpret legislation according to what a minister has said in the debate on the bill in question may have a chilling effect on parliamentary debate. Thus a state government might pass a law restricting political demonstrations, knowing that it may ultimately be ruled unconstitutional, but relying on the impact it will have until that time. The German legislators, on the other hand, may be restrained from trying to carry out a policy even if it might turn out to be acceptable to the court, because of the political embarrassment of being overruled. The British government minister may give a very narrow interpretation of a proposed bill in a speech to the House of Commons for fear of how the Law Lords may use anything said in a later interpretation; this will then become a self-imposed restriction, possibly preventing the government from doing as much as it wants, for fear of being taken to intend to do even more than it wants. Recognition of chilling effects accepts that much of the impact of any law or administrative policy depends on the uncertainty of law because of the importance of judicial **discretion**.

Choice of occupation

The right freely to choose and exercise an occupation is most clearly stated in the **German Constitution**; Article 12 provides that 'All Germans have the right freely to choose their occupation or profession, their place of work, study or training.' This right is not absolute, as there are limitations; for example, the regulation of professions by the government, and the 1956 amendment allowing conscriptive military service, which is subject to a very strong protection for **conscientious objection**. Some other countries have come close to recognizing the right to choice of occupation as a specific human right, and where it has been recognized, in Israel for example, the right can have quite extensive applications. The main aim in protecting such a right is to prevent a system where people are directed into that work which the state feels it needs; where it is threatened, such a **liberty** is indeed precious given that one's work forms so large a part of one's entire identity. In these terms it is seldom threatened outside national emergencies in modern states. However, the right to practise a profession can easily run into limitations imposed by the state for otherwise legitimate reasons, and it is in this context that the right has been recognized and proven to be politically controversial in the USA. The **Fourteenth Amendment** protects 'property rights' in a very broad sense, which in the 19th century was held to include the right to practise one's trade. In one of the classic cases of US jurisprudence, known as the Slaughterhouse case, a very strong minority voted to overthrow a state law setting up a monopoly in animal slaughtering, on the grounds that the right to labour as animal slaughterers on their own account was thus violated. Although the case in question was lost, this extensive definition of property proved to be extremely important in the development of the US concept of substantive **due process**. The right to choose and exercise any trade or profession, subject only to regulation in the public interest (for example, licensing of doctors or lawyers by professional bodies), is a prime example of how a right can be simultaneously an economic interest right and a personal development right, with inevitable problems for its justification and definition. (See also **forced or compulsory labour**).

Citizenship

Citizenship is a legal status defining the relationship between an individual and the state, defining both rights and duties each bears to the other. Although the classical world understood the idea of citizenship, with both Greek and Roman legal systems giving complex definitions, it largely lapsed during the post-Roman Empire era and was revived, with a new meaning, by the American and French revolutions. The notion of citizenship is in sharp contrast to the historically rival notion of being a subject. In countries ruled by a powerful monarch, subjects owed their sovereign unquestioning obedience and allegiance, and could even be said to be his property. A citizen, on the other hand, is himself part of the sovereign, when sovereignty comes to be seen as a collective attribute of the people. Thus in ancient Greece there was a clear distinction between citizens and non-citizens, namely women, slaves and resident aliens, who nevertheless lived legitimately in the city state and were obliged to obey its laws. Citizens had duties, sometimes more arduous duties than residents, but also enjoyed political rights, within a form of participatory democracy, denied to non-citizens. The Roman Empire originally restricted citizenship to free-born descendants of the original population of the city of Rome, and only in AD 212 was Roman citizenship extended to all free-born males in the Empire. Nowadays citizenship is the norm: it is the usual relationship between a native inhabitant of a country and its state even where monarchies still exist, and citizenship carries the political rights to vote (see **voting rights**), to be elected, to serve on juries, and generally to engage in the political system.

As a rule citizenship is acquired by birth, although this can as easily mean inheriting the citizenship of one's parents or acquiring the citizenship of the country of birth. Citizenship law is, however, everywhere complex and usually controversial in marginal cases. Some countries allow their citizens to acquire citizenship of other states, while others regard such acquisition as effectively renouncing the original citizenship, which can cause considerable problems for the children of marriages between citizens of different countries. Most countries allow some methods of acquiring their citizenship other than birth, such as by naturalization of legal immigrants or by marriage, but the conditions placed on such acquisition can be very restrictive. Furthermore, European countries with a significant colonial history have all inherited problems from that past relating to the extent to which they are legally or morally obliged to offer the protection of their citizenship to inhabitants of their former colonies (see also **asylum**).

The connection between the words 'city' and 'citizenship' is not accidental; citizenship as a legal relationship of mutuality of duty and privilege developed in the small face-to-face societies of classical city states where some actual degree of equality was found. When these were swept away in the creation by conquest of much larger empires the mutuality, based on the society of equals, was replaced by the domination of power which turned most people into subjects. Only as the Middle Ages saw the development of cities as centres of real power in rivalry to the church and the nobility did citizenship again become an important, and highly desirable, status.

In most countries, either by constitutional right or common law expectation, a citizen cannot be stripped of that status, whatever other punishment may be imposed. There exist thousands of people without citizenship, however, 'stateless persons' in technical language; hundreds of thousands of people have been expelled from their homelands, which have come to be governed by states which are unprepared to grant citizenship, or to which the refugees dare not, or will not, return and to whom no other state is prepared to grant full citizenship.

Civil liberties

The term civil liberties is mainly used, as it is throughout this book, as a synonym for civil rights. The idea of a 'liberty' rather than a 'right' is used to stress that the freedoms covered in the civil libertarian tradition are seen as part of mankind's ideal fundamental and complete **liberty**, which, in the general interest, needs to be constrained in political systems, or in what some political philosophers have liked to call 'civil society'. The only difference is a matter of nuance; civil rights can give the impression that each right stands alone, rather than being derived from some general state of total liberty. Some of the major pressure groups, such as like the **American Civil Liberties Union (ACLU)** and the British organization **Liberty** (formerly the National Council for Civil Liberties), have preferred the title, possibly in part because the language of 'rights' has sometimes seemed slightly alien in the positivistic legal culture of the common law world. There is some sense in which the liberties of the individual recognized in the concept civil liberties have to do with the public sphere of life, and especially with people's involvement in the political or 'civil' sphere, and in a related way that they include group rights rather than purely individual entitlements. Thus **freedom of speech**, or the right to run for electoral office, are perhaps more properly called civil liberties, while the right to **religious freedom** might be more properly described as a human right.

Civil Rights Acts (USA)

Since the late 1950s there has been, in the USA, a series of important federal legislative assaults on discrimination, particularly **racial discrimination**. The most important have been: the Civil Rights Acts of 1957, 1960, 1964 and 1968; the 1965 Voting Rights Act; and the 1968 Fair Housing Act (see **voting rights** and **housing rights**). The 1957 Act was passed by only one vote in Congress, prompted largely by the courts' attack on educational discrimination in **Brown v. Board** *of Education of Topeka*. The only right specifically mentioned in the Act was that of voting, which was not to be effectively ensured for blacks in the South until the 1965 Act. It did, however, establish a Civil Rights Division in the Department of Justice, and a fact-finding body, the Civil Rights Commission. These institutional developments ensured the existence of a professional body with an interest in developing the reach of whatever legislation may come into being. The three acts of the mid-1960s, part of President Lyndon B. Johnson's 'Great Society' programme, itself a response to President John F. Kennedy's short-lived reforming administration, remain the core of US civil rights protection outside court-developed doctrines. The 1964 Act struck at overt discrimination such as segregated provisions in public services, while it and later acts outlawed the often more insidious discrimination in employment and access to voter registration. The US Constitution, with its federal structure and general respect for private **property**, often makes it difficult for the federal government to take direct action, and much of US civil rights legislation functions indirectly, by withdrawing federal funding from any programmes that practise what the Attorney-General has certified to be widespread discrimination. This strategy was at the heart of civil rights legislation in the 1960s, and, for example, the 1968 Fair Housing Act prohibits discrimination in the sale or rental of housing where any federal funds are involved. The weakness is obvious; if an institution, say a college, is capable of doing without state funding at all, there is no effective way of preventing discrimination. Nevertheless, these acts, and later ones like the Equal Educational Opportunity Act of 1971, and acts banning discrimination in the provision of financial credit, have done much to eradicate not only racial but also **sex discrimination**. (See also **equal opportunities**.)

Clear and present danger

The phrase 'clear and present danger' refers to a legal test developed by the US Supreme Court to decide when a governmental attempt to punish someone for saying or advocating something can be legitimate despite the **First Amendment** protection of **freedom of speech**. It originated in an opinion of 1919 by one of the leading figures in Supreme Court history,

Oliver Wendell Holmes (1841–1935), in 1919 and was developed as a test by him and others over the next four decades. Ironically the first usage was actually in an opinion supporting the constitutionality of the 1917 Espionage Act, under which the government was attempting to imprison socialist anti-war protesters who had distributed leaflets to conscripts. As later used it came to mean that an infringement of free speech could only be justified when the offending actions constituted a clear and present danger of something that the government was otherwise entitled to ban. In most uses it meant that there had to be an immediate likelihood of the offending speech causing a criminal act. It has not been used very much since the 1950s, the Supreme Court developing other and more complex theories to handle freedom of speech cases, but it has become established in US political culture as a general statement of when some government action which would generally be wrong, immoral or illegal can nevertheless be justified.

Collective bargaining

Although not directly listed as a basic human right in many documents, collective bargaining, lying as it does at the heart of industrial relations, is, by implication at least, a protected practice in most liberal democracies. Most modern rights documents, such as the **European Convention on Human Rights** (in Article 11), specifically protect the right to join a trade union. Others, drafted before the modern organized labour movement became established, may do so only by language which has had to be interpreted to include such a right, via protections on other freedoms. Nevertheless, collective bargaining *per se* is seldom mentioned, because it falls into a category of rights arguments that pose considerable problems. The right to collective action is effectively a group right, not an individual right, and civil rights theorists are not universally happy with the idea that groups can in themselves be granted rights. The **German Constitution**, for example, has specifically granted civil rights protection to 'artificial' or 'legal' persons in order to make sure that bodies like churches, and presumably trade unions, have legal protection. The distinction between individual action and collective action is precisely how the early anti-union legislation in much of Europe operated. In the United Kingdom, for example, it was held that while no individual could be forced to report to work for his employer, any combination of people collectively withholding labour was guilty of a criminal conspiracy. Any supposed right to collective bargaining would impose a duty on the employer to negotiate with organized labour, rather than to insist on individual contractual negotiations with each worker, and this duty, along with the legal validity of collective industrial action, was recognized in legislation such as the US **National Labor Relations Act**.

Commission on Racial Equality

The Commission on Racial Equality (CRE) was created by the British government under the 1976 Race Relations Act, to replace the ineffective machinery of the Race Relations Board and the Community Relations Commission which had operated the weak acts of 1968 and 1965. The general duties of the CRE are to work for the elimination of **racial discrimination** and to promote equality of opportunity for racial minorities and good relations between racial groups generally. It can issue codes of practice for attaining **equal opportunities** in employment and housing, and although these codes do not have direct legislative effect, they are taken into account by the courts when dealing with cases arising under the 1976 Act. Perhaps the most important aspect of the CRE's work is one that sounds fairly innocuous, the carrying out of formal investigations. There are two sorts of investigation; firstly into the behaviour of a 'named person' (which can obviously be a legal person, that is, an institution or corporation) and secondly into an area of activity, for example, banking. In the former instance the CRE must inform the suspected person that they intend to investigate him, and why, and to give him a chance to make representations as to why this should not happen. Unlike its predecessor bodies, the CRE has full **subpoena** powers in carrying out the investigations. If the investigation does disclose unlawful discrimination the CRE can issue a non-discrimination notice requiring the behaviour to cease and, if necessary, requiring the discriminator to report to the CRE on changes in procedure he has carried out to ensure that discrimination ceases. If the CRE has reason to believe that the discriminator is not complying with the notice, it may than apply to the courts for an order requiring compliance. Although the immediate legal consequences of disobeying such a court order are not great, because it does not constitute **contempt of court** as would be the case with an **injunction**, it is rare for any organization or individual to persist. The CRE has the additional function of aiding individuals to make their own complaints to courts; earlier versions of the Act did not allow such individual actions, which was one of their principal weaknesses. It is vital that the CRE should play this role, because a complainant under the **Race Relations Act** does not qualify for **legal aid** until the appeal stage. In practice the CRE itself will often act as the *de facto* plaintiff to ensure that cases involving important legal principles receive adequate legal attention.

Compensation

One of the weaker areas of the legal protection of human rights comes when the issue arises of how people should be compensated for infringements on their rights and liberties. In general, of course, what a plaintiff claiming that his rights have been infringed really wants is for the state to be told to stop infringing them, or, more generally, for the court to enunciate that a particular form of state action is actually prohibited. This latter remedy is what is often legally called a **declaration**, and is available in one form or another in most liberal democracies, as are the equivalent to the various English common law writs like **mandamus** and prohibition, which prevent or require administrative action. In some cases, however, the damage caused by a breach of civil rights may be ongoing, even if the state's unconstitutional actions have ceased. In an ordinary civil law situation, say the breach of a contract or a negligent injury, damages would indeed be given. Even where, as in the case of physical injury, monetary compensation may not be capable of truly making up for the loss incurred, money has a remarkable capacity for easing suffering and indignation. It is not, however, normally possible to sue a government for financial compensation for an infringement of one's rights, unless the infringement has a very clear pecuniary effect, in which case an ordinary civil suit may be appropriate. For this reason it has always been seen as one of the stronger points about the **European Court of Human Rights** that it has the power to, and does, award damages against offending states to give the complainant what the **European Convention on Human Rights** describes as 'just compensation'. Such awards, as well as being of value to the sufferers, have even greater value in marking the general public disapprobation of the offending state's behaviour.

Conference on Security and Co-operation in Europe (CSCE) (see Organization for Security and Co-operation in Europe (OSCE))

Conscientious objection

Conscientious objection usually means a person's refusal to engage in military service on the grounds that it is contrary to his conscience as a pacifist to take part in military activities. So much of human rights thinking is based on the primacy of the **right to life** that forcing someone to take life seems one step further than a state can legitimately demand. There is a widespread recognition in modern society that killing, even in a collective form of self-defence such as a defensive war, is on the margin of justifiability, and yet the duty to fight for one's country is usually seen as a primary obligation of the legal status of **citizenship**. Thus there is an unresolvable clash between two absolutely primary considerations. Most states recognize conscientious objection, some even in times of actual war, but it is usually made dependent on proving a deeply rooted general objection to military actions, and traditionally it has been hard to establish such an objection without recourse to religious arguments. It has also proved virtually impossible to justify objection to some specific war, rather than to war in general.

Among major human rights documents only the **German Constitution** expressly recognizes the right to conscientious objection, in Clause 3 of Article 4; the article, which otherwise deals with **religious freedom**, is one of the few protected from any constitutional amendment or legislative curtailment. In Germany there is no requirement at all to justify a refusal to render what the Constitution calls 'military service involving armed combat', and the state has not tried to substitute for such service any other form of military service. Instead, those wishing to exercise the right have to do some other, entirely non-military, form of public service. Towards the end of the Cold War this option had become so popular that the German Defence Ministry feared serious future manpower problems. Neither the **European Convention on Human Rights** nor the **European Court of Human Rights** fully recognizes a right to exemption from military service on grounds of conscience, although the Court has been relatively sympathetic in cases involving the claim. By contrast both the Council of Europe's Committee of Ministers and the UN Commission on Human Rights have pressed for an international recognition of the claim.

In principle one could conscientiously object to obeying any law, but successful attempts to make this argument are rare. They have not succeeded where, for example, those opposed to war on general grounds have tried to insist that they need not pay that part of their taxes which go to military expenditure. Occasionally such claims do succeed in contexts where someone has a religious objection to some form of medical treatment and the state tries to enforce it, but there is no guarantee that even this argument will gain a court's support.

Conseil Constitutionel

The *Conseil Constitutionel* is an institution set up by the makers of the Constitution of the Fifth French Republic, promulgated in 1958, to play something like the role played in other written constitutions by a supreme or constitutional court. However, it is a unique legal body and is neither officially a court nor, in fact, very much like one. The very existence of the *Conseil* is remarkable because the entire political history of post-revolutionary France is adamantly opposed to the involvement of courts in politics, a legacy of the hatred felt for the courts and the legal *parlements* of the monarchical regime. French constitutional thought has always stressed the absolute sovereignty of the National Assembly as the only true representative of the will of the people. The idea that a non-elected legal body should interfere with the Assembly's right to legislate whatever it likes would, in the past, have been anathema. The writers of the Constitution, however, believed that the previous republics had encountered problems precisely because the National Assembly wielded too much power, and set out to restrict it in several ways. They did not intend the *Conseil* to exercise any positive power; its function was expected to be that of ensuring that the Assembly did not try to trespass on the powers of the executive, and did not seek to legislate in areas, and in ways, forbidden to them by the Constitution. It was expected to be very much the creature of the executive, which it duly was for the first 15 years or so of the Fifth Republic. Partly this was a matter of its personnel. The *Conseil* consists of nine members, who need not, and originally usually were not, lawyers. The President of the Republic and the Presidents (i.e., Speakers) of the two houses of the National Assembly each appoint three members, and initial appointees were typically former ministers or others with political experience. Unlike a court, the *Conseil* does not hear appeals in actual litigation. Its power is restricted to ruling, if invited, on whether a bill which has been passed by both houses of the Assembly, but has not yet been promulgated by the President, is in conformity with the Constitution. This is the only time that the *Conseil* may act; existing laws may not be brought before it, and no court may refer a matter to it for resolution. Initially the only people who could refer a bill were the three officers who could appoint to it, and the Prime Minister. As all of these posts were in the hands of the same party or coalition in the early years of the Republic, it was hardly surprising that the *Conseil* had little to do. The only important issue to come before it in these years demonstrated its subservience to the executive; in 1962 President de Gaulle tried to change the constitutional rule on how the President was elected by a declaring a referendum in a way which was itself clearly unconstitutional, but the *Conseil* refused to rule that it was improper, even though Article 60 of the Constitution charges it with ensuring proper procedures for referendums.

In 1974 the power of the *Conseil* was considerably strengthened by the introduction of a new system under which a bill could be referred to it by any group of 60 Deputies or Senators, enabling the parliamentary opposition to make a last ditch attack on legislation they had unsuccessfully opposed. Since then many bills have been referred, and the *Conseil* has found about half of them to be, at least in part, unconstitutional. Consequently what might usually have been a weakness, that the Fifth Republic's Constitution contains no equivalent to a **bill of rights**, has actually proved to be a strength. The *Conseil* has developed a very wide-ranging approach by which all sorts of documents, especially the revolutionary era **Declaration of the Rights of Man and of the Citizen** and the bill of rights in the Fourth Republic's Constitution, are seen as sources of fundamental constitutional principles.

Membership of the *Conseil* has come to be more like that of some other constitutional courts, with the appointment of leading legal experts, though not usually judges, and also of former ministers, who themselves have valuable legal experience in offices such as the Ministry of Justice. On the whole the *Conseil's* track record has been fairly even-handed. For example, although it found part of the Socialist nationalization programme of the early 1980s unconstitutional, it also faulted part of the successor privatization programme under the Gaullists. Unlike a real court, it has felt able to play a more proactive role when it finds legislation unconstitutional, and will often explain how the aims of the law could be achieved in ways it would accept. In terms of protecting human rights it has been fairly liberal for a political culture that has always tended towards the executive, and it has supported **freedom of speech**, **freedom of assembly**, freedom for broadcasting and union rights fairly effectively. The *Conseil* has been surprisingly supportive of **religious freedom** given the Republic's traditional anti-clericalism. As, however, it does not exercise the supervision of executive actions, which in France is left to a separate court structure culminating in the *Conseil d'Etat*, and has no role in determining the constitutionality of administrative decrees, it cannot exercise much of the human rights protection available to a real constitutional court.

Conseil d'Etat

The French *Conseil d'Etat* (Council of State) is probably the most famous of the European **administrative law** tribunals. As part of the Napoleonic model of legal systems, it was created in 1799, and it has been the inspiration for much of Europe's approach to legal control over the executive. Despite its general importance as the summit of administrative law, it is probably unique in its structure, being simultaneously a court and a government department, and as a court it acts mainly as the supreme court of the French administrative law structure. France, like most European countries, has quite separate court hierarchies for civil, criminal and administrative law, and only in the administrative courts can the actions of the executive be challenged. Because of the huge caseload in this system, with around 10,000 cases a year brought before it in the late 1980s, a new intermediary tier of regional administrative appeals courts was set up in 1989. Subsequently the *Conseil* has heard only the most important cases—but this has not reduced its significance. The French tradition of hostility to courts being involved in politics has only recently, in 1958, allowed the creation of a constitutional court in the shape of the *Conseil Constitutionel*. Consequently civil rights have been protected mainly in terms of this control over the administration, and the *Conseil d'Etat* has an admirable record for keeping the government firmly within the bounds of whatever powers it has persuaded Parliament to allow it. In fact, because much of French legislation is not properly parliamentary statute at all, but decree legislation, the power of the administrative law structure has been vital.

The *Conseil* owes much of its influence and authority as a court to its other function, as the official legal adviser to the government, which passes all draft legislation through the *Conseil* for its advice. As such it is one of the most prestigious of the formidable *Grand Corps* of the French civil service élite, selecting the cream of the graduates of the *Ecole Nationale d'Administration*. With such people both staffing the court section of the *Conseil*, and advising the government on its actions in the first place, whatever protection the élite wishes to give to human rights within the sphere of government behaviour is more or less guaranteed. As members of the *Conseil* also serve the *Conseil Constitutionel* as its secretariat, the general overview of human rights protection is strengthened. Nevertheless, it has to be said that the *Conseil* is, in the end, a prime example of the French statist tradition as well as the population's main bulwark against excesses in that tradition, with inevitable strains and conflicts of loyalty.

Contempt of court

There are two versions of contempt of court, civil and criminal. Criminal contempt is the one best known to the public, consisting of insulting the court (contempt in the face of the court) by indulging in behaviour outside the court which risks damaging the process of law, such as by publishing material that may make a **fair trial** difficult or by interfering with witnesses. Civil contempt is disobedience to an order of the court or breaking a commitment made to the court. It is this latter instance where the court has the power to give effect to its decisions, particularly in civil rights cases where the issue for the court is not just to declare the state to be in breach of the law, but to stop it continuing to do so. In the United Kingdom it has even been held that a cabinet minister can be declared in contempt of court where his department, unknown to him, and without intentional malice, ignored a commitment they had made not to deport an asylum seeker until judicial procedures were finished. Theoretically contempt can be punished by summary imprisonment by order of the court, but it is more usual for a government department to face a fine.

Contraception

The right to practise contraception would now usually be discussed under the heading of **reproductive freedom**, and is, in any case, no longer a matter of importance in liberal democracies. Even Ireland, the last developed country to try to enforce the teaching of the Roman Catholic Church by constitutional means, no longer attempts to enforce this particular ban. Historically, laws forbidding contraception were not, however, limited to Catholic-dominated areas; US states with very diverse religious cultures had such legislation in the 19th century. Indeed, some of these laws lingered on into the later part of the 20th century, and it was the overturning of one such law in 1969 that allowed the US Supreme Court to develop the constitutional right of **privacy**, which shortly thereafter was used to uphold the constitutionality of legal **abortion**.

Convention for the Protection of Human Rights and Fundamental Freedoms (see **European Convention on Human Rights**)

Criminal civil liberties

Many of the most important **civil liberties** relate to the state's treatment of those suspected of criminal activity, not only because a civilized society treats even its criminals with some degree of decency, but because the criminal law is the main interface between the power of the state and the individual. Such civil liberties fall into three broad categories: restrictions on the state in criminal investigation and the enforcement of **public order**; rights of the accused during the trial and pre-trial phases of prosecution; and rights relating to the punishment of those convicted of crimes. The first category focuses largely on aspects of the right to **privacy**, involving, for example, protections against being arbitrarily stopped and questioned or searched (see **stop and search**), against entry into one's home, and **privacy of correspondence**. They can be summed up as preventing the state, without good cause, invading the private space of an individual, and because of the age-old fear of oppressive state action to intimidate its political opponents, these are usually older than rights falling into the second two categories. The French **Declaration of the Rights of Man and of the Citizen** and the US Bill of Rights (see **Bill of Rights (USA)**), for example, both contain prohibitions against unjustified 'searches and seizures'. All liberal democracies have more or less stringent controls on the state's rights to intercept mail or tap telephones, and the development of modern methods of electronic communication regularly cause court cases defining these limits further; the British House of Lords recently ruled that for the police to use a radio to pick up the signals between the hand set and the base unit of a cordless telephone did not constitute an illegal version of telephone tapping. Perhaps the most important question about this first type of civil liberties is what should be done when it is shown that the police have infringed them. The US tendency has been to treat any evidence gained by such unjustified invasion of privacy as invalid, thus attempting to control the police by preventing them getting convictions. This, sometimes known as the fruit of the poisoned tree doctrine, is not followed very far by European courts, which argue that the actual probative value of the evidence is not tainted, and that the injured party has full recourse to the law in an action for damages if the police have misbehaved. Other rights intended to offset the dangers of misuse of power include the right to a speedy trial, which causes a considerable amount of litigation under the **European Convention on Human Rights**, and related questions about **pre-trial detention**.

Civil rights during the trial and pre-trial phase focus upon the **fair trial** idea, especially in Anglo-American common law jurisdictions reliant on the accusatorial system. Some such rights, like the **right to counsel** to help present one's case, and to have it provided free where necessary (see **legal aid**), follow directly from the inequality inherent in the state versus the individual conflict. Similarly, rules on what sort of evidence can be raised, and on the selection, where appropriate, of a jury are intended to redress this power imbalance (see **jury trial**). Others, though deeply rooted in our expectations, are not as easy to explain theoretically. The **right to silence** both after **arrest** and during the trial seems to raise questions of conflict with the need to arrive at the truth.

The final category of rights presents perhaps the most basic of all tests of a nation's human rights record, because the very fact of conviction and punishment means that many, if not most, civil rights are being taken away. The focus here is on the nature of the punishment itself, and is one of the oldest concerns, often revolving around the core prohibition on **cruel and unusual punishments**. Most **bills of rights** have some such prohibition, but the assessment of what may be cruel or unusual varies tremendously from culture to culture. It is notable that the death penalty itself is retained as not being in conflict with this axiom even in some states which otherwise take rights very seriously, and where all sort of questions of when, how and on whom death is inflicted are nevertheless considered important (see **restrictions on death sentence**). Finally, attempts are made to retain procedural civil rights (see **procedural rights**) as far as further administrative decisions, over eligibility for parole for example, or discipline inside a prison, are concerned. These are seldom as restrictive on the state as those pertaining to someone as yet not judged guilty, but can still be important.

Cruel and unusual punishments

One of the earliest constitutional prohibitions on cruel and unusual punishments is found in the Eighth Amendment of the US Bill of Rights (see **Bill of Rights (USA)**). Earlier human rights documents, for example, **Magna Carta**, restricted when and how punishments might be applied, but were necessarily silent, given the violence of the days, on what could be done; even today 'cruel and unusual' may have more to do with matters of procedure than substance. Thus the US Supreme Court has always recoiled from finding the death penalty in itself to be cruel and unusual. The nearest the Court has ever got to banning capital punishment has been to rule that the methods for selecting when the death penalty rather than imprisonment was to be the sentence were so haphazard and biased as to be cruel and unusual. Other Western courts and human rights documents have tended to concentrate on matters like the length of time a person may remain in prison while awaiting execution, either because they have been reticent to ban the death sentence itself, or because they do not have the authority to do so. In the case of certain Caribbean Commonwealth countries, which retain the death penalty, the final court of appeal is the Judicial Committee of the Privy Council in the United Kingdom. In 1993 the Committee ruled that if a death sentence were still pending after a period of five years then it should be reviewed and commuted. The ruling came in the wake of an appeal on behalf of two men in Jamaica, who had been convicted of murder in 1979, and had effectively been on 'death row' ever since; the Judicial Committee commuted the sentences on the grounds that it was 'an inhuman act to keep a man facing the agony of execution over a long extended period of time'.

Cruel and unusual, or less evocatively 'inhumane', punishment is banned by the main human rights conventions, including the **European Convention on Human Rights**, and would certainly cover all obvious forms of **torture** or extremely harsh imprisonment conditions. There is some suggestion in the jurisprudence of the Convention that life imprisonment in its full sense may come to qualify as an inhumane sentence. (See also **degrading punishment** and **restrictions on death sentence**.)

D

Death sentence (see **restrictions on death sentence**)

De facto discrimination

Relatively little discrimination, racial, gender or otherwise, in the modern world is overt and formal. Such discrimination, where laws or regulations specifically treat people differently according to some particular characteristic, is usually referred to as *de jure* discrimination. Far more often, patterns of behaviour occur where people's life chances are in fact unequal because of their religion, colour, age or whatever, but this follows from correlated sociological or personal facts rather than openly discriminatory behaviour. The classic modern example is racially-based educational disadvantage in the USA arising from residential patterns. Long after *de jure* racial discrimination in education, practised almost entirely in the South, had been outlawed in the celebrated case of **Brown v. Board**, blacks were systematically getting inferior education in northern states because the highly-localized funding basis for school districts meant that neighbourhoods where blacks were in a majority delivered inferior education because of their relative economic deprivation; and because of these racially segregated residential patterns, blacks were still educated almost entirely in nearly all-black schools. To remedy this *de facto* discrimination the Supreme Court developed the policy of **busing**, whereby schools had to be artificially integrated. *De facto* discrimination can occur in any institutional context. A typical example has been in sex discrimination where, despite nearly a generation of legislation, women still tend to earn lower average salaries than men. It is hard for legislation to penetrate these patterns. An example is the British **Sex Discrimination Act** of 1975, which attempted to make it illegal to treat women differently from men not only directly, but by applying criteria which will pertain to substantially fewer women than men. Only continual pressure by legislation to affect decision-making mechanisms can hope to prevent such discrimination. For example, policies making it illegal to ask candidates for jobs about their marital situation, requirements to have women and minority members on all selection committees and so forth can help, but only the slow process of changing entire cultures of decision-making in industry and commerce, as well as the state and educational institutions, will abolish *de facto* discrimination. (See also **age discrimination** and **racial discrimination**.)

Declaration

A declaration, given by a court, is a statement of what the law is in a particular situation. As a remedy it may seem very tame, as granting a declaration does not, in itself, either award damages for an injured party, nor, like an **injunction**, constitute an order to cease to do an illegal act. In English law the power to grant declarations, usually described as giving a declaratory judgment, is a discretionary power which has only relatively recently become commonly used in **public law** cases. It originates in a statutory power granted in the 19th century, but the revival of English public law with the creation in 1978 of the procedure of **judicial review** has made the granting of a declaration a more common, as well as a more powerful, remedy. It does have considerable effect, however, when, as is common in cases touching on human rights, one party to the conflict is the government or a local authority. Here effective remedies may not easily be available, particularly because of the difficulty of enforcing injunctions against the state itself, but a mere statement that what the government is attempting or proposing to do would be illegal may be all that is needed to protect rights.

Declaration of Independence (American)

The American Declaration of Independence of 4 July 1776 was both the effective announcement of the American War of Independence, and the starting point for most American constitutional theory. It was written, with only the slightest amendment from a committee, by Thomas Jefferson (1743–1826), although he himself denied that it was in any sense original, stemming as it does both generally from John **Locke's** theories of government, and more specifically from previous American statements such as that of the slightly earlier Virginia Declaration of Rights. It falls into two parts: an initial statement which has become famous, asserting the theory that government exists only to protect mankind's inalienable rights to 'life, liberty and the pursuit of happiness'; and a set of some 30 indictments against the British Crown for offences ranging from the deeply constitutional to mere policy disagreements. As a constitutional document it has a very vague status, and neither the US Supreme Court nor constitutional theorists are very willing to use it to support arguments in court, as it has less effective force than the preambles typically found at the beginning of all **written constitutions**.

In part this is because it is, overtly, a revolutionary document and therefore hardly suitable as part of a constitution, which is a description of an ongoing political system; and partly it is because the rights enshrined in it are so broad as not to be justiciable. The most interesting right guaranteed is the right to pursue happiness, not the right to achieve it nor be granted it.

Declaration of the Rights of Man and of the Citizen

This human rights document, passed by the French National Assembly in 1789 at the height of revolutionary fervour, is one of the earliest in legal history, being only two years younger than the US Constitution itself. It is treated with great veneration by the French, and indeed is used extensively by the French *Conseil Constitutionel* as a source of constitutional doctrine. It was indeed radical in its day, but can seem curiously disappointing when read against 20th-century expectations of what rights such a document should protect, and how trenchantly it should protect them. Its radicalism is, perhaps, demonstrated more in its egalitarianism than in its protection of liberal rights. Article 1 states: 'Social distinctions may be based only upon considerations of general usefulness', and other articles ensure the French dream of 'a career open to the talents'. Executive power is restricted to what the legislature ordains, but there are virtually no limitations on what legislation can achieve. Indeed, Article 7, while providing that no one can be accused, arrested or detained except as provided by legislation, goes on to say that anyone charged under legislation must immediately obey, and that 'he renders himself culpable by resistance'. Even the protection against persecution for opinions and religious beliefs in Article 10 makes an exception if the manifestation of them disturbs public order. Furthermore, even the egalitarianism enshrined in the Declaration is limited, because **property** is defined as an 'inviolable and sacred right' in the final article, and indeed the article's requirement for compensation if property is taken for public purposes has been used by the *Conseil Constitutionel* to limit nationalization legislation in the Fifth Republic.

In fact the Declaration represents the ambitions of what was essentially a rising capitalist class, and protects such a group from the sort of extra-legal attacks of the previous monarchical state, but has none of the sense of a need to protect against the **tyranny of the majority** that suffuses the slightly older US Constitution. (The full text of the Declaration of the Rights of Man and of the Citizen is given in the Appendix.)

Degrading punishment

Many constitutions and **bills of rights** have some provision to forbid the imposition of what the US Constitution terms **cruel and unusual**

punishment, and the ban on degrading punishment is typical of these. While a ban on cruelty, whether or not obeyed, depends on a very general and consensual moral code, the idea of degradation as unacceptable punishment is rather more recent, and related to a rather specific strand in humanitarian thinking. Essentially the idea that it is improper to degrade another human being comes from the current of thought often described as 'dignitarian', and best represented best by the first article of the **German Constitution,** which states: 'The dignity of man is inviolable. To respect and protect it shall be the duty of all public authority.' In such a view a person may deserve punishment, it may be necessary for deterrent purposes that he be punished, and it may be in his interests, through reform, to be punished, but at all times he remains a human being entitled to be treated as the equal of all others except in the limited way caused by the punishment. Yet degrading someone, intentionally reducing him in public respect, has at times been seen as exactly what punishment can and should do. In fact criminological research suggests that it is the very fact of being held up to public dishonour by being put on trial that accounts for much of the deterrent effect of criminal law. Certainly modern states do at times intentionally use what can only be called degrading punishment; the return to the chain gang as a punishment in some US states has precisely this intention, and much of military discipline, until recently, at least, has been based on the principle. There is, in fact, a contradiction at the very root of the concept. Unless degrading punishment actually does not mean anything more than cruel punishment, it may be logically impossible to punish at all without degrading the recipient.

Detention

Detention is the forcible removal of a person to a place where he can be prevented from leaving, and his being kept in this state of absence of personal **liberty**, subject to whatever regulations the detainer may impose. It is similar to imprisonment, but imprisonment is technically restricted to a legally-sanctioned punishment for a criminal offence; hence the English common-law offence of 'false imprisonment', where the imprisonment is a form of detention, which is 'false' because it is not an act of the state pursuant to criminal law. Detention can therefore be either legal or illegal, depending on who does it and the justification. The term is commonly used to cover acts of the state either before an actual prison term has been set but in anticipation of one, as in **pre-trial detention**, called 'remand' in the United Kingdom, or where the deprivation of liberty is the consequence of the detainee's criminal act, but for some reason the state is unwilling to acknowledge that he is being imprisoned as such. Thus it is common to refer to what amount to prison terms for juvenile offenders as 'periods of detention'.

In a somewhat similar way, someone forcibly deprived of freedom and forced to reside in a hospital or treatment centre because of mental health problems is likely to be described as undergoing 'detention'. However, in human rights law, for example in the **European Convention on Human Rights** and its ensuing case law, detention covers all those contexts in which a person is forced to reside in a set place under discipline, whether as a punishment or for other reasons. Although this is logical, it raises problems with regard to legitimate conditions imposed during detention; harsh conditions, which may be acceptable in the actual imprisonment, might not be legitimate in the case of someone being detained, for example, while awaiting deportation as an unsuccessful applicant for political **asylum**. (See also **arrest**.)

Development of personality

Many civil liberties or human rights relate primarily to sheer physical survival or safety, or to other basic human needs, and require very little in the way of philosophical justification. Thus the right not to suffer **torture**, however often abused, and however much, in consequence, it needs to be recognized and enshrined in civil liberty law, is not difficult to justify. The complexities attached to this right are largely about either the conditions, if any exist, under which the right can be abrogated by the state, or the scope of definition. Is it, for example, legitimate to torture a terrorist who has planted a bomb in a school somewhere in a city and will not say which? Can a punishment regime which restricts diet to bread and water be classified as torture? The arguments for other rights, however, are more complex, and require some more general justification; the right to **freedom of speech** cannot be justified on the grounds that a person's life is threatened because he cannot air his views. This sort of right tends to take its justification as a 'civil right' from a procedural necessity; hence the courts have imputed the right to freedom of speech from the prerequisites of parliamentary democracy. There is still another group of widely recognized rights, however, which are neither physically necessary for survival, nor procedurally necessary, such as **religious freedom** and education, yet many human rights codes regard education as a basic right, and go further and demand for parents the right to considerable control over the content and nature of the education (see **parental rights**). There is a strong tendency to link these, and indeed other rights less obviously appropriate, to a justification based on the idea of human personal development.

The language of personal development is 20th-century in origin, but the idea is one of the likely meanings of the famous phrase in the American **Declaration of Independence** that: 'all men . . . are endowed by their creator with certain inalienable rights; that amongst these are life, liberty and the pursuit of happiness . . .' Before the Enlightenment, states took their justification from largely theological grounds; the authorities were there not only to keep the peace, but also to establish the conditions for living a life according to religious values for the transcendent ends of religion. With the diminution of religion to the private realm, states still need some overarching justification, and this is seldom offered as pure hedonism. The liberal state, however, is by definition a value-free state in its aims; it cannot promote any particular vision of life as morally superior, for this would be regarded as itself a breach of rights to equality and independence of faith. States which do not claim to be free of values have a ready basis for their constitutions; the various constitutions of the former USSR made it clear that their purpose was to guarantee a Marxist-based economy, and the Preamble to the 1977 Constitution is a short essay in applied Marxist philosophy. By contrast the liberal democratic state has no such means to justify those rights which go to the purpose of the state itself. The French Fourth Republic's Constitution contrasted itself to the recently overthrown tyrannies, which it described as states seeking to 'degrade the human personality'. The **German Constitution**, drafted for a state to succeed a tyranny, opens with the statement that 'The dignity of man is inviolable', and starts its second article with 'Everybody has the right to self-fulfilment . . .'

Almost any human rights question can be linked to the development of personality. The real force of the commitment on the part of the liberal state is to allow its citizens to exercise choice; the state may not prefer one particular route, and all options that do not infringe another must be allowed to flourish, hence not only rights to educational and religious freedom, but rights to **privacy**, speech rights and so on. Nor is the difficulty restricted to liberal societies in this way. A state may be more directive, or wish to be more associated with a particular creed without wishing to crush all individuality, and will still need some generalized explanation for protecting some rights that do not seem absolutely basic in a physical sense. The particular problem for liberal democracy, however, is that it rests on an antithesis; as liberal values are not necessarily, and not even often, majority preferences, a democratic pressure to intolerance may need to be curbed by human rights legislation. For the justification of these values, the development of human personality serves as a sufficiently impressive concept, while being sufficiently innocuous to serve this function.

Disability

Rights for the disabled are steadily becoming accepted in legislation in most countries, although they do not take their force from inclusion in any generalized codes of human rights. They are **positive rights**, but fall into two categories: rights dealing with provision, which cannot be covered by legislation, and rights relating to discrimination, which are justiciable. In the first category, where disablement rights are held to cover special steps taken to make life easier for the disabled, although like any welfare right they must be regarded as positive rights, they call for actual provisions to be made by the state or other institutions, and as such necessarily clash with all other calls on the public purse. It is generally accepted that such positive provision, however it may be rhetorically lauded by a human rights document, cannot be made justiciable because it would involve the courts in public-policy decisions.

In the second category these rights can be expressed legally as a ban on discrimination against disabled people where the discrimination is irrational. If, for example, a company refused to employ as clerical staff people confined to a wheelchair when there was not serious difficulty in allowing such access to an office, the company would probably be in defiance of a generalized duty not to discriminate in employment. Whether in fact a disabled person managed to get redress for such an act of discrimination would depend on the extent to which supportive legislation, or court **interpretation** of constitutional rights, had developed in his particular jurisdiction. The obvious problem with an approach like this is the over-simplifying of the 'making provisions' as opposed to 'failing to discriminate' dichotomy. Is an employer who could, with some but minimum difficulty, rearrange work schedules to facilitate the employment of the disabled, entitled to claim that any steps that had to be taken which would not be taken for a non-disabled person absolved him of discrimination? Compare the situation where an employee who follows a minority religion is allowed time off on a day when others would not be allowed to take time just because they felt like it. This right to time off, which may well be implied in the **European Convention on Human Rights**, is based on something special about the individual, his specific religious beliefs, which entitle him to a consideration not paid to his co-workers. Such a logic must surely apply to someone who, in all but specified respects, is equally capable of doing a job where the specific difference can be made irrelevant by employer action. Whether such a claim would succeed before, say, the **European Court of Human Rights** or the Canadian Supreme Court is a matter of speculation, but it is clearly within the possible ambit of judicial **discretion**.

Discovery

The right of discovery is not normally seen as a civil liberty or human right in the usual sense. Though discovery rights are an essential part of all legal systems, they are subordinate or pragmatic rights that derive either from statutes or common law as necessary legal tools. Discovery is a litigant's right to see documents and other material in the possession of his opponent that he needs in order to argue his case before a court. As such it is as much a routine matter of civil or criminal law as of civil rights law. Corporate lawyers, for example, spend a huge amount of time trawling through the papers and memos of businesses their clients are suing, looking for material on which to base their case. Discovery in this sense can also cover, for example, the right to force employees of such an opposing company to answer questions about their doings, and to swear to such accounts in affidavits; the amount of material a court will authorize a litigant to demand in discovery is usually a discretionary matter, and can have a major impact on a trial. In the context of civil liberties discovery is equally vital, most obviously in criminal trials, where a defendant's right to see the material the prosecution is going to rely on can vitally affect the fairness of the proceedings (see **fair trial**). Consequently any doctrine of **natural justice** or **due process** may entail very extensive discovery rights for defendants, and there has been a tendency to make these rights asymmetric in criminal trials in a way that would never be acceptable in civil litigation, because traditionally the prosecution has not been accorded equal rights to know details of the defendant's case. This comes from the general doctrine of the **right to silence**, and also from more general constitutional protection of the right to **privacy**, and such matters are delicate balances which can change from time to time. The United Kingdom has recently shifted considerably towards giving the prosecution what amounts to stronger discovery rights in the abolition of the complete right to silence, as displayed in the new police caution (see **caution on arrest**). In other areas of human rights litigation discovery against the government is both vital and contentious. Governments everywhere try to keep much of their working secret on grounds of national security or executive privilege, involving in the UK, for example, the extensive use of Public Interest Immunity certificates. Yet without the ability to see what information a minister had when making a decision, perhaps a decision to deny political **asylum**, or to refuse release on license to a prisoner serving a life sentence, it is almost impossible to demonstrate that an abuse of discretion has taken place.

Discretion

Discretion exists in all legal systems to a greater or lesser degree. Sometimes it is intentional, as when the law recognizes that a particular decision can, in the end, only be a matter of human judgement and nominates a specific individual or office holder to exercise this, with only the sketchiest guidance, or none. One example is the prerogative of mercy exercised by heads of state in criminal law systems, especially over capital punishment; the special nature of this discretion often leads it to be described not as a legal power, but as a power to be applied when the legal system has run its course. A more common example would be in family law, where decisions over whether a child can be taken from its natural parents for its own good come in the end to be matters of judgement, where a judge exercises his discretion in a way that cannot, if he acts in a formally proper way, be challenged. A similar type of discretion is when a legal system gives certain powers to be exercised by a court in a discretionary mode; that is, no one has a right to insist on action by a court, but they may apply for it. So the right to have a decision of an administrative body reviewed by a court as a matter of the court's judicial review power is discretionary in the United Kingdom (see **judicial review (United Kingdom)**, and there is no absolute right to such a review.

The core sense in which legal discretion becomes a matter for human rights is when a person challenges the decision of an executive body to refuse to grant him some right, under welfare legislation perhaps, or in some area involving **freedom of speech** or **freedom of assembly**. Such decision-making is sometimes seen as **quasi-judicial**, and courts may intervene to ensure that proper procedures have been used, although they will not make a different decision on the content of the case. The English **public law** doctrine here is to apply a test of 'reasonableness'; could the official, if he had considered everything he should by law consider, and had properly understood his duties, have reached his conclusion about the applicant's case reasonably? The court does not need to think he has come to the right decision, and may not substitute their own judgment for his, as long as his decision, however wrong-headed, is one a reasonable office-holder could, in this sense, reach (see **Wednesbury reasonableness**). Clearly such discretion, and modern states to a large extent run by such discretion, can all too easily be exercised in a prejudiced or discriminatory way. It is particularly a problem where state powers curtail basic rights of assembly, of free movement into and out of countries, of speech and so on, but it effects **positive rights** under legislation even more so. The principal tool courts have is to insist that administrative decision-makers give written reasons to justify their actions, based on this test of reasonable connection between the facts and the decision. In the USA the concept of rational connection between a governmental aim and policy as a test of when rights are unfairly abridged has been developed with considerable forensic skill.

Discrimination (see **age discrimination**, *de facto* **discrimination** and **racial discrimination**)

Divisional court

All three divisions of the High Court in England, the Chancery, Family and Queen's Bench Divisions, can be the basis of a divisional court. In the realm of **civil liberties** a reference to 'the divisional court' means a bench of two or more judges from the Queen's Bench Division. This is the most common forum for a civil rights challenge to the executive, where a complainant will seek either a writ of **habeas corpus** (though this can be issued initially by a single judge), or one of the remedies available under the judicial review process, namely the writs of **mandamus**, prohibition or *certiorari*, or an **injunction** or **declaration**. Appeal lies from a divisional court to the Court of Appeal, and a divisional court also hears appeals in some circumstances from magistrates courts.

Double jeopardy

Double jeopardy means that a person can neither be tried nor punished twice for the same offence. It is extended to mean that no one can be forced to face charges twice for the same actions, unless the crimes are clearly different and not alternative ways of prosecuting for substantially the same offence. So one might possibly be tried for murder, acquitted, and then tried for the robbery during which the victim died, but one could not be tried once for actual bodily harm, acquitted, and then tried again for common assault, both arising from the same street fight. The right in question is not as clear cut as it seems, because trials can be halted and dropped, and the same charge brought up again. Furthermore, one can face a civil case for an offence after having been acquitted of the relevant criminal offence, as many crimes are also civil offences. This is more than an idle possibility, because the standard of proof required in a civil case, that the guilt be demonstrated 'on the balance of probabilities', is notably lower than the 'beyond reasonable doubt' test in a criminal trial. The importance of the right against double jeopardy is that it prevents oppressive behaviour by a state which might be prepared to keep on trying to imprison a dissident. There is no logical reason why, if one can ask an appeal court to hear new evidence and reverse a conviction, the state should not be able to re-try someone acquitted the first time because of paucity of evidence, but it is traditionally felt that asymmetry is legitimate when there are historical reasons to doubt the *bona fides* of the state. The right is specified, among other places, in the **Fifth Amendment** to the US Constitution and by Protocol 7 (Article 4) of the **European Convention of Human Rights**, and is recognized in most other **written constitutions** or common law systems. It should be noted that the right not only prevents a second trial for someone acquitted, but also for someone convicted, so the state cannot decide to re-try on a more serious charge having gained a conviction on a lesser charge.

Dual citizenship

Some states allow their citizens to acquire or retain the **citizenship** of another state, and the most common source of dual citizenship is by birth to parents of different nationalities. Some states, including the USA, automatically treat anyone born within their borders as having their citizenship, regardless of the citizenship status of the parents. Dual citizenship can be restricted by incumbent legal obligations, so, for example, someone initially enjoying two citizenships may lose one if he refuses to return to that country to do national service. Other countries will accept duality of citizenship from birth until the age of maturity, but require a choice to be made in their favour, and the renunciation of the other nationality, if their citizenship is to be retained. This was the situation in the USA until such an automatic loss of citizenship was deemed unconstitutional. Having a citizenship in a country other than that in which a person resides as a national may confer little in the way of rights in that country, and in particular will not usually allow voting registration there. A new sense of dual citizenship is developing, where an individual can have both a national citizenship and a citizen-like legal status in a supranational entity such as the European Union, and this may come to be as important as dual citizenship in two states. In this sense US citizens have dual citizenship, belonging both to the state in which they reside, and to the USA itself.

Due process

The term due process is fundamental to the nature of relations between the individual and the state, and therefore to all human rights jurisprudence. It comes from the **Fifth Amendment** to the US Bill of Rights (see **Bill of Rights (USA)**), which states that nobody shall 'be deprived of life, **liberty**, or **property**, without due process of law', and is reiterated in the **Fourteenth Amendment**, forbidding any of the US states from abrogating the right. Applications of the due process clause refer to **procedural rights** and are refered to as procedural due process, while the term substantive due process is used for the legal theory by which the US Constitution is taken to protect a set of rights (the set varies from judge to judge), which are seen as in some way fundamental and logically prior to the Constitution itself, in which they are not mentioned. Procedural due process, governing matters like the entitlement to a **fair trial**, with all its implications, and rules governing proper decision-making procedures by administrative agencies, is what the idea of due process would normally mean to anyone outside the US legal tradition, and arguably all that was intended by the framers of the Constitution. Since the late 19th century US jurists have developed the due process clause into a complex substantive code of what actual ends the state may not pursue, rather than a merely procedural code about how to pursue them.

Substantive due process as a formulated doctrine derives from a powerful dissenting opinion by Justice Stephen J. Field (1816–99) in the Slaughterhouse case of 1873 (see also **choice of occupation**). The case involved a challenge to the US state of Louisiana's attempt to give a monopoly to a particular slaughterhouse so as to centralize animal slaughtering on public-health grounds. The majority of the court accepted this as a legitimate exercise of the state's inherent power to regulate on public-health grounds, but the dissenters held that the action was a breach of the due process clause in the Fifth and Fourteenth Amendments. This clause had previously been interpreted as a matter of procedural rights, but Field argued, and the court held in later cases, that certain basic unwritten rights pre-existed the Constitution, and were essentially 'packaged' into the 'life, liberty and property' trio. In the Slaughterhouse case the right Field discovered was the right to exercise one's trade freely, which was denied where a state created a monopoly. Whether freedom of occupation is part of one's property or a basic liberty did not need to be spelled out; the point is that virtually anything can be loaded into the phrase in this way. Essentially the argument was that such a deprivation could be applied only as a punishment for a specified crime, hence the 'due process of law' aspect. Taken to an extreme such an argument could be used to hold income tax unconstitutional, and indeed some theorists, such as Robert **Nozick**, have argued that income tax is forced labour, which would indeed be forbidden by the Constitution except as a criminal penalty.

After Slaughterhouse the Court regularly, though not invariably, struck down state legislation which regulated the economy using this technique, in pursuit of the goal of a free enterprise culture. Naturally not all regulation could be seen as unjustified, and the Supreme Court struggled to find a regulating principle. It adopted a rough idea of 'reasonableness', which questioned whether the state (or occasionally federal) law was reasonably connected to a legitimate aim, but the Constitution is no more specific on legitimate aims than it is on appropriate methods, and the doctrine was inevitably both patchy and, throughout, deeply ideological. Substantive due process as applied to economic regulation died away as the pressing need for economic regulation after the First World War, and more particularly the Great Depression of the late 1920s and 1930s, persuaded a new generation of judges that only legislative and executive agencies were suitable for this sort of policy-making. In particular the clash between the Supreme Court and President Franklin D. Roosevelt's 'New Deal', with its host of federal regulatory laws, was one the Court could not win, and the economic substantive due process era ended in 1937 when a minimum wage law was upheld in an opinion in which the Chief Justice specifically noted that 'the Constitution does not speak of freedom of contract'.

In other areas substantive due process as a way of recognizing rights that seem fundamental but cannot be found in the text has certainly survived, especially for social rights such as the right to **privacy**, and **abortion** rights.

These are justified on the grounds that the Bill of Rights has a number of 'penumbral' rights, and the Ninth Amendment, which states: 'The enumeration in the Constitution of certain rights shall not be construed to deny or disparage others retained by the people' is cited in support of this. In some ways the substantive due process doctrine takes the place of the technique of **imputation** used by other courts interpreting documents which are inadequate in their precision about human rights. The history of the doctrine goes to show, however, how very much subject to cultural interpretations apparently consensual rights may be. Given this history, it is not surprising that many otherwise highly 'liberal' thinkers on the political left are deeply suspicious of entrenched **bills of rights** as potential tools for conservative courts.

Dworkin

Ronald Dworkin (1931–) has been the Professor of Jurisprudence in the University of Oxford since the equally famous H. L. A. **Hart** retired in 1969. The irony of this is that Dworkin's claim to fame as a legal philosopher, and his reputation is unmatched in Western legal cultures, is largely built on his outright opposition to Hart, who in his own time was the international standard bearer of legal positivism. Dworkin's legal philosophy is rich and complex, and is set out in a series of major books, the earliest of which is *Taking Rights Seriously*, with *Law's Empire* arguably the most important of later works. Rich though it is, Dworkin's thought has often been characterized as amounting to the working out in detail of the values of East Coast US liberalism, and there is certainly a considerable amount of congruence between his views and that strand of thought, not only in substantive values, but also in methodology. US legal thought is relatively comfortable with the role of the US Supreme Court in interpreting the Constitution, particularly when it is in one of its counter-majoritarian modes of upholding human rights and **civil liberties**. Dworkin has spent much effort in justifying such judicial law-making, and in protecting it from attack as an exercise of mere and uncontrolled **discretion**. For Dworkin, and this is where he most conflicts with legal positivism, there are, in some sense or other, 'correct' answers to all legal problems; for him, although judges naturally can make mistakes, their actions in interpreting vague rules, or ambiguous, even silent, constitutional texts, are not the making and enforcement of private values through discretion, but the uncovering of these correct answers.

Dworkin's ideas on the nature of law itself bring him into conflict with the legal positivism expounded by Hart in his classic book *The Concept of Law*. In keeping with the original Benthamite ideas expressed by John Austen (see **Bentham**), Hart had defined law as consisting of various types of rules, with the implication that rules can sometimes clash, and that they may 'run out', that is, they may fail to give any answer to some problem not covered by legislation. In contrast, Dworkin insists that law consists primarily of principles, not rules. Principles, according to Dworkin, do not clash, but have varying weights, so that where two principles would appear to give different answers, the one with the greater weight is the guiding one, but the other is not 'broken'. Secondly principles can always be derived from various sources, and are not limited to formally recognized rules in statute or common law, so that a judge can always generate an answer. The problems with Dworkin's theories are manifold, though to his supporters in the **rights jurisprudence** school he is favoured for giving a secure foundation to human rights, which he regards as absolute limitations on legislation, thus dismissing utilitarian tendencies to see rights merely as short-hand policy statements. He is also popular with those who are uncomfortable with the apparently undemocratic implications of positivism, in which unelected judges, through the use of barely controlled judicial discretion, act as legislators in their own right.

Although Dworkin's work may fit modern US liberalism, he is no closer to traditional American legal thinking than to European positivism, because much 20th-century US legal thought has been committed to a distinctly positivist position of their own under the label of judicial realism. At the same time European currents of rights jurisprudence, which treat rights as fundamental and pre-dating political systems, are not necessarily happier with Dworkin's approach, because they base themselves on a natural law tradition which is often at odds with liberalism.

E

Entrenchment

Entrenchment is the process of making a law or code harder to repeal or amend than ordinary legislation. A constitution cannot, usually, be altered by its own provision for the legislative repeal of statutes made under it, and most theorists would question whether a document subject to the legislature were really a constitution at all. There are, however, examples of such constitutions: the Constitution of the French Third Republic was just a single act of the National Assembly, and what passes for the Israeli Constitution is a set of laws passed by the Knesset, originally set up as a constitutional convention and later transmuted into a governing legislature. In the same way there have been many attempts to treat some basic laws, typically codes of human rights established by a normal legislative process, as more fundamental and less alterable than other acts of the same body, and afford them special protection. Most typically a parliament will pass a piece of legislation which itself demands that the law to be entrenched should be altered in the future only by a two-thirds vote of the parliament, or whatever proportion would suffice to make it harder to repeal than an ordinary law.

Logically entrenchment is impossible. As long as the constitutional rules of a system include, *de jure* or *de facto*, the rule that a parliament may not bind its successors, then all that a future, less civil-libertarian, parliament has to do is to repeal, by an ordinary vote, the entrenching legislation, thus making the law sought to be entrenched itself vulnerable to repeal by an ordinary majority. In substance entrenchment is little more than an empty piece of legal formalism. If a parliament once goes through with an attempt to entrench, a great deal of political symbolism would be invested in the special legislation, and an attempt to change it would be a very weighty act, something no government could attempt unless it was very sure indeed of the popularity of undoing the civil rights in question. Ultimately, however, human rights protection always depends on public support, and a public uninterested in protecting civil rights would be quite unmoved by parliamentary game-playing. Entrenchment is useful in preventing a government with only weak support from casual infringement of **civil liberties** or other constitutional rights, but it cannot protect those rights or liberties as effectively as a constitution quite separately created by an extra-parliamentary process.

Equal opportunities

Equal opportunities are protected by legislation in most developed countries, and by some supranational organizations like the European Union, and this is best developed in the area of **equal pay** for equal work. Equal opportunities, however, must be understood in the technical legal sense of a ban on *de jure* discrimination according to race, religion, ethnic origin, sex, and increasingly in the USA, age, marital status and sexual orientation (see also **age discrimination**, **racial discrimination** and **religious freedom**). The term equal opportunities does not, however, refer to what has been its historical origin as a political goal ever since Napoleon and his idea of the 'career open to talents', that is, a guaranteed equal starting point for everyone regardless of their class or socio-economic status. Until and unless some attempt is made to promote a legislative guarantee of genuine equality to develop one's talent, or prohibitions on methods, like private schooling, which give some a much better starting point than others of the same talent, the overwhelmingly most important source of social inequality and discrimination will go uncorrected. Yet it is extremely difficult to see how such **positive rights** could ever be incorporated into either **bills of rights** or equal protection doctrines that have become increasingly successful at fighting *de jure* discrimination based on externally visible physical characteristics.

Equal Opportunities Commission (EOC)

The Equal Opportunities Commission (EOC) was set up by the British government under the **Sex Discrimination Act** of 1975, to counter sex discrimination in a similar way to the work of the **Commission for Racial Equality (CRE)** against **racial discrimination**. The EOC may be asked directly by the government to carry out research or investigation on some policy area or problem of sex equality, or it may set itself such targets. Its primary duty is to monitor the workings of the Sex Discrimination Act and the **Equal Pay Act** of 1970, and to offer suggestions for amendments. Recently, however, the EOC has assumed an additional role, to the considerable displeasure of the government, claiming standing before the courts to bring cases against the government for failing to implement properly European Union legislation on sex equality matters. Somewhat to their own surprise, the House of Lords accepted the EOC's right to standing, and in a major case agreed with them and found for the EOC and the original plaintiffs in a case involving the rights of part-time women workers to full pay-equality with men. The more the EOC develops this role of public champion the more effectively equality provisions will be implemented. The CRE has, from its inception, taken on this role, and many of the more important court victories on the racial discrimination front have been fought at its instigation. The difference between the two bodies is that while both are simply creatures of legislation, and therefore controllable by the government, it would be politically much harder for a government to risk being seen as opposed to the CRE than the EOC which, by the nature of its work, runs the risk of assuming the role of a champion of the European Union as much as of underpaid women.

Equal pay

Of all the practical steps made towards attacking discrimination in society, the idea of a right to equal pay for equal work for men and women is both the longest-established as a political goal, and the one most concretely legislated for, at least in Europe. Even if they did not otherwise wish to do so, all member countries of the European Union now have to implement effective equal pay acts under European Commission regulations. Long before the Commission had made serious moves to insist on this, the **European Court of Justice**, in a relatively early case, had interpreted the **Treaty of Rome** itself to require equal pay between men and women. In the United Kingdom the basic legislation is the 1970 **Equal Pay Act** and the 1975 **Sex Discrimination Act**, which has a complex set of tests to identify not only direct but also indirect discrimination, which occurs when an employer pays two groups differently, with the groups not overtly defined on gender lines. If far fewer women than men can satisfy the discriminating test, the resulting differential treatment will be a breach of the Act unless a good reason can be demonstrated for the test result which does not itself revolve around gender. Equal pay is governed in the USA and Canada both by legislation and by constitutional implications drawn from the US Bill of Rights (see **Bill of Rights (USA)**) and the **Canadian Charter of Rights and Freedoms**. In the USA the main thrust to equal pay comes from the Equal Employment Opportunity Commission set up by the 1964 **Civil Rights Act**. Equal pay is a portmanteau term for equality of economic recompense for work, because the legislation in most, if not all, cases also requires equality of pay-related matters like pension rights and retirement ages, though protection of these has required more forceful intervention from the European Commission and Court of Justice than the basic pay principle.

Equal Pay Act

The Equal Pay Act of 1970 and the **Sex Discrimination Act** of 1975 are the two major pieces of British legislation introduced in an effort to tackle the problem of sex discrimination. In addition, there is a set of directives from the Council of Europe which has legislative force in the United Kingdom. Originally the Equal Pay Act required that women be paid the same as men when doing 'the same or broadly similar work' if one of two conditions applied: either the man and woman must be covered by common terms and conditions, or the men and women are doing work rated as equivalent by a study carried out by the employer to measure this under various headings like effort, skill, decision-level needed and so on. There have been a host of court cases before both the British courts and the **European Court of Justice** to work out the details of this essentially simple legislative requirement. Amendments were adopted in 1983 because of European Commission pressure on the UK properly to fulfil the terms of the Equal Pay Directive of 1975, which had been intended to reinforce the existing equal-pay obligation under the **Treaty of Rome**. Subsequently the employer could not avoid the obligation to pay similar but different jobs equally by failing to carry out the job-evaluation study, though such studies have often been used for the opposite purpose of demonstrating that jobs are not equivalent, to avoid an obligation to give **equal pay**. The original version of the Act was a political compromise; employers, represented by the Confederation of British Industry (CBI), wanted to conform to the minimum Treaty of Rome definition, which was equal pay for equal work, while the trade unions called for equal pay for work of equal value, the standard recommended by the **International Labour Organization (ILO)**. Although the Act did immediately make a considerable difference, problems of comparability continue to plague the issue, and it will be a generation, by some estimates, before true parity of wages is achieved. The Equal Pay Act covers only contractual terms, and consequently many peripheral issues arise under the Sex Discrimination Act.

Equal protection

Equal protection by the laws is guaranteed by the **Fourteenth Amendment** to the US Constitution, which provides in Section 1 that no state shall 'deny to any person within its jurisdiction the equal protection of the laws'. This apparently simple phrase, along with the **due process** of law clause, has played a crucial role in developing and protecting human rights in the USA ever since. Initially the Amendment, passed to protect former slaves in the Southern states, was interpreted in a highly restrictive and purely procedural manner. Legal protection was limited to outright and intentional discrimination, and the legislation was easy to circumvent. This was more than adequately demonstrated by the history of racial segregation, especially in the issue of education in the Southern states; the impact of the equal protection clause was initially blunted by the Supreme Court, whose ruling in *Plessey v. Ferguson* in 1896 held that it was constitutionally acceptable for states to insist on racial segregation as long as the facilities provided for both blacks and whites were equal. Although *Plessey* involved segregated public transport, the main implication of the ruling was on education, and *Plessey* was not properly overruled until **Brown v. Board** in 1954. The equal protection clause had little impact in protecting minorities, therefore, in the first 50 years or so of its existence, though it had significance in another area; because it protects 'persons' rather than citizens it could be used, along with the due process clause, to protect corporations, which in law are persons, from state economic regulation. It was the heightened awareness of **racial discrimination** and persecution during the Second World War that helped revive the clause, and from the 1940s onwards it became an increasingly sharp tool against discrimination, with the development of complex tests regarding the **level of scrutiny** which courts will apply to prima facie discriminatory legislation. Not until the 1960s, with the passing of the 1964 **Civil Rights Act** and its support in the Supreme Court, was racially-segregated education completely ended *de jure*, although it continued for some time as a *de facto* practice.

The equal protection doctrine has emerged as a powerful weapon against all forms of discrimination because the clause came to be used as a method for examining the internal structure of policies. Essentially it works by holding up any categorization used in a statute to distinguish between people and asking whether the basis for the categorization, sex, age, race, ethnic origin and so on, is either illegitimate altogether, or, if legitimate, sufficiently closely related to a sufficiently important public policy goal. The main thrust of the doctrine is to treat all categorization as dubious and requiring justification, as demonstrated in a commonplace test case. In *Craig v. Boren* (1976) two young men challenged an Oklahoma law which allowed women over the age of 18 to buy beer with a low alcohol content but forbade men to do so until they were 21. It was claimed that this age categorization was an unconstitutional infringement of the equal protection clause. The state defended its policy on the grounds that it was aimed at drink-related car accidents and that men in the 18–21 age group were many times more likely to be involved in such accidents than women. The court upheld the men's claim on the grounds that there was not sufficiently strong a relationship between the method of the policy and its aim. Technically the court was raising the stakes of what has come to be known as the level of scrutiny test where gender classifications are involved. Generally a statute involving classifications which have become politically sensitive will be held to breach the equal protection clause more easily than one that does not. The absolute bar is on racially-based classifications, which are seen as intrinsically denying equal protection, with gender-based distinctions coming a close second.

Equal Rights Amendment

The Equal Rights Amendment, usually referred to simply as the ERA, was a proposed amendment to the US Constitution advocated by women's rights and feminist groups in the USA during the 1970s. **Civil liberties** actions in the 1960s by women's rights groups like the National Organization of Women (NOW), established in 1966, had aimed to persuade the courts to grant the same **level of scrutiny** status to gender that they have to race. As the ERA would have been a full constitutional rule, and as it would have been more specific than any judicial pronouncement could be, sex would have been even more firmly entrenched as an unacceptable basis for any legislative policy than race. A similar amendment had first been introduced in Congress in 1923, but had made no progress. The ERA was passed easily by Congress in 1972, boosted by a wave of support for feminist issues, and went on for ratification by the states as required by the Constitution. In the early 1980s the US political climate began to turn more conservative, and when the final deadline for ratification was reached in 1982, the amendment failed to get the necessary three-quarters majority, with only 35 out of the necessary 38 states voting in favour, some having rescinded their former approval. Apart from the political move to the right, the amendment encountered a problem common to attempts to abolish sex discrimination: equal rights would mean overturning policies, administrative practices and legal doctrines already in operation, such as earlier retirement ages, preferential motor insurance rates and alimony orders from courts, specifically designed to protect womens interests. Many US women were unwilling to put their practical interests second to a status issue, and preferred the, arguably, patronizing protection to the absolute abandonment of gender labelling in policy. Despite the failure of the ERA, however, many US court decisions have come close to imposing a standard equivalent to its proposals.

European Commission on Human Rights (see **European Court of Human Rights**)

European Convention on Human Rights

The Convention for the Protection of Human Rights and Fundamental Freedoms, normally referred to more simply as the European Convention on Human Rights, was drafted by the Council of Europe and adopted in 1950. Acceptance of the Convention, of the jurisdiction of the **European Court of Human Rights (ECHR)** in interpreting it, and of the right of individuals to petition the ECHR for protection, are now obligations of membership in the Council. All but two member states, the United Kingdom and Ireland, have incorporated the Convention into their domestic law so their own courts can apply it where an individual claims a breach of one of the rights it contains. (In 1997 it appeared likely that the election of a new Labour government in the UK would lead to the Convention being incorporated in that country.) As a citizen can petition the ECHR itself only after all remedies available in his home country have failed to satisfy him, in a state where the Convention has not been incorporated he may not be able to get final judgment of the case against his government until years after the event; this also accounts, in part, for the large number of cases in which the UK has been found at fault by the ECHR. An unusual feature of the Convention is its wide scope, which allows one state to petition the ECHR about the actions of another state. Though seldom used, this procedure was one of the main aims of the drafters, who, in the aftermath of the Second World War and conscious of the nature of the pre-war fascist regimes in Europe, saw the Convention as a form of alarm system to alert European states to wrongdoing by one of their members.

The Convention consists of 66 Articles in five Sections and a series of protocols further defining and extending the authority of the Convention and the ECHR. However, it is the Preamble and Section 1, which consists of 11 substantive Articles protecting broadly defined rights, and seven procedural Articles ensuring the viability of the protections for the basic rights, which are of most interest. (The remaining four Sections of the Convention concern institutional matters.) The rights protected vary in theoretical nature, in broadness of definition and in detail. The full text of Section 1 of the Convention is included in the Appendix. Its rights and freedoms include: the **right to life**, freedom from **torture** and **slavery**, the right to **liberty** and the **security of the person**, rights to a **fair trial** and other **due process** rights, and a set of more **positive rights**, including **freedom of assembly**, **freedom of speech**, **religious freedom** and the **right to family life**. The rights are not expressed in absolute terms, and some Articles, both in the Convention itself and in its Protocols, contain a phrase permitting the right just defined to be breached where necessary for national security or public interests. Article 15 expressly allows the rights to be put in abeyance during times of national emergency, but defines such steps very carefully.

In practice the ECHR has been expansionist rather than restrictive in its interpretation of rights on most occasions, and has not seemed unduly worried by holding governments in breach of those rights. Nevertheless, the articles of the Convention are necessarily often vague, because of the problem of expressing values which may vary considerably between member states according to their cultures and historical experience, and the ECHR has tried to allow for this without making the rights entirely relative. As intended, the Convention has developed naturally through both formal changes to its authority and also interpretation by the ECHR, and is steadily growing in importance. The recent extension of Council of Europe membership to Eastern European states, themselves recently recommitted to liberal legal values, can only enhance its status. Most important of all, the **European Court of Justice** has effectively incorporated the provisions of the Convention into European Union law, giving them added impact on those states who are members of both the Union and the Council. From its initiation the Convention has had more practical effect than the UN **Universal Declaration on Human Rights** or the other regional conventions, largely due to the ECHR's power to award damages to plaintiffs, as well as the need of member states to reform their legislation to retain membership of the Council when found in breach of the Convention. (See also **incorporation, treaty rights**.)

European Court of Human Rights

The European Court of Human Rights (ECHR) and the European Commission of Human Rights (the Commission) are the two parts of the enforcement machinery of the **European Convention on Human Rights**. The Court consists of one judge for each of the member states of the Council, sitting in benches of nine; the state arraigned before the court always has its judge on the bench. Decision is by majority voting on the bench, but dissents usually number no more than one or two judges, with the judge from the country which is a party more often than not in dissent if the majority finds against his country. This situation is quite usual in international law bodies, and has not detracted from the authority of the Court, because when a state is held to be in breach of the Convention and its national judge sides with the majority the impact is all the more marked. Judges are elected by the European Parliament, which chooses one from a list of three names presented by the member state, and they serve for nine years. The nominees are usually either distinguished lawyers or judges in their own countries, and may not serve in their national governments or judiciaries during their term of office.

The ECHR is the last stage of a petition under the Convention. A petition is first examined by the European Commission of Human Rights, usually described as a group of independent experts, but essentially comprising professionals of similar experience to the judges. They first vet petitions to see if they appear, on the surface, to merit examination, and reject a good number at that stage. On average only about 15% of the petitions submitted pass this first stage, but that still leaves some 200 cases each year. Once a case has been admitted, the Commission examines the facts and law, and seeks to arrive at a friendly settlement. If this is not possible it publishes a formal report, including its decision as to the rights, and its recommendations. Once the report is published either the Commission itself or any party to the dispute may refer the case to the ECHR, which is not bound to agree with the Commission, though in the majority of cases it does. It was agreed in October 1993, through a new protocol (11) to the Convention, that the ECHR and the Commission would be replaced by a single Court of Human Rights, and, in October 1997, the Council of Europe announced that the new Court would commence work in November 1998.

The ECHR has taken pains to establish that it is not to be treated as yet a further stage of appeal within the national court hierarchies. It will not overturn a national court decision just because it seems to be wrong, and is unwilling even to impose its own interpretation of national law. Only if the member state appears clearly to be in breach of the Convention will it act, and its rulings are declaratory of this breach. The Court does not try to tell member states what they must do to remedy the defect in their law, considering that to be legitimately only the concern of the state itself, though it does award damages, and its decisions are binding in international law. Technically decisions of the ECHR are binding only on the country in question, and there is no strongly developed doctrine of precedent, but most member states will examine their own legislation and try to bring it in line with the new understanding of the Convention rather than wait to be judged themselves.

In its interpretation the Court tries to apply generalized values and standards seen to be more or less universally accepted among all liberal democratic states, while being as tolerant as possible of the different legal and political cultures represented. Despite this it necessarily shows a bias in methodology, and arguably in substance, towards the code law rather than common law understanding of human rights law, given the preponderance of members from that tradition in the Council of Europe.

European Court of Justice

The European Court of Justice (ECJ) is properly known as the Court of Justice of the European Communities, formerly of the European Economic Community, and was created by Article 4 of the **Treaty of Rome** in 1957 as one of four equal institutions, along with the Council, the Commission and the Parliament. It has developed so that, in its own sphere, it is equally powerful with the first two, and notably more powerful than the Parliament. The Court has one judge appointed from each member state, and several Advocates-General. These latter have no equivalent in the court structure of the common law world, but act in a similar way to various officers known to code law countries, such as the *Commissaire du gouvernement* in French

administrative law. They vet each case accepted for hearing and give an independent reasoned opinion to the Court on how the case should be handled. The idea is to have arguments made to help the Court, in addition to those made by counsel on behalf of the litigants. Though in no way binding, the opinions of the Advocates-General are very frequently followed and always treated with great respect by the Court; several Advocates-General have subsequently been appointed as full judges.

The ECJ has a rather complex jurisdiction, because its rules on *locus standi*, though not as generous as those of the **European Court of Human Rights**, are nevertheless more open than many national supreme courts. Any member state may take any other member state to the Court and complain that it is failing to abide by its treaty obligations, and similarly the Commission may take any member state to the Court on the same grounds. In addition, any one of the other three institutions can bring a case against another for trespassing on its treaty role, and, though rare, such cases have been brought; in the latter instance the ECJ acts rather as a constitutional court does in a country with a separation of powers doctrine in its constitution. None of these examples of the Court's jurisdiction directly involves individual citizens of the member states.

There are two routes by which citizens can bring matters to the Court. One, of little interest in the context of this book, is where an individual (legal or real) challenges a regulation or directive of the Commission which is directly addressed to him. Thus were the Commission to issue a rule that directly affected, say, a livestock transporter under the Common Agricultural Policy, the transporter company could challenge it. The most relevant part of the jurisdiction for the purposes of this book, however, comes under **Article 177**, and such matters are often referred to as 'Article 177 proceedings'. Under this Article a citizen involved in litigation in a national court against either another person or his government, may ask his court to refer some matter involving an **interpretation** of the Treaty or of Community legislation to the ECJ for a preliminary ruling, which, if granted, is binding on the national courts. Agreeing to do this is usually optional for most national courts, but becomes compulsory if the case has reached the limits of appeal in the national system. While this procedure may sound innocuous, it can be very powerful because it entails asking the ECJ if a national law adequately protects rights the citizen has under Community law. Where relevant Community standards exist, say on matters like **equal pay**, a decision of the ECJ may impose a duty on a government to recognize and protect a citizen's rights more fully than they have been prepared to do. In this way a form of **judicial review** by a supranational court has come into being and, in the case of the United Kingdom which completely lacks an internal doctrine of judicial review, a major, if limited, constitutional change has been effected. The national courts have, in the main, not sought to avoid the overarching power, even though they have thereby become less sovereign than previously.

75

Initially the French higher courts attempted to avoid such references, but even they have now come into line. An example of how powerful the ECJ can be is given by the Factortame case in the UK in 1990, where a foreign company from another member state protested against a British statute, which they claimed breached their rights. They insisted that the House of Lords not only hear the case, but grant an **injunction** against the government preventing the act being implemented until a judgment from the ECJ had been obtained. Much against their will, the idea of an injunction against the government at that time being quite novel in English law, the House of Lords nevertheless issued one, and in due course the ECJ ruled that the English statute was in breach of treaty obligations, so it could never be put into effect.

As yet, the only kind of rights clearly protected by the ECJ's jurisdiction are economic in character, as fits the origins of the European Union. However, the ECJ has announced that it regards the **European Convention on Human Rights** as having binding force in the interpretation of Community legislation, and therefore in questions of clashes between national legislation and Community-based rights, and this can result only in a further strengthening of the standards encapsulated in the Convention. The ECJ has made no attempt to hide the fact that it sees itself as effectively a supreme court for Europe, and is fully intent on developing a European-wide common law on all matters within its ever-increasing remit. Though unpopular with some member governments, the ECJ's powers have, if anything, increased with the Maastricht Treaty, which now gives it direct powers to fine offending member states, as well as awarding damages.

F

Fair Trial

The idea of a fair trial is central to human rights doctrine, not only as a right in itself, but because without this one right, all others are at risk; if the state is unfairly advantaged in the trial process, it cannot be prevented in the courts from abusing all other rights. It is not easy to reach agreement on what constitutes fairness in trials, although some elements are common to most definitions of **due process** (the more generalized category of rights covering fair trials). Thus the natural-justice doctrines of an impartial judge (and, where applicable, jury) and the right to be heard, to make one's defence, are obvious. Disagreement arises over the exact procedure. Some insist that it must involve **jury trial**, but, outside the criminal process of the common law, juries in the English sense are rare, and this does not lead to serious doubts about the fairness of all other trial processes. Allowing the accused in a criminal trial the right to make a defence is often equated with the right to be heard, which in itself is often taken to imply the right to be legally represented, through some system of **legal aid** if necessary; however, most legal-aid systems cannot begin to afford the quality or sheer quantity of legal talent open to the state in its prosecuting team (see also **right to counsel**). For much of the history of English criminal law the defendant was not allowed to give evidence in his own case, giving rise to the development of the doctrine of the **right to silence**, and it could be argued that the advent of free legal aid to defendants has made the right to silence no longer necessary to a fair trial. The problems, and there are many more, arise because, despite its surface plausibility, the idea of 'fairness' in a trial should not be taken literally, in the sense of there being a 'level playing field' on which the best side will win. This analogy is inevitable given the Anglo-American adversarial trial system, where the aim is not to find the truth, but to select the better of two arguments against some doctrine of weight of evidence. What a fair trial means therefore depends on a prior choice between inquisitorial truth-finding and adversarial case-testing.

Federalism

It is not purely a historical accident that the countries where liberal democratic protection of human rights is most advanced have often been federations. Federations, like the USA, modern Germany, and one of the possible futures for the European Union, necessarily require **written constitutions** to set out the division of responsibilities and powers between the subordinate provincial-level governments and the national government. Equally they need some form of constitutional court to decide on disputes between these governmental units. In such a context it is highly likely that constitution drafters, already committed to the idea of limits on legitimate government power, will append some form of a **bill of rights**, placing further limits on what one or more levels of government can do even within what would otherwise be their legitimate sphere of activity. This does not have to be the case. Australia is a federal system with a High Court empowered to carry out **judicial review**, indeed one deliberately modelled in part on the US Supreme Court, but the constitution-makers there chose not to have a bill of rights. This has led, in recent years, to the High Court indulging in judicial **interpretation** to try to read one into the Constitution. Nevertheless, once the idea that government power must be limited is part of the political culture, along with the idea that it is acceptable for a non-elected court to decide fundamental political questions, it is highly probable that human rights will come to be protected more efficiently than in a political system where the idea of uncontrolled central power is taken to be the constitutional norm. The various forms and doctrines of federalism are, however, largely irrelevant to human rights; whether the centre has all powers not specified to the provinces or vice versa, or whether there can be co-ordinate or overlapping jurisdictions, are all technical details to the central rights-protecting notion that government is man-made for a purpose, and therefore can and should be limited.

Felony

Felony was originally a crime in common law sufficiently serious to involve forfeiture of a felon's property to the crown, and included such offences as murder, rape and robbery. The equation of felony to serious, and **misdemeanour** to less serious, crimes was never precise, and in large part the difference was one of criminal procedure, especially after forfeiture was abolished in 1870. In the United Kingdom the distinction was replaced altogether in 1967, the new distinction, reflecting seriousness more directly, being between a non-arrestable and an **arrestable offence**. Other common law jurisdictions continue a version of the felony/misdemeanour distinction, especially the separate criminal jurisdictions of the US states. There the distinction is usually based on the penalty for the offences, with felonies carrying a prison sentence, normally a minimum of one year.

Fifteenth Amendment

The Fifteenth Amendment is one of the post Civil-War amendments to the US Constitution, the others being the Thirteenth and Fourteenth Amendments. It is a straightforward ban on denying the vote to anyone because of race or colour, or because he was previously a slave (see also **voting rights**). Although a fundamental principle, it has been of no further theoretical or practical importance in US human rights history, unlike the **Fourteenth Amendment** which has been the source of much more extensive human rights protection.

Fifth Amendment

The Fifth Amendment to the US Constitution is possibly the most famous part of the US Bill of Rights (see **Bill of Rights (USA)**) because the clause against **self-incrimination** has been immortalized in US gangster movies. In countless scenes a person has responded to a district attorney with the phrase 'I take the Fifth!', meaning: 'I am advised to rely on my Fifth Amendment rights and to refuse to answer the question on the grounds that the answer may tend to incriminate me'. What the Amendment actually says is that no person 'shall be compelled in any criminal case to be a witness against himself'. It has been left to Supreme Court interpretation to widen this immunity to the point that it can be used, for example, when interrogated by a Congressional Committee because the testimony might, at some later date, be used in a criminal trial. It is a very strong version of the **right to silence** found in some form or other in all legal systems based on adversarial trial processes, and historically arose because of the practice of courts like the English Star Chamber, where there was compulsion to give evidence. It is also part of the very logic of the adversarial system, where the aim of a trial is for the prosecution itself to prove guilt, not for the defendant to assume the **burden of proof**.

The whole of the Fifth Amendment is about controlling the use of state power, mainly in the context of criminal law. It contains a prohibition on **double jeopardy** trials, as well as a more or less technical requirement for the use of a grand jury in criminal trials. The most important clause, however, is that stating that nobody may be 'deprived of life, **liberty** or **property**, without **due process** of law'. This due process clause, repeated in the post-Civil War **Fourteenth Amendment** to make it apply to the separate states as well as to the federal government, is at the heart of **rights jurisprudence** as it relates to criminal law and, through the idea of substantive due process, these protections against arbitrary state power have gone far beyond the criminal sphere. In some ways this is foreshadowed by the last clause of the Fifth Amendment itself, which forbids the state to take private property for public use without 'just **compensation**', an early protection against some forms of redistributive politics contained also in the slightly earlier French **Declaration of the Rights of Man and of the Citizen**.

Final Act of the Helsinki Conference

The Helsinki accords were international agreements covering three areas, referred to as 'baskets'; basket three covered human rights and humanitarian issues, baskets one and two covered, respectively, security issues and economic matters. The whole process, which started in 1972 and was to grow into the regular meetings of the Conference on Security and Co-operation in Europe (CSCE—later renamed the **Organization for Security and Co-operation in Europe**), arose out of the USSR's desire to secure acceptance for its political and military role in Europe. As part of wide-ranging discussions involving, initially, all European states (with the exception of Albania) plus the USA and Canada, the Western allies were able to secure public acceptance of basic human rights principles in return for what amounted to little more than recognition of a *de facto* situation on the security front. Initially the human rights emphasis was the result of Western European initiatives, as the USA at this stage was little more willing to tie human rights matters to security issues than was the USSR. Human rights was very broadly defined in basket three, and much of the subject matter was more directly political, involving an acceptance of the legitimacy of pluralism and basic democratic rights. Although the signatory nations from the Warsaw Pact changed little, if anything, of their domestic practices as a result of publicly accepting basket three, the fact that they had signed it acted as a rallying point for humanitarian-oriented dissidents. In particular, **Charter 77** in Czechoslovakia was able to bring some pressure to bear on the communist regime, and 'Helsinki monitoring groups' sprang up in most signatory states; ironically, the persecution of these groups in the Eastern bloc countries helped further to draw world attention to the behaviour of the states. As part of the agreement itself required the publication of the agreement in all member states, and acceptance of the legitimacy of international surveillance of human rights issues, the recalcitrant states were actually forced to aid the process.

First Amendment

The First Amendment to the US Constitution, which is also the first article of the US Bill of Rights (see **Bill of Rights (USA)**), is a portmanteau statement containing protections for three quite separate sets of rights. Their joint selection to be of first importance reflects the mood of the times in which they were drafted. The first section covers **religious freedom**, and breaks down into what US constitutional lawyers call the 'establishment clause' and the 'free exercise clause'. The first clause states: 'Congress shall make no law respecting an establishment of religion', responding to very specific anxieties expressed in many of the new states which had been settled by religious dissenters from Europe. There was considerable fear that the new federal government would attempt to create an established church as a mirror to the role of the Church of England. This clause has been interpreted very strongly by the Supreme Court both against the federal government, and, after the **incorporation** of the Bill of Rights to the states, against state governments. No government ever has attempted establishment, though some of the states did initially have established churches; instead the Court has been involved in striking down almost any form of state aid to religion. This goes so far as to prohibit a state government allowing its funds to be used in partial support of the Christian Student Movement on university campuses, and has always been held to prohibit tax concessions for parents who send their children to religious schools instead of free state-provided schools. Any governmental support for religion, however indirect, as in allowing Christian symbols like nativity scenes on public property, has been outlawed, and the impetus for such bans has come usually not from members of some other religion, but from what Europeans would call 'free thinkers', and others 'militant atheists', often supported by the **American Civil Liberties Union (ACLU)**. The 'free exercise' clause has been slightly less important, largely because no state power has ever seriously tried to influence people's religious behaviour in a country noted for both the intensity and the pluralism of religious sectarianism. It has been used to prevent the state forbidding religious education, and indeed to defend one religious group, the Amish, from the obligation to send their children to formal schools at all after the eighth grade (roughly equivalent to the age of 14), but has not prevented, for example, laws against bigamy nor, in some cases with Christian Scientists, compulsory medical treatment. (See also **separation of church and state**.)

The second concern of the First Amendment has been with **freedom of speech** and press, which Congress is forbidden to 'abridge'. Though this clause has been interpreted more strongly than similar protections elsewhere, as for example with the **European Convention on Human Rights**, it has never been taken to be absolute, though some members of the Court have fought for a very strict interpretation. Instead the Supreme Court has recognized an area of what is often called 'protected speech', and allowed acts of communication outside that area to be subject to some limitations; the US law on **libel** is weaker in important respects than its counterparts in most European countries. Out of a sense of the political importance of free criticism of authority, the Court has fashioned a libel law where what otherwise would be a libel, a false statement damaging to the reputation of a public figure, may not be treated as such unless actual malice, rather than negligence, can be shown; the idea is that those choosing to enter the public arena must take the consequences. Similarly there are laws restricting speech which is labelled **sedition**, but only where the government can show a **clear and present danger** of serious and dangerous unrest. The Court has been very unwilling to allow censorship in the form of 'prior restraint', and although a newspaper may possibly be prosecuted for some form of security offence if it publishes national security matters, it will not be prevented from the publication itself, as was demonstrated during the Vietnam War when the *New York Times* published the highly damaging Pentagon Papers. The area where there is the least clarity is in state prohibition of pornographic or obscene material, because, not raising any sort of clear and present danger, such material has largely been treated as part of protected speech. The Court has at times tried to craft some form of test, famously along the lines that such material must be 'utterly without redeeming social value', before it can be prosecuted, but with little long-term success. Speech has been widely interpreted to include virtually every form of symbolic communication, including, in a famous example, the right to burn the national flag as part of a political demonstration.

The final provision in this very political set of human rights is the right 'peaceably to assemble and to petition the Government for a redress of grievances' (see **freedom of assembly**). As with the free speech and free exercise clauses, state authorities have been allowed obvious public safety regulating powers, but with very limited scope, with the consequence that some of the crowd limitation powers regularly enjoyed by European police forces would be clearly unconstitutional in the USA.

Forced or compulsory labour

The **European Convention on Human Rights** declares in Article 4 (Clause 2) that 'No one shall be required to perform forced or compulsory labour'. The article already prohibits, in Clause 1, **slavery** or servitude, and in Clause 3 it sets out a range of areas not covered by the prohibition, which include military and other national service, work in prison, emergency work, and work forming 'part of normal civic obligations'. Consequently it is not entirely obvious what the prohibition does cover. The relatively few cases brought before the **European Court of Human Rights** have all been marginal, where people have attempted to evade socially desirable duties the state has associated with their profession, such as the obligation to give some legal services free to poor defendants, the obligation to charge less for professional services given to a charity, and so on. Clearly the prohibition would apply to any attempt to set up a highly directive labour system in which people were told what jobs they could and could not undertake, but it has not, for example, been held to invalidate the requirement to take a suitable job when offered or lose unemployment benefit. There are rough equivalents elsewhere; the **Universal Declaration of Human Rights** provides, in Article 23, the right 'to free choice of employment', as does the **German Constitution**, among others, but these have more to do with banning discriminatory entrance conditions to occupations, and it is notable that the ban on slavery and servitude in the Universal Declaration does not include an equivalent to the European Convention's forced labour clause. The prohibition, apart from clearly pre-empting radical economic policies of labour-force direction, indicates that part of the pressure behind the Convention was grounded in a fear of a return to policies characteristic of the German Nazi period, rather than being an essentially forward-looking plan for a liberal European future. (See also **choice of occupation**.)

Fourteenth Amendment

The Fourteenth Amendment to the US Constitution, ratified in 1868, could be described as the single most powerful legal instrument in the history of **civil liberties**. Along with the Thirteenth Amendment and **Fifteenth Amendment**, of 1865 and 1870 respectively, it represented the North's legal attempts to ensure the fruits of its victory in the Civil War (1861–65). The legal power of the Amendment lies in subsequent interpretations of two clauses in Section 1, amounting altogether to only 51 words. They are known respectively as the **due process** and the **equal protection** clauses. The former asserts that no state may 'deprive any person of life, **liberty**, or **property**, without due process of law', the latter continues 'nor deny any person within its jurisdiction the equal protection of the laws'. At first sight these would hardly seem to be very radical restrictions on government action, and the Supreme Court's interpretations have not been uniformly liberal over the whole period; but on many occasions the Fourteenth Amendment has, in practice, been vital to civil libertarians. Historically there have been two reasons for its importance.

In 1791, three years after the official adoption of the US Constitution, a Bill of Rights (see **Bill of Rights (USA)**), consisting of the first Ten Amendments, was added, establishing a series of fundamental civil liberties, including, among others, rights to **freedom of speech** and **freedom of assembly (First Amendment)**, the protection against **self-incrimination** in criminal trials (**Fifth Amendment**) and against **cruel and unusual punishment (Eighth Amendment)**. Because the USA is a federal system, and this was the Federal Constitution, the Bill of Rights did not apply to state governments. In practice most of the legislation and executive actions that might infringe these rights were inevitably going to take place at the state level; for most of US history, for example, there had been very little federal criminal law. The Fourteenth Amendment was used by the Supreme Court over a period of several decades in a process known as **incorporation** to apply the Bill of Rights to the states. The argument was that the due process clause of the Amendment meant that anything in the Bill of Rights which could be seen as absolutely essential to due process, must thereby now apply to each state. In the words of Justice **Cardozo**, one of the intellectual leaders of the Supreme Court of the 20th century, any right which was 'essential to any concept of ordered liberty' could now be held to protect a citizen against a state government.

The other reason for the importance of the Fourteenth Amendment to civil rights has been the use made of the equal protection of the laws clause, which has been fashioned into a powerful theory about when and how different treatment of individuals by legislation is legitimate, covering areas as diverse as sex discrimination, sexual orientation, equal **voting rights**, **welfare rights** and educational policy. Little, if any, of this development was anticipated, let alone desired, by those who wrote the Fourteenth Amendment. Like the other post Civil-War amendments, it was primarily intended to prevent a re-emergence of the political influence of the Democrats in the South. Indeed, the earlier decisions interpreting the Fourteenth Amendment were models of restrictive interpretation, such as *Plessey v. Ferguson*, which was not successfully overruled until the landmark decision in ***Brown v. Board***.

Fourth Amendment

The Fourth Amendment is the part of the US Bill of Rights (see **Bill of Rights (USA)**) which deals with police powers to search persons or property. The fact that these powers are so clearly and specifically circumscribed in a Constitution which is, in general, both short and often vague is a testament to the fears of the population. The Bill of Rights is in part a revolutionary document, drafted after a violent war of independence against a colonial government which many considered not merely inconvenient but tyrannous. Under colonial rule wide and unchecked search powers had been granted, with their coverage general rather than aimed at specified people or crimes, to stop the extensive smuggling necessary to evade the strict colonial controls of American trade. The Amendment states that the right against 'unreasonable searches and seizures, shall not be violated', and that no **warrant** shall be issued 'but upon **probable cause**'. These clauses have been interpreted in two different ways. One holds that almost any search not backed by a warrant is unreasonable and therefore illegal, while the other reverses the thrust of this, and bans all unreasonable searches, which are mainly defined as those without probable cause, and then treats any search for which there is a warrant as more or less automatically reasonable. On the whole the first, more restrictive, interpretation has been adopted, but some commentators feel that the Supreme Court is ready to revert to an interpretation which would allow warrantless searches, certainly where an **arrest** has been made, much more readily. This would accord more closely to the practice in Europe, and particularly in the United Kingdom. The Supreme Court has always taken its time in developing the Fourth Amendment restrictions as technology changes; for some time the Amendment was thought not to control electronic eavesdropping by the police, though now warrants may have to be issued for this purpose. The greatest problem in interpretation has been in defining what is to count as probable cause. Unless the judge who issues the warrant is entitled to be given some good reason for doing so, the process becomes uselessly automatic, but it is obviously too strong to demand that the police offer evidence that would stand up in a trial. Similar problems occur in any country with a warrant procedure, and little more can be done than to rely on the experience and discretion of a magistrate.

Fox's Libel Act

The Libel Act of 1792 instigated by Charles James Fox was one of the earliest protections for political free speech in the common-law world. On the surface it is a relatively technical piece of legislation which does not seem to change much. Until the British Parliament passed this act **libel** cases went before a jury, but the jury was not allowed to decide whether the accused intended to commit the offence of libel. All the jury could decide was whether or not the accused had in fact published the matter in question; if they decided he had, it was for the judge alone to decide whether or not it was actually libellous. Fox's Act made the jury responsible for deciding whether or not the accused had actually intended to commit a libel. The reason it was so politically important is that the offence of criminal libel covered all seditious matter including, as it does today, the offence of **blasphemy**. Consequently a judge, who might well be over-sympathetic to the establishment, was able to hold someone guilty of **sedition**, even if the jury would not have done so. Criminal libel, at least for blasphemy, still exists in the United Kingdom, and even the protection of Fox's Act has not prevented a number of successful private prosecutions of writers.

Freedom of assembly

Freedom of assembly, is protected in, *inter alia*, the **First Amendment** to the US Constitution, the **European Convention on Human Rights**, the

German Constitution and the **Universal Declaration of Human Rights**, and is one of the earliest rights to be recognized. It stems directly from the sense that collective assemblies of the disenchanted protesting about government behaviour are a vital protection against tyrannical executives, and the First Amendment defines the right as 'the right of the people peaceably to assemble, and to petition the Government for a redress of grievances'. The right has been carefully defined because just as 'the people' have, throughout history, seen their right to assemble together in protest as a vital protection, governments have equally traditionally thought of them as lawless mobs when they do so, and sought to control them by the common law restrictions on crowd behaviour, including laws against riot and conspiracy. Consequently all rights statements invariably qualify 'assembly' with the word 'peaceful', and definitions of allowable executive restrictions on assemblies, marches and protests are always controversial and problematical.

One version of the right of assembly that has continued to cause legal problems has been the implied right to **picket**, where protesters stage themselves at the entry of a place, most commonly a place of work, in order to persuade others not to enter. The intimidating effect of even the best controlled picket-line is enormous, and, without any obvious breach of criminal law against assault or threatening behaviour, a picket can easily deter others from going about their business, which has to be an infringement of some very basic right of those who have to submit to such treatment. Laws on industrial picketing vary enormously, but it is by no means only trade unions which picket. Where other groups or associations picket to try to influence either the views or the behaviour of other members of the public, rights of **privacy** at the very least are infringed. Most legal systems still give considerable weight to freedom of contract, and to the problem of restraint of trade, and so in a case where pickets attempted, for example, to dissuade customers from entering a shop selling a product currently politically controversial, they would run the risk of the shop-owner seeking legal protection in the form of an **injunction**. Similarly the fairly well-defined **freedom of movement**, usually seen as a restraint on government restrictions on freedom of residency, can clearly be affected by the actions of those exercising the freedom of assembly in the form of picketing. The problem with picketing is that it cannot avoid invading the rights of others even when it is exercised strictly within the law.

Freedom of association

The freedom of association is recognized, in one form or another, by most statements of human rights, and, in varying degrees of restriction, in common law. It is one of the more clearly political rights sometimes regarded as **civil liberties**, and is clearly a group, as much as an individual, right. Its purpose is to enable the creation of political parties and other social movements, and, by extension, to legitimate the creation of trade unions, though the right to form or belong to a trade union is often recognized separately. Many important associations are of neither status, of course, whether they be for the preservation of the interests of their members, as with a professional association, or the interests of others, as with a cause group like the **National Association for the Advancement of Colored People (NAACP)**, and their freedom is equally vital in a pluralistic democracy. Freedom of association is also often linked with **freedom of assembly**, and as long as **bills of rights** include one or the other entitlement the courts are likely to interpret them as having a parcel of such rights. Thus, while the **First Amendment** to the US Constitution protects freedom of assembly, there is no US constitutional document which specifically protects freedom of association; this right would be a strange omission in a society so given to forming and joining associations, and the US Supreme Court has always treated it as covered by the assembly right. The **European Convention on Human Rights** is clearer than most, in specifically recognizing, in Article 11, all three rights: peaceful assembly and 'freedom of association with others, including the right to form and to join trade unions for the protection of his interests.' In France the **Conseil Constitutionel**, in one of its earlier and most creative judgments, derived a sufficiently strong right from 'the general principles of the French Republican Tradition' in order to overrule part of a law aimed at curtailing the ease with which associations could be formed.

Since freedom of association is in part a group right, associations can sometimes be treated as legal individuals with rights of their own, and real individuals may have rights against such association-individuals, although civil rights law varies considerably on these issues. For fully functioning democracy it is probably necessary that some of the **privacy** rights associated with search and seizure and **privacy of correspondence** also be granted to associations. Questions on individual relations with associations revolve mainly around membership. Do individuals have a legal right to join any association whose terms of reference would otherwise disqualify them? Can membership of such an association be made compulsory, as with professional associations and with trade unions under 'closed shop' arrangements? Do associations have the right to discipline, and ultimately to expel, members? There are no obviously correct answers to these questions from a civil rights perspective, but they all involve the public/private distinction that runs through both law and, increasingly, social and political theory. The general right to freedom and autonomy would suggest that associations as purely private activities should be left alone, but if they have a strong impact on public life, or on the personal life of individuals in a public manner, there is likely to be a clash of rights. With regard to trade union membership, there has always been a problem of what is sometimes called 'negative association', the right not to join without suffering any consequences. This right is not formally contained in the European Convention, but is written into the **Universal Declaration of Human Rights**. Within the field of **natural justice in English law** some doctrines have developed specifically because the courts had to deal with the disciplinary powers of associations. The most interesting example of the public/private problem has come about recently in the USA, where legal challenges were brought to the right of private clubs, like those for the graduates of major universities, to remain men-only organizations. The argument was made that important business, and perhaps political, arrangements were conducted and contacts made in such settings, and therefore they were public bodies in so far as the career prospects of women excluded from them were damaged.

Freedom of combination

Freedom of combination is rather archaic language for a sub-set of those rights covered by the concept of **freedom of association**, and refers especially to the right to form and join trade unions. The name comes from early anti-trade union legislation in Great Britain known as the Combination Acts of 1799 and 1800, which were repealed in 1824, although trade unions were not made fully legal until the Trade Union Act of 1871. The Combination Acts were justified by the idea that they involved an illegal interference with freedom of contract, and actually included clauses, never enforced, forbidding combinations of employers.

Freedom of conscience

In **bills of rights** clauses on freedom of conscience are frequently linked to **religious freedom**, or freedom of thought, and the concept has several dimensions. Above all, freedom of conscience must guarantee that no one will be discriminated against or persecuted for any belief he or she has and declares publicly. There is little point to a freedom of conscience if this has to be exercised in private, and public expression of one's beliefs is often explicitly, and always implicitly, guaranteed where the right is recognized at all. Thus the **European Convention on Human Rights**, which is more precise in its language than many similar declarations, in Article 9 combines thought, conscience and religion, and explicitly defines the right as including the freedom to change such belief, to hold the beliefs in public or private, alone or in community with others, and to manifest the belief 'in worship, teaching, practice and observance'. Another article provides that no one can be discriminated against for exercising any of the other prescribed rights.

The definition of freedom of conscience raises certain questions where an individual or group's belief impinges on their behaviour towards others or the state. The right must include that a person be allowed not only to hold and exhibit a belief, but also to have some say in how beliefs are transmitted to the children of the family, hence raising questions of educational freedom. Problems arise from compulsory activities in work or in terms of civil obligation: if a person sincerely believes, but for humanist rather than religious reasons, that all war is evil (see **conscientious objection**), can he, in conscience, pay taxes that may go towards buying nuclear weapons? Can the state require a person to swear an oath in court? Can it force someone to give consent to some form of medical treatment to a dependant which they oppose on grounds of conscience? There can be no clear and permanent answers to such questions, and they have to be left to the courts, through judicial **discretion**, to craft a pragmatic approach fitting the social culture of the period. The right, like so many, is tied to the fundamental right of autonomy, or, as it is more often described, the right of free **development of personality**.

Freedom of expression

Freedom of expression is essentially another, and perhaps more accurate, way of referring to the composite of rights usually labelled **freedom of speech**. Some constitutional documents do draw a distinction, or use it instead of the phrase freedom of speech: the **Universal Declaration of Human Rights** provides, in Article 19, that 'Everyone has the right to freedom of opinion and expression' and to 'impart information and ideas through any media and regardless of frontiers'. The only problem that arises in this distinction is that its greater width, though avoiding definitional problems about forms of media, does mean that all forms of expressive behaviour may be thought to be protected. While this may be the intention, and may be desirable, there are those who do wish to draw a distinction between formulated speech, either in writing or broadcast, and purely visual symbolism. It can be argued that speech is a way of expressing ideas that limit the emotional and therefore possibly irrational aspects, and favours calm and reflective consideration of argument. There can be some reasons for wishing to limit the excitability of, and also to protect against the subliminal impact of, some forms of expression.

Freedom of information

Freedom of information is sometimes regarded as a human right, and it is clearly a desirable characteristic of a political system to avoid excessive secrecy in government processes. It is vital in protecting **civil liberties** that anyone who suspects that the government is infringing his rights, especially by practising discrimination, should be able to prove his case, and anyone accused of criminal activities should have access to any relevant government documents which might tend to support his innocence. However, freedom of information only comes close to being a right when it refers to an individual's entitlement to know what information about him may be held by powerful agencies, not only of the government but in private organizations. This latter right is slowly being recognized in statute, though it is not contained in any major formal statement of human rights, and is important as much of this sort of information can be highly unreliable, and people's life chances can easily be damaged by, for example, faulty credit ratings. The easy availability and transmission of such information raises a serious threat to the acknowledged human right to **privacy**. In Europe there have been attempts to protect the confidentiality of personal data held in electromagnetic form, but there is no generalized right to see files on oneself, and even less of a right to see government material unless as part of the **discovery** process in litigation.

In general, the power of discovery enables civil litigants to obtain such information from a person or corporation they suspect of unfair practices. So, for example, in a case to stop sex discrimination it will usually be possible to force an employer to disclose employment and payment records which would help to establish the complaint. It is usually much more difficult to establish the basis for governmental action, because governments everywhere tend to try to prevent their inner workings from being disclosed, often under the pretext of either national security or the efficient working of government. Demands for freedom of information are demands for institutional policies to make it much harder for the government to withhold information, and generally to make the working of government much more open. National practices vary widely. The USA, which has had a Freedom of Information Act since the 1970s is the world leader in this respect. Under the Act most material held by federal agencies, including CIA and FBI files, may be seen by a concerned citizen, with relatively minimal security restrictions. So powerful is this Act, and so weak are similar provisions in the United Kingdom, that British journalists have often gained information on domestic British political matters by making a freedom of information request to US departments involved in monitoring the issue. The UK has a strong tradition of withholding information, exemplified in the Official Secrets Act, which makes it a criminal offence to disclose very broad areas of information to any unauthorized person. Other practices, like the use of Public Interest Immunity certificates (PIIs), by which ministers can try to prevent the disclosure of sensitive documents in court hearings, increase this tendency to secrecy. PII certificates were used by the government in two criminal trials concerning allegations of illegal arms trading during the early 1990s, even though they showed the innocence of several people charged with arms trading offences. Though this was the first time the public became widely aware of the practice, it had been employed for some 30 years.

Freedom of movement

In so far as a right to freedom of movement can be defined, it is certainly a highly circumscribed one. The **European Convention on Human Rights**, in the Fourth Protocol of 1963, does include a version of this right, in that it guarantees the right of anyone to leave any territory, and the right to enter the territory of which one is a national. It also claims that anyone legally resident in a country has 'the right to liberty of movement and freedom to choose his residence'. However, these rights are so circumscribed by the right of the state to interfere with its citizens' enjoyment for reasons of public interest that it is unclear what exactly is being protected. Furthermore, the European Court of Human Rights' interpretation of the rights in the cases it has dealt with has almost always upheld any restrictions on movement imposed by the state in question. More generally, the right to freedom of movement is impossible except within one's own country because of the increasingly tight **immigration** controls applied by all modern states. Like the provision for freedom from **forced or compulsory labour** in the Convention, freedom of movement would appear to be a relict of concern about the tyranny characteristic of the 1930s and 1940s, rather than a serious concern for the future. The only obvious applicability would be some long-term government policy of forcible resettlement of minorities, which is thus a group right, if it exists. It is unlikely, for example, that an order requiring a convicted person to reside in a certain area for a fixed time, the modern equivalent of internal exile, would be introduced into European criminal law, and even if it were, it is equally unclear that the language of the Fourth Protocol would ban such a punishment.

Freedom of the press (see **freedom of speech**)

Freedom of speech

Freedom of speech is one of the core **civil liberties**, in the sense that certain rights can be said to be more political, and a version of it in some form or other, often including freedom of the press, is protected in all rights documents. The **First Amendment** to the US Constitution puts freedom of speech and press second only to **religious freedom**; it is in the **Declaration of** the Rights of Man and of the Citizen of 1789; both the **European Convention on Human Rights** and the **Universal Declaration of Human Rights** contain the right to free speech in strong forms; the **German Constitution** places it fifth in order of rights, and incorporates it in three clauses, one of which expressly states: 'There shall be no censorship'. Even countries like Australia and the United Kingdom, which have constitutions without **bills of rights**, have had freedom of speech highly protected by judicial **imputation**. In 1992 the Australian High Court overthrew a parliamentary statute aimed at restricting the ability of rich candidates to buy extra broadcasting time in election campaigns, on the grounds that Australia was a parliamentary democracy, dependent on party competition for informed votes, and thus, by necessary imputation, though the Constitution was otherwise silent on the matter, that freedom of speech was vital. It is this link to democratic politics, where an informed public can choose between rival rulers, that makes freedom of speech so necessary, and so, because freedom of speech helps the governed to control the government, it may be seen as the key freedom on which all the others depend.

Beyond their role in the political arena, freedom of speech and **freedom of expression** play a key role in the **development of personality**, which, along with the idea of human dignity, is seen in many human rights documents as the end values towards which modern society aims. It is, however, very hard to treat free speech as an absolute value, and most codes in fact attach rather vague restrictions to it. The French Declaration of 1789, for example, while stressing freedom of speech as 'one of the most precious rights of man', nevertheless warns, slightly ominously, that a citizen 'may have to answer for the abuse of that liberty in the cases determined by law', and Clause 2 of the freedom of expression clause in the German Constitution warns that 'these rights are subject to limitations embodied in the provisions of general legislation . . . and the citizen's right to personal respect'. Personal honour is a rather grandiose way of talking about the law of defamation, known as **libel** and slander in the common law world, which exists everywhere and is the most obvious limitation on freedom of speech. Another limitation to free speech arises from the demands of national security. Both publication which risks giving information away, and publication which affects morale or support for the government, the latter often referred to as **sedition**, have frequently been seen as grounds for restricting freedom of speech, and clearly there is a delicate balance to be drawn, one that occurs also with the related right to **freedom of information**.

Finally, freedom of speech can also be abused when it leads to hurt and suffering to holders of values and beliefs attacked in perhaps insensitive or unnecessarily cruel ways. Traditionally societies have protected feelings, at least in religious matters, against such speech by, *inter alia*, **blasphemy** laws, and criminal sanctions against pornography and obscene material are common, though much diluted since the 1960s. This is the most controversial area, because it deals with judgements so subjective, in a context where social desires for conformity can be so repressive, that many think any diminution of free speech to be too dangerous. Nevertheless, even the **European Court of Human Rights** has upheld convictions for blasphemy, and has allowed states to censor religiously offensive films.

G

General principles of law of civilized nations

The idea that there are some very general principles more or less spontaneously adopted by all civilized, or 'developed', nations is a legal doctrine used to defend the legitimacy of supranational courts like the **European Court of Human Rights** or the International Court of Justice. The problem is that all laws, perhaps especially broad statements like conventions on human rights, require **interpretation** when applied to concrete circumstances. A national court can rely on a cultural agreement about basic values, or perhaps refer to the intention of constitutional founding fathers, and may be in less need of interpretative techniques because a national parliament can be expected to keep the status of its laws under observation, and fill in gaps which social development shows up. An international body, however, cannot as easily refer to such material in justifying answers it may give to vague declarations, or in closing legal loopholes. Thus a reference to something seen as a cultural constant, something any country would more or less automatically agree to by virtue of being an advanced society, can give legitimacy to what might otherwise be thought of as naked judicial power. It is, of course, essentially a legal fiction, not an invitation to counsel to engage in a sociological enquiry as to what principles are, empirically, to be found in all civilized nations. When applied with anything like an empirical basis, as sometimes by the European Court of Human Rights with reference to Europe-wide principles, there is a marked tendency to take a 'lowest common denominator' approach, and not to hold a government to the highest standards of human rights to be found in Europe.

Geneva conventions

So many vital agreements in international law have been negotiated and signed in Geneva that it is easy to be confused by the title 'Geneva conventions'. There were four Geneva conventions signed in 1958 alone, for example, in this case dealing with matters of international maritime law. When the term Geneva conventions is used with no qualifier it usually refers to the various international conventions on warfare. The earliest of these was an agreement signed in 1864, as a result of negotiations instigated by the newly-formed International Committee of the Red Cross (known as the International Committee for Relief of Wounded until 1880), called the First International Convention for the Amelioration of the Condition of Soldiers Wounded in Armies in the Field. It was extended and modified in a convention more widely ratified in 1906 (the Second Geneva Convention), and was brought to include maritime warfare by a separate convention signed at The Hague in 1907 (the Hague Rules). Finally a Convention Relating to the Treatment of Prisoners of War (the Third Geneva Convention), perhaps the one most usually referred to, was added in 1929. These conventions were so widely flouted by all sides in both world wars that a new start was made in 1949, when these original conventions were further extended and defined and became very widely ratified. These four new conventions cover: wounded and sick in armed forces in the field; a similar convention for armed forces at sea; treatment of prisoners of war; and protection of civilians in time of war. Much of the conventions follows time honoured (or dishonoured) principles of warfare following from the classic 'just war' theories. As such the basic thrust is that killing or wounding are not the aim of war, and must be minimized, and that the only legitimate target of force is an armed soldier offering resistance. There is an ongoing effort to control the nature of warfare, and an increasing tendency to incorporate general human-rights theory into the discussions. In 1974 the UN set up a Geneva Diplomatic Conference on the Reaffirmation and Development of International Humanitarian Law Applicable in Armed Conflicts.

Genocide

Genocide was defined in the Convention on the Prevention and Punishment of the Crime of Genocide, which was adopted by the UN General Assembly on 9 December 1948, as the crime of destroying, or committing conspiracy to destroy, a national, ethnic, racial or religious group. The reason for the crime's recognition in international law was the systematic effort carried on by Nazi Germany during the 1930s and 1940s to destroy the Jewish population of Europe, and the immediate legal justification was that the International Military Tribunal hearing cases against prominent German war criminals at Nuremberg during 1945–46 had established the principle of individual accountability of those who were responsible for Nazi extermination policies. The Convention itself recognizes that the Nazis did not invent genocide and that often in history 'genocide has inflicted great losses on humanity', so it must be tackled through international co-operation. Article 1 of the Convention makes genocide a crime whether committed in time of peace or war, raising inevitable questions about the international community's obligation to invade national sovereignty where such a crime is being committed; Article 4 establishes the principle that punishment for genocide shall apply not only to guilty 'constitutionally responsible rulers' and public officials, but also to private individuals; and Article 5 imposes on the signatory nations the obligation of enacting legislation to give effect to the provisions of the Convention and to provide suitable penalties for persons found guilty. Article 7 denies to persons accused of genocide immunity from extradition, while the previous Article provides that anyone accused of genocide 'shall be tried by a competent tribunal of the State in the territory of which the act was committed', or by an international tribunal with jurisdiction. Unfortunately the former is often fairly pointless, as the state itself is very likely to be implicated, and the latter raises afresh the whole question of jurisdiction in international law. Inevitably genocide is punished only where the oppressing nation loses, and the Convention might have been said to do little more than put a seal of respectability on victors. In 1993 and 1994 international tribunals to prosecute persons accused of genocide and war crimes in former Yugoslavia and Rwanda, respectively, were established. The outcome of these trials, particularly that they were of individuals representing states and military forces which had not necessarily been subjected to utter military defeat, was likely to be of more lasting significance than that of the Nuremberg trials in fostering a sense of international crime against humanity.

German Constitution

Technically, the document known as the German Constitution was not originally intended to have quite the permanent status of a constitution, as its title in German, Grundgesetz, or Basic Law, implies. At the time of its ratification by the 10 Länder in West Germany in 1949 (that is, excluding the Länder of East Germany and Saarland, which was not reintegrated with the other West German territories until 1957), the ensuing Federal Republic did not embrace all Germans, and the politicians in the Constituent Assembly did not wish to be seen as accepting this as a permanent state of affairs. (The Preamble to the Basic Law specifically stated that the German people 'have also acted on behalf of those Germans to whom participation was denied'.) Nevertheless, the Basic Law has been a very successful constitution, has always been treated and interpreted as one, and is extremely unlikely ever to be radically changed. More than most **written constitutions**, the German one concentrates on the protection of human rights, and Article 1, entitled 'Protection of human dignity', making the firm declaration that 'inviolable and inalienable' human rights form the 'basis of every community, of peace and justice in the world'. What follows, though tailored naturally for German cultural expectations and historical concerns, is a model of human rights protection which has been furthered by a very active constitutional court (see **German Constitutional Court**) absolutely committed to protecting and even extending such guarantees. There is no other European document similarly specific as well as extensive in its listing of protected rights, and, with the exception of the **Canadian Charter of Rights and Freedoms**, an even more recent attempt to entrench liberal values, there is probably no national document in the world to compare with it. Even the UN and European human rights conventions compare unfavourably, mainly because they necessarily cannot have the same degree of specificity. Not all of the rights are absolute; for example, Article 10 guarantees **privacy of correspondence**, but allows, in Clause 2, that the right may be restricted by law, and even then the clause itself sets up safeguards against abuse. This is a typical pattern. Some rights are absolute: Article 4, providing for freedom of faith and creed, contains no permission to pass restrictive laws. Some rights are absolute in part: Article 8 guarantees **freedom of assembly**, including the right to assemble without prior notification, but allows this right to be regulated by law, though only in cases of outdoor meetings. Some rights are recognized, by their nature, to carry their own limitations: the Article 2 right to **liberty** states that 'everyone shall have the right to self-fulfilment *in so far as they do not violate the rights of others or offend against the constitutional order*' (author's italics; see also **development of personality**). It is this very pragmatic approach which really distinguishes the German Constitution, and which, for example, permits such an admirably liberal document nevertheless to allow the Constitutional Court to ban extremist political parties. (The full text of the Articles 1 to 19 of the Basic Law, which form the human rights code, is given in the Appendix.)

German Constitutional Court

The German Constitutional Court, or *Bundesverfassungsgericht*, sits in Karlsruhe, and was established under the **German Constitution**, properly known as the Basic Law or Grundgesetz of 1949. Germany does not technically have a constitution as such, because, in the context of the post-Second World War divided state, it was deemed to imply a long-term acceptance of this division to enact a formal constitution. Despite this the Basic Law has always been interpreted by the Constitutional Court as operating exactly like a full written constitution, and the Court has never been reluctant to exercise its very considerable political power. Unlike some constitutional courts it is precisely and only that defined by its title. Some courts with constitutional powers, such as the US and Canadian Supreme Courts and the Australian High Court, are the senior appellate court for all branches of law, the exclusive pinnacle of a judicial pyramid. There are several other superior courts in Germany, and the Constitutional Court hears cases only if they touch on constitutional matters. Thus a criminal law case might go to the Constitutional Court, but only because some fundamental question of the constitutionality of a law, or a constitutionally-based complaint about police or prosecution behaviour, was involved. It would deal with a straightforward matter of interpretation of the criminal law in itself, or the adequacy of evidence.

There are three main ways that an issue can come before the German Court. Firstly, a citizen may make what is called a 'constitutional complaint', directly challenging an action by any level of government or administration on the grounds that his rights, mainly those contained in the first 19 Articles of the Basic Law, have been breached. Several thousand such complaints are made each year, and they are all given at least preliminary investigation by a committee of the Court, though only about five per cent are actually upheld. Secondly, a judge in an ongoing case which is not prima facie about a constitutional matter, may refer a point of law for constitutional interpretation. Indeed, the judges of whatever would be the ultimate appeal court in the matter are obliged to make such a reference if the point has not already been adjudicated by the Constitutional Court, a procedural rule found to be necessary because the Court's unique right to make such determinations is sometimes resented by members of the ordinary judiciary. Finally, the Federal Parliament may refer an act directly to the Court for what is known as a 'prospective' or 'abstract' ruling as to whether it will be regarded as constitutional if promulgated.

The Court has been very active and has not hesitated to strike down legislation coming before it, especially in this third mode. Among other major pieces of legislation, it has twice refused to accept legislation permitting **abortion**, making it clear that it regards the protection of human life and human dignity in the Basic Law as paramount, and specifically stating that Germany's past record in such areas requires extreme vigilance. The relatively few successful appeals to the **European Court of Human Rights** by German citizens suggest that the Constitutional Court has been effective in protecting human rights in Germany. The country has developed a rich and complex **rights jurisprudence**, amounting to a subtle philosophy firmly grounded in Article 1 of the Basic Law, entitled 'Protection of human dignity', as demonstrated in particular by its strong interpretation of both **religious freedom** and **parental rights** to control their children's education. In structure, the Court consists of a mixture of political appointees and independent professionals. Appointments are made by the two houses of the federal legislature, but internal codes of conduct have nearly always ensured a partisan balance. Judges are appointed for a fixed and non-renewable 12-year term. Though some have been career lawyers, and though all have to hold the qualifications for an ordinary judgeship, many are academic lawyers or former politicians. The Court is rare in Europe in allowing identifiable dissenting judgments to be published, although in practice it has always demonstrated a considerable internal consensus.

Golden rule

In legal discourse the golden rule is generally a reference to one of the standard rules of statutory **interpretation**, also called the 'plain words' rule. No judge is completely obedient to the golden rule, but in essence it requires a statute to be interpreted to the ordinary dictionary meaning of words and the correct grammatical rules, provided the resulting interpretation is neither absurd nor illegal (see also **strict construction**). The golden rule is designed to counter strained interpretations given to derive something from an act that it was not originally meant to provide, and is a denial of what is sometimes called 'purposive' interpretation, the method in which the judge takes words and phrases to mean whatever is necessary to carry out the obvious intent of the legislator or the overall purpose of the act. (The forerunner of the modern notion of purposive interpretation was the 'mischief' rule, under which acts should be interpreted so as to prevent the 'mischief' their authors had intended to correct.) Those who advocate interpretation of the law by the golden rule are attempting both to restrict judicial **discretion** as far as possible, and also to voice a general principle of law that ordinary people should be able to understand the laws they are required to obey. Thus if a word has to be given an unusual meaning, or the ordinary range of some action restricted from what a phrase might normally be thought to cover, the golden rule will strike down such interpretation on the grounds that ordinary law-abiding people would have no way of knowing that was what the law meant. The exception that even adherents of the golden rule would allow it where a word is a 'term of art', that is, it has taken on a special technical meaning as a piece of legal jargon. Some very common words have become 'terms of art' because of their frequent use in very complex legislation; the words 'reside' and 'occupy', because of their use in statues covering tax, rates, planning matters and even nationality rights, have come to have restrictive judicial meanings, leaving the golden rule little room in interpreting, for example, a taxation statute, or a rule on who can qualify for university grants from local education authorities.

Grotius

Hugo Grotius (1583–1645) is often regarded not only as the founder of modern international law, but, because of his intellectual stance, as in effect the founder of modern natural law argument, and hence is of vital importance to much civil liberty and human rights law. He was a diplomat and civil servant for much of his life, but, because of his own involvement in the religious disputes of the period, was *persona non grata* in the Netherlands intermittently throughout his career. Grotius's first published work was *Mare liberum* (1609), a treatise on maritime law in which he defended a ban on any state claiming ownership of the open seas by a form of natural law argument that was later to become familiar to human rights theorists through the writings of John **Locke**. His most important work, a general treatise on international law, *De iure belli et pacis* (On the Law of War and Peace) was published in 1625. The connection between international law theory and human rights law is closer than might at first appear. The logical problem is the same in both: how to deduce principles controlling the right of a sovereign state to do whatever the rulers of the state perceive to be in its interest. Grotius tried to blend prudential morality (rules based on enlightened self-interest) with an essentially theologically-derived notion of natural law which would have little appeal today, but he did open up the entire question of rationally-derived constraints on state power. Furthermore, he clearly took the interests of citizens as ultimately superior to the interests of states or rulers, which had not been an automatic position in legal thinking before him. As one personally involved in religious intolerance he was aware of human rights in a more modern conception than might otherwise have been possible from an early 17th-century perspective, and his work might, *inter alia*, be seen as an early discussion of the role of human rights intervention in international law.

Grundgesetz (see **German Constitution**)

H

Habeas corpus

The writ of habeas corpus is very old, certainly pre-dating **Magna Carta**, though redefined several times by legislation. Literally meaning 'you have the body', it is a prerogative writ which can be issued nowadays by any High Court judge. The writ is an order to the person in charge of someone's **detention**, typically a prison governor, to deliver the named person so the court can investigate the legality of his imprisonment. In the United Kingdom it cannot be used as an alternative to an appeal in a criminal trial if some appeal mechanism already exists or has been used unsuccessfully, but otherwise can be issued in a wide variety of contexts; a common current human rights application in the UK is in **immigration** appeals where someone is held in prison awaiting deportation. It is similarly used against detention under non-criminal statutes like the Mental Health Act. It is a common misunderstanding to believe that a detained person can have a series of applications made from judge to judge until one is successful, as subsequent applications may be made only when based on new evidence. The writ has been suspended during various emergencies in the past, but never in the 20th century. It is specifically protected in the US Constitution, in Article 1 (Section 9), which states that it may not be suspended except during periods of emergency; it has been suspended only once, when, during the Civil War, President Abraham Lincoln (1809–65) ignored a judicial pronouncement that only Congress had the power of suspension. In the USA it has a particular use in enabling federal courts to test the constitutionality of state criminal laws under which someone is imprisoned. Technically, the writ commonly used is *habeas corpus ad subjiciendum*; there are other habeas corpus writs, largely obsolescent, for particular technical circumstances.

Harassment

Harassment, by state power or by individuals, has emerged as a central human rights concern, with daily news reports of allegations of, for example, sexual harassment in the work place, or racial harassment by the police. Most complex organizations, such as corporations or universities, now have codes of behaviour to control harassment, which is often left undefined, as though it were a very obvious and natural concept. In fact proper legal controls in statutes very seldom use the concept, let alone the word, precisely because it is too wide. Where harassment can be given a sufficiently concrete definition to enter a parliamentary statute, it usually turns out to be perfectly well-covered by one or more terms which already define crimes. There are two core meanings to harassment. One, typical of what is meant when police or other authorities are accused of harassing someone or some group, refers to someone or some group deliberately using their proper powers and authorities in such a way as to pick on a particular target unnecessarily, with the aim simply of making life miserable for the victim, rather than achieving whatever the purpose for which the powers were originally granted. Thus police harassment of, say, black youths might consist of them regularly and automatically using **stop and search** powers to interfere with the legitimate movements of the youths when there is no real ground for suspecting them, and when some more favoured but equally potentially suspect group, white football fans, for example, are left untroubled. The difficulty in controlling harassment under this meaning is that the powers which are being misused are necessary for legitimate law and order tasks, and the claim of harassment becomes a judgement on operational police matters, with the ready defence that civilian investigators cannot possibly understand the problems experienced in the course of everyday police work.

In a way, the logic of the other core meaning of harassment is the same. This usually refers to persistent behaviour which is not in itself illegal, and could not easily be made so, but is targeted at a victim in order to persecute them. Sexual innuendo and persistent unwelcome sexual invitations addressed towards a junior staff member of the opposite sex by a manager, or by the staff member's workmates, can lead to destructive feelings of insecurity, and clearly constitutes harassment. The difficulty is how to isolate the offending ingredient in the behaviour sufficiently closely to ban it when, innocently carried out, the behaviour, language or whatever is part of common daily life. What all forms of harassment have in common is the motive of the harasser, to hurt, inconvenience, embarrass or whatever, and the fact that harassment, as opposed to actually illegal behaviour, involves a misuse of powers or an excessive indulgence in what is otherwise legitimate.

Hart

H. L. A. Hart (1907–92, who seems never to have been publicly known other than by his initials), was Professor of Jurisprudence in the University of Oxford until 1969, when he was succeeded by the man who has done most to try to overthrow his philosophy of law, Ronald **Dworkin**. Hart was the last of the great exponents of legal positivism, and generally an exponent of a particular, highly utilitarian, conception of Liberalism associated with John Stuart Mill (1806–73). He was equally influenced by the general positivism of the Oxford 'analytic philosophy' tradition of his day. His major work, *The Concept of Law*, published in 1961, is still treated as an authoritative statement of legal positivism, and has by no means ceased to have influence. To a large extent one could characterize legal philosophy in the last part of the 20th century throughout much of the common law world as an ongoing debate between Hartians and Dworkinians. It is characteristic of positivist thinking in any field that it is deeply suspicious of any truth claims based on non-observable grounds. The application of this scepticism to law is that much talk of rights requires acceptance that they are, at root, based on personal intuitions of natural law or moral beliefs, even if these are claimed to be universally held.

In contrast to such theories, Hart recognizes only two sorts of legal rules as valid. These he calls primary and secondary rules. Broadly speaking a secondary rule is what others might call a constitutional rule, which sets out for a legal system who can make other rules, and how they are to be legislated. This secondary rule is in some ways tantamount to a sociological observation, and indeed Hart subtitles his book 'an essay in sociological jurisprudence'. The secondary rule is the rule which is recognized and followed by those who need to follow it for the system to work, such as legislators, judges, police and so on. All other valid law consists of primary rules, intentionally made by those operating under the secondary rule, which is also called a 'rule of recognition'. They need not actually be statutes; Hart is happy to accept that common law contains judge-made rules, but they must all be identifiable by the rule of recognition. It follows from this position that the only rights that exist, human, civil or whatever, are themselves primary rules identified by a rule of recognition, and there can be no absolutely valid human rights mankind has by virtue of being human. To the extent that internationally recognized rights, such as those applied by the **European Court of Human Rights**, exist at all, they do so by virtue of being 'recognized', that is, validated, by the positive rule-making machinery of each national state. Hart's legal philosophy, despite being positivist, was highly liberal in other ways, as witnessed by his celebrated literary debate with Patrick Devlin (1905–92), a distinguished Law Lord, on the legitimacy of legal enforcement of sexual morality. In this Hart followed the line taken by John Stuart Mill that moral values could never be enforced except to protect others from harm.

Helsinki Accords (see **Organization on Security and Co-operation in Europe**)

Housing rights

Rights such as housing rights fall into the general category of **positive rights**, which does not fit well into the traditional theories of human rights or **civil liberties**. A right to a certain standard of housing, like a right to medical care or to employment, puts demands on the state which may be impossible to satisfy at any given level, and which inevitably involves policy choices in terms of public expenditure. As such they cannot have the neutrality towards overall political ideology which liberal democracy strives for in its general definition of human rights. Housing rights are problematic in particular because they touch on the conditions necessary for the full enjoyment of other rights more typical of modern rights charters. For example, the **right to family life**, which in one way or another is widely recognized in post-1945 rights documents, is largely meaningless unless a family is able to live securely together. Because homelessness is a recurrent social problem even in the most affluent societies, housing rights have assumed a prominence among positive rights. Though most modern states are unwilling to recognize an absolute right to be housed, pressure from many sources led to a UN conference recognizing, in 1996, that such a right was at least a prescriptive duty on all member states. As with all positive rights, it is difficult to see how such a right could become the subject of a trial, although the legal control over land and real estate is everywhere complex. One way in which a general recognition of a housing right may have an effect is by acting to limit the freedom of property owners to evict squatters (people residing in a previously unoccupied property, without permission from the owner), or to encourage legislation against second home owning.

Humanitarian intervention

Humanitarian intervention is the relatively new doctrine under which one or more states may take military action inside the territory of another state in order to protect those who are experiencing serious human rights persecution, up to and including attempts at **genocide**. Until very recently the understanding of national sovereignty in international law has largely meant that there were no legal measures by which anyone could prevent a government doing whatever it liked to its own citizens, or certainly not any measures which involved direct force within the borders of the offending state. Thus there could have been no question of the European nations sending troops into Greece, during its period of military rule (1967–74) to protect the rights of the enemies of the regime, even though the military take-over was met with a revulsion that led to Greece being suspended from the Council of Europe. The restriction on such intervention clashed, after the Second World War, with a general sense of international obligation. In the case of genocide, for example, the signatories to the Convention on the Prevention and Punishment of the Crime of Genocide (1948, came into force in 1951) were clearly under an obligation to intervene, presumably with force if necessary, to prevent such a policy being applied. The first clear-cut abandonment of the pure sovereignty doctrine in favour of humanitarian intervention was probably the UN action in Iraq after the Gulf War of 1991 to protect both the Kurds in the north and the Marsh Arabs in the south. The original UN mandate for military force to be used on Iraq after its invasion of Kuwait (Security Council Resolution No. 678) had not authorized such intervention, but clearly it was easier to extend military protection in the context of Iraq's partial defeat by a UN-authorized contingent. Further UN and multinational humanitarian interventions were made during the 1990s in former Yugoslavia, Somalia and Rwanda. How far the doctrine may extend in the future is very unclear, because the attraction of sovereignty as an absolute national right is very strong, and is strictly incompatible with the idea of intervention, even where the motives are quite altruistic.

I

Immigration

The right to immigrate is not recognized in international law. At most, the international conventions on refugees (such as the UN Convention relating to the Status of Refugees) grant to some, political **asylum** seekers for example, the right not to be deported to a particular country where they may suffer persecution. The extent to which rights to immigrate are recognized in any nation's domestic law is less clear. Some countries, notably Israel with its openness to any Jewish person born anywhere, create rights for a broad definition of 'their own people'. Thus West Germany allowed entry to virtually anyone who could claim prior German national identity after the Second World War, and Ireland has very generous and extensive rights to an Irish passport for anyone with a clear Irish national heritage. These instances, however, are not strictly exceptions to an absence of rights to immigrate but rather a special definition of pre-existing **citizenship**.

As immigration has grown to be a perceived serious problem for richer nations in the last few decades, previously sympathetic host countries have revised their policies, and most now have very tight restrictions on immigration. In most cases, unless there is some prior right to at least a form of citizenship within recent family history, there are only two criteria which qualify a person for entrance and residence in a country. The first, and most common, is as the spouse of someone with uncontested citizenship, although some countries treat even this as a privilege that may not necessarily be granted, rather than a strict right. The second is where a would-be immigrant has a job to go to and where the employer can pass very stringent tests of the necessity of employing the applicant rather than someone already a citizen. Where human rights problems arise is either in assessing the fairness of the machinery for granting right of residence to the comparative few who may have a claim, or, increasingly vital, in controlling the treatment of illegal immigrants. In practice, entry to many countries which do not encourage immigration is usually very easy. Even an island nation like the United Kingdom is readily accessible under the guise of tourism, and Western European countries and the USA, with long and undefendable borders, are easily entered. The treatment of an illegal entrant if later discovered is a particularly sensitive human rights issue. As a non-citizen, and indeed as someone who has, *de jure*, broken the law by being in the country at all, it is tempting to say that an illegal immigrant has no rights at all. After all, if the most basic of political rights, to be a citizen, is denied, as it must be, any rights remaining must adhere to someone solely as a human being; that is, they are of the most basic survival nature, concerned with the minimum of human dignity we owe to anyone. It is not clear that any Western liberal democracy achieves even this standard with most illegal immigrants.

Imputation

Imputation is an interpretative technique often used in constitutional adjudication, though it is not always so labelled by the judges who use it. Imputation is used where a constitution is silent on some question, either through vagueness or, for example, because the constitution contains no explicit bill of rights and a human-rights issue arises. The judge 'imputes' the answer to the question from the structural features of the constitution itself, or as a logically necessary consequence of what is stated. It was very frequently used, and highly developed as a technique, by the first generation of judges on the Australian High Court to work out details of the power balance between the federal government and the states. Where, as was common, the Australian Constitution did not adequately delineate which federal powers could be used in areas where the states also wished to act, the answer was said to follow from the necessary imputation of a working federal system. In this way much that had happened in the early days of the US Constitution was replicated in Australia, and indeed the writers of the Australian Constitution had intentionally chosen the system in the hope that the US Supreme Court would act as a methodological precedent. In the USA the question of whether the federal government could tax a state government, a question not directly addressed in the Constitution, was answered in the negative by imputation, on the grounds that to allow such taxation would weaken state independence; the famous doctrine was enunciated that 'the power to tax is the power to destroy'. Although the use of imputation was officially abandoned by the Australian High Court in the 1920s, it has recently been revived specifically for human rights issues because of the absence of a bill of rights. The classic civil right of freedom of the press was imputed by the Court in 1992, when it struck down a federal act regulating political advertising during election campaigns (see also **freedom of speech**) on the basis that, as the Constitution clearly set up a democratic system based on competitive party elections, complete freedom of the press could be imputed as a logically necessary condition. A very similar argument was made in 1993 in the United Kingdom by the House of Lords when it held that a local authority could not be libelled, because freedom of press comment was necessary. Where an overt statement of human rights exists, such a methodological technique is much less useful.

In camera

Trials held in camera allow no access to the press or public. Only very rarely can this method be used for criminal trials, and then only where state security is at risk. It is generally considered that secret trials are an affront to the right to a **fair trial**, even though all the other protections, such as the right to appeal, and the various procedural rights about legitimate evidence, the **right to silence** and the **right to counsel** still apply to the defendant. However, given the increasing concern for **privacy**, and the difficulties of ensuring a fair trial under intense media speculation, there is growing hesitancy over the real advantages of public trials.

Inalienable rights

Political theorists have often talked about rights as being inalienable. The American **Declaration of Independence** refers to life, **liberty** and the pursuit of happiness as rights which are inalienable. Thomas Hobbes (1588–1679), in *Leviathan* (1651), thought that the right of self-defence was inalienable, and there is a strong tradition throughout liberal political theory that the core right of personal freedom is also inalienable. To alienate a right is to give it up, to divest oneself of the entitlement to require some action or forbearance on the part of another. It is unclear whether the adjective 'inalienable' actually adds anything at all to the noun 'right', because the conditions in which it makes sense to see basic 'human' or 'civil' rights as alienable is obscure. Some statutory rights can clearly be alienated; a statute may provide citizens with the right to some degree of employment security, and an employer may offer a short-term contract, one of the terms of which is that anyone signing it will not press his rights against dismissal when the contract expires. Some political rights are clearly alienated when a person takes a post in a civil or military service which has, attached to it, the obligation not to stand for election, or not to publish anything in the newspapers without clearing it with the department. Both the latter examples are intentionally ambiguous: it is not at all clear that a court would interpret employment law as actually depriving the short-term contract holder of employment rights were he to disown the fact that he had tried to sign them away; a constitutional court could well hold that the civil servant could not, in fact, be required to give up his rights to political involvement.

There is a certain logic in declaring such rights alienable, given a sufficiently precise context, but it is questionable whether a basic right, say the right to

freedom of speech, can be alienated. If an individual were unable to complain against the censorship of his writings, then this loss of rights would have to be perpetual; a right, to be effectively alienated, must be beyond recall, or else all that has happened is that someone has privately decided not to protest about the government trampling on his rights, which is quite different. Rights are corollaries of duties. If several of us give up our right to **religious freedom**, does that entitle the government to force us to attend a church? A properly alienated right would involve the proper assumption of countervailing power, yet private decisions cannot legitimate a power the state ought not to have, and one thing we mean when we say the citizen has a right to do something is that the government has a duty not to prevent that action. The actual purpose of the 'inalienable' language is to make a much broader political statement about what forms of government can be legitimate. To say that the rights to life, liberty and the pursuit of happiness are inalienable means that only governments dedicated to these ends are legitimate, and that, whatever the appearance, no body of citizens can ever be seen as consenting to be governed against these interests. The entire language of rights in this context comes from the long-abandoned social-contract style of argument in political theory, where people are conceived of as originally living in a state of anarchy; because of the inconvenience of such a state they set up a government by contract, agreeing to transfer certain powers they had in the anarchic state to a central authority. Inalienable rights are ones they could not give up, because to do so would subvert the very purpose of setting up the government. There has been a rebirth of interest in social-contract thinking in recent decades, particularly relevant to rights discussion in the work of authors like Robert **Nozick**.

Incorporation

Incorporation is the process by which one legal code is taken into another and made a fully functioning part of it. It takes place where a code has a jurisdiction which does not include the jurisdiction of the system into which it is going to be incorporated, and cannot therefore be used by litigants or courts unless formally incorporated. The main current example is the status of the **European Convention on Human Rights** which, though signed by Ireland and the United Kingdom as by the other members of the Council of Europe, has not been incorporated into the domestic law of either country, as it has been by the other signatories. The result is that though the Irish and British governments are ultimately bound to abide by the Convention, this can only be enforced as a last resort by taking the governments to the **European Court of Human Rights**. The Convention cannot be cited in a British or Irish court, and the citizens of the two countries therefore lack day-to-day legal recourse against human-rights violations in ordinary first level courts, unlike, say, a Dutch citizen who can seek protection from all tiers of his own court system. Consequently there has been considerable pressure in the United Kingdom to incorporate the Convention and make it directly applicable (and these demands seemed likely to be met by the new Labour government elected in 1997), as is the case with directives of the European Union, following the incorporation of the **Treaty of Rome** in the early 1970s. The most notable historical example of incorporation of a human rights code is the process by which the **Fourteenth Amendment** to the US Constitution incorporated what had previously been civil liberty standards applicable only to the federal government into the legal systems of the separate states. (See also **Incorporation of the Fourteenth Amendment**.)

Incorporation of the Fourteenth Amendment

The US Bill of Rights (see **Bill of Rights (USA)**), the first Ten Amendments to the US Constitution, was originally intended to apply only to the federal government, because states were deemed entitled to make their own provision for matters like **religious freedom**, where practices in the original colonies had varied widely. One consequence of this was that discriminatory patterns, above all the legal protection of **slavery**, were able to flourish in parts of the Union when they were abhorred elsewhere. After the Civil War the North felt that it had to enforce minimum standards to protect the former slaves, now freed by the Thirteenth Amendment of 1865, from the inevitable vindictiveness of the whites in the South, and that this could not be done unless the federal courts could apply to state legislation the standards that it had developed from the Bill of Rights. Consequently the **Fourteenth Amendment** was passed in 1868, and introduced two pertinent measures. Firstly, it defined everyone born or naturalized in the USA as citizens of the USA and of their state of residence; slaves, of course, had not previously counted as citizens, and merely abolishing slavery did not, of itself, grant them this status. Secondly, the Amendment provided that no state could pass a law that would 'abridge the privileges or immunities' of a federal citizen, and, in the famous **due process** and **equal protection** clauses, incorporated the developing federal jurisprudence of **civil liberties** and human rights into the state law. Now no state government could do anything that the federal courts would not allow the federal government to do, effectively standardizing human rights across the USA.

What this meant in detail took decades to work out, because the vital clause, the due process clause, is too cryptic to be a code in itself. In a whole series of cases from the late 19th century until the 1960s the US Supreme Court held due process to have more and more content. The test, developed by the prominent Supreme Court Justice Benjamin **Cardozo**, came to be that due process incorporated all those standards which were essential to 'any scheme of ordered liberty'. An example is the **right to counsel** in a criminal trial. The Sixth Amendment in the Bill of Rights provides that the accused in a criminal prosecution shall have, *inter alia*, 'the assistance of counsel for his defense'. However, the Fourteenth Amendment does not say, in so many words, that the Sixth Amendment now applies to the states, only that the states must abide by due process of law, raising the question of whether protections like the right to counsel are part of the very meaning of due process, or just a specific Sixth-Amendment right that still applies only against the federal government. At first the Supreme Court was prepared to insist only that the states should provide counsel for those too poor to afford them in capital cases, and it was not until the landmark case of *Gideon v. Wainright* in 1963 that Cardozo's test was held to imply that no one should face any sort of criminal trial without legal counsel. Each of the various due process rights had to be brought into application piecemeal, and the entire process came to be known as the incorporation process. The **incorporation thesis** was never easily accepted in a context where the right of each state to develop its institutions along its own lines was at the heart of the very doctrine of federalism, but *Gideon* is often regarded as the last battle, and it is now rare for a state to try to argue that it should be held to different standards than the federal government itself.

Incorporation thesis

The incorporation thesis refers to an argument of great importance in US **rights jurisprudence**. The original US Bill of Rights (see **Bill of Rights (USA)**) was demanded by several of the separate states as security against the new federal government invading the individual rights of their citizens. So, for example, the **First Amendment** prohibition against established churches was written into the Bill of Rights in a context where some states did have established churches which they wished to protect against any federally backed rival, while others already prohibited, or simply lacked, such establishment and wished to preserve the **religious freedom** of their citizens. In a pluralist society of separate states both positions were compatible with restrictions on the new central government. However, after the Civil War the **Fourteenth Amendment**, passed to ensure that **slavery** was eradicated in fact as well as legally, guaranteed to all US citizens both **due process** of law and **equal protection** of the laws. This seemed to many to imply that some, at least, of the civil rights guarantees in the Bill of Rights must now apply against the several states, if the citizens of states with different traditions were in fact to have equal protection, and if due process, which must have some standardized core meaning, was to be everyone's right. The history of the Supreme Court's development of civil rights jurisprudence is in large part the history of this 'incorporation', as more and more of the first Ten Amendments were held to be incorporated by the Fourteenth Amendment into the overall constitutional limitations on the actions of the states. The process of incorporation took nearly a century, with the last details, largely to do with **criminal civil liberties**, not being considered as fully covered by the due process clause until the 1960s.

Inherently suspect category

The complex jurisprudence of civil rights in the USA has been closely associated with working out the legal limits to discriminatory practices. Discrimination *per se* cannot be outlawed, because legislation works against the very logic of discrimination, which singles out certain groups to have treatment different from others. The problem has been cast in terms of what categories of person may legitimately be discriminated, either negatively or positively, and for what sorts of policy ends. As part of the development of these tests there has been a pressure to rule that some categorizations are simply always unacceptable, however benevolent the policy aims may be. The US Supreme Court has recognized three levels of such categories. Most possible classifications, for example one based on wealth or place of residence, are acceptable as long as there is a rational policy connection; thus a city income tax on commuters who live outside the city boundaries would be acceptable. Other forms of discrimination, notably gender, are seen as being too politically sensitive to be used in legislation unless there is a very good reason, even though it is not unconstitutional to treat men and women differently. One classification however, that based on race, has come to be identified as 'inherently suspect'; essentially there is no government aim, however vital, which the Supreme Court will allow as justifying a racial classification, because of the whole history of racial degradation. Pressure groups for other minorities or categories, especially feminist groups, have struggled, so far without success, to have their categorization promoted to this 'inherently suspect' status.

Inheritance

There is no formal right either to inherit or to bequeath in any modern rights document, although through most of modern history the rights have been assumed to be virtually inviolable. Their omission as specific rights is due to the fact that the right to own **property** is well entrenched in most rights documents, and it would never have occurred to thinkers of the great age of constitution writing that property rights might not entail the freedom to inherit one's parents wealth nor to pass it on to future generations. In some respects the main legal developments of the 16th and 17th centuries in England (the historic heart of the common law world) were the derestriction of regulations on how property could be disposed of after death. Indeed the invention of the equitable trust, which many legal historians consider one of the single greatest inventions in English legal history, was entirely intended to allow the rich to determine in some detail how their wealth would be inherited and used. In at least one of the fundamental documents of 18th-century rights philosophy, John **Locke's** *Treatises on Civil Government* (1689–90), part of the very duty to obey the government is derived from the fact that it ensured the protection of the wealth you have inherited. Only with the advent of Marxist-influenced socialism in the late 19th century did anyone doubt the moral validity of inheritance, indicating the way in which classic doctrines of human rights are only with difficulty adjusted to modern more egalitarian social doctrines.

Injunction

Injunctions are a form of court order originally derived from the equity jurisdiction of courts. They are orders a plaintiff can seek from a court, ordering someone or some group either to do or to refrain from doing some specific act. Injunctions come in two forms, interlocutory or perpetual. Interlocutory injunctions, which are most often of importance in the area of **civil liberties**, are orders to prevent or enforce some action with immediate effect, to remain in place until the issue can be fully litigated; they have the effect of preserving the status quo until some later date. Perpetual injunctions tend to be less important because they are given only in a situation where an ordinary order for damages, or for the performance of a contract, is for some reason insufficient or inappropriate.

Interlocutory injunctions can be vital, because the plaintiff may feel that once the damage he fears is done, nothing can compensate him, even if he ultimately wins a case against the defendant, and in human rights contexts they can prevent a government from doing something that would abridge a freedom or right in a way which cannot afterwards be compensated for. For example, in the 1993 English civil rights case of *M v. Home Office*, an injunction was issued against the Home Office to prevent them deporting a supposedly illegal immigrant who claimed political **asylum**. The argument was that, if the Home Office were allowed to deport him, as threatened, before his case were fully adjudicated, he might be killed in his home country. In this case the Home Office, arguably accidentally, ignored the injunction, and the Law Lords made legal history by ruling that the Home Secretary himself could be held in contempt (see **contempt of court**). Injunctions do not necessarily work in favour of the weaker party in civil rights cases; temporary injunctions, often known as 'gagging orders', can be used by the government, or by the rich and powerful generally, to prevent publication of material on the grounds that it may later turn out to be libellous or seditious (see **libel** and **sedition**). The immediate prevention of publication may be all that the plaintiff in the case is concerned about, either because the matter may not even come to full trial, or because it will cease to be newsworthy before that can happen. Similarly, injunctions gained by employers against trade unions were, by blunting the strike weapon, particularly dangerous in industrial relations; the employer might not later be able to demonstrate that the strike would have been illegal, but, even if he ended up paying costs, it might well be economically worthwhile. For this reason industrial relations law in the United Kingdom has considerably limited the use of injunctions.

International Covenant on Civil and Political Rights

This Covenant, which was intended to make more precise, and therefore justiciable, the rights listed in the UN's **Universal Declaration of Human Rights** of 1948, was passed by the General Assembly in 1966, and came into force in 1976. By mid-1995 130 states were party to the Covenant, thus making it part of international law as far as they are concerned. Like the **European Convention on Human Rights** of 1950, the Covenant provides for an optional enforcement machinery, known as the Optional Protocol, which by mid-1995 had been signed by 84 states. Under the Optional Protocol the Human Rights Committee set up by Part IV of the Covenant is accorded jurisdiction to investigate complaints made by individuals against any state for abridging the rights set out in the Covenant. Unlike hearings by the **European Court of Human Rights**, the consequences for a state of having such a complaint upheld are purely in the realm of publicity as no further enforcement machinery exists; there is no power to award damages nor a duty to amend national law to bring it in line with the Committee's recommendations.

Part II of the Covenant, which opens with a general justificatory section, serves as an essential methodological preface, requiring each state to establish internal mechanisms to protect the enumerated rights, and to protect them in a non-discriminatory way. It contains two further notable protections; firstly it specifically states that other rights already existing in member states cannot be taken away on the pretext that the Covenant does not recognize them. This is equivalent to the Ninth Amendment to the US Bill of Rights (see **Bill of Rights (USA)**), which stresses that mention of some rights in that document does not invalidate other pre-existing rights. It is a necessary tool when states at varying levels of political development, as was the case with the colonies of North America, try to form an all-embracing agreement. Secondly Part II, by accepting that, in periods of emergency, states may not be able to guarantee all the rights possible and desirable in peacetime, actually increases the general level of protection, because it lists those rights which cannot, in this way, be derogated. These specially protected rights are mainly rights to **security of the person** and bans on, for example, **slavery** and **torture**, but also, more surprisingly, include the **freedom of conscience** and thought rights encapsulated in Article 18 of the Universal Declaration of Human Rights.

The main part of the Covenant is Part III which, in 22 articles spells out the **negative rights** of the Universal Declaration. These are often drafted not only with more precision, but with much substantive detail. For example, instead of a bland guarantee of the **right to life**, Article 6 adds four clauses severely restricting the use of the death penalty, and one replicating the UN's prohibition on **genocide**, supported fully in other conventions. Similarly the Article 9 protection for **due process** and the Article 10 protection of **liberty of the person** are very detailed, applying standards at least as high as those enforced by the US Supreme Court or the European Court of Human Rights on matters like speedy trials, and rights to know precisely what one is charged with. Indeed, Article 9 (Clause 3), stating 'It shall not be the general rule that persons awaiting trial shall be detained in custody . . .' may imply a standard that some liberal democracies, not excluding the United Kingdom, would find it hard to meet. These **criminal civil liberties** are yet further developed in Article 14, so that the Covenant in total completely protects, and in great detail, any right a British or US citizen could claim to have under either common or constitutional law, and may, given certain problems of legal **interpretation**, actually exceed some versions of rights protection in code law countries. It is not, for example, generally thought to be a basic human right to be compensated if it is found that one has been wrongly convicted of a crime, though some states make *ex gratia* payments in such circumstances. Most of the other rights are presented in ways that more closely resemble their equivalent in the Universal Declaration, and cover **freedom of association**, **freedom of speech**, **religious freedom**, **privacy** and the **right to family life**.

The one Article in the Covenant that reflects its international concerns and which could seem to clash with, or at least stretch, ordinary national rights codes is Article 27, the last in Part III, which provides that: 'In those States in which ethnic, religious or linguistic minorities exist, persons belonging to such minorities shall not be denied the right, in community with the other members of their group, to enjoy their own culture, to profess and practise their own religion, or to use their own language.' The problem is not that such rights are impossible, if narrowly defined, to guarantee, but that any purposive interpretation by an activist court might well turn such protections into claims that required special privileges. As the Article presents these as group rights, a concept with which western rights theory is generally unhappy, the article might be thought less consensual than the rest of the document. In order to avoid these problems of positive versus negative rights, **positive rights** are dealt with separately under the **International Covenant on Economic, Social and Cultural Rights**. (The text of the Preamble and Parts I to III of the International Covenant on Civil and Political Rights is given in the Appendix.)

International Covenant on Economic, Social and Cultural Rights

Like the **International Covenant on Civil and Political Rights**, also promulgated by the UN General Assembly in 1966, but not entering into force until 1976, the International Covenant on Economic, Social and Cultural Rights was intended to enhance and supplement the **Universal Declaration of Human Rights**. It was deemed necessary to separate these two areas of rights because member states would not be willing to accept, in the economic and social sphere, anything like the degree of enforceability that is required if a civil or political right is to mean anything. Necessarily, the social and economic covenant is more in the nature of a set of commonly agreed goals for socio-economic progress. Notably missing is any strong conception of duties the richer states may have towards the poorer; such an idea might have been useful in a document which, as a treaty, is capable of conferring duties and rights in international law. At most, parts of some articles imply a transnational duty. Article 11 (Clause 2), for example, declares that 'The States Parties to the present Covenant, recognizing the right of everyone to be free from hunger, shall take, individually and through international co-operation the measures, including specific programmes, which are needed . . .' Then follows a list of the technical measures to improve world agriculture. The clause ends with a statement of a general duty, though not addressed to any particular states, 'to ensure an equitable distribution of world food supplies in relation to need'. This section apart, there is almost no external duty imposed on any state. Indeed the clearest duty call, written into the Preamble, is still in the best of Western individualist traditions, stating that the States Parties agree upon the Articles of the Covenant, 'Realizing that the individual, having duties to other individuals and to the community to which he belongs, is under a responsibility to strive for the promotion and observance of the rights recognized in the present Covenant'.

Like the second chapter of the Universal Declaration from which it derives, and unlike the first chapter of that document and the civil and political covenant, there is an uncomfortable looseness of drafting and repetition in the economic, social and cultural covenant. There is no obvious reason, for example, why sex discrimination needs an entire Article (Article 3) banning

116

it specifically, when it is already banned under Article 2 (Clause 2), along with every other conceivable basis for discrimination. The actual rights are enumerated in Part III, in only ten Articles; consequently the substantive part of the Covenant accounts for less than half of its length. Most of the enumerating articles follow roughly the same pattern. First a general right is announced, and then it is either delineated with greater precision, or various steps likely to effect it are listed. Thus Article 6 sets out a 'right to work', (see also **right of employment**), including the right freely to choose one's work, and then suggests means to this end, to include: 'technical and vocational guidance and training programmes, policies and techniques to achieve steady economic, social and cultural development and full and productive employment under conditions safeguarding fundamental political and economic freedoms to the individual.' As there is no known government which would not follow such measures were it to be able to think of them, it is entirely unclear what Article 6 can be thought to achieve. Article 7 in a sense goes the other way, combining similar generalized values with oddly specific details. It again refers to work, and is intended to ensure good working conditions and decent wages, but is unclear as to what exactly it is mandating. 'Just and favourable conditions of work' are defined to include 'fair wages and equal remuneration for work of equal value without distinction of any kind, in particular women being guaranteed conditions of work not inferior to those enjoyed by men, with **equal pay** for equal work . . .' The language is rebarbative and unclear, to a greater extent than can be explained by the fact that the document is not intended even remotely to endow people with justiciable claims. The Article suddenly becomes clear and highly specific in subsection (d) when it requires 'remuneration for public holidays', which is surely the sort of detail, however desirable, that cannot be taken to be some form of universally valid entitlement.

Most other articles follow this pattern of vagueness and sudden clarity. They include, *inter alia*, social security rights, trade union rights, rights of the family familiar from all the universal and regional rights declarations, the right to good health provisions and rights to education. The contrasts are stark: Article 9 guarantees the right to social security in only 18 words, while Articles 13 and 14 on educational rights take up 30% of the entire substantive section of the Covenant. Much of Article 13, Clauses 3 and 4, may, in fact, be misplaced, and belongs more naturally to the domain of the civil and political covenant, protecting as it does freedom of choice in education. The curious rag-bag nature of the Covenant is demonstrated nowhere so well, perhaps, as in the fact that it replicates a specific very narrow right from the Universal Declaration, one that most people would not regard as a basic right at all, which is the copyright protection under Article 15 (Clause 1c). It is possible to imagine very good reasons for a state denying legal protection to copyright without abridging anything whatsoever of a fundamental nature. Parts IV and V of the Covenant set up an elaborate reporting mechanism for each state, and delegate the Economic and Social Council to monitor performance in attaining the goals set out.

The principal weakness of the International Covenant on Economic, Social and Cultural Rights is not that it tries to set out universally valid goals of economic development, nor even that it calls them rights, though it is unclear how the appellation 'rights' in such a context helps; it is that the document is unsystematic, neither everywhere precise and offering measurable scales of development nor adequately broad and general to compel real assent. It is not clear why 132 states had ratified the convention by mid-1995: although in some areas it actually commits them to nothing they would not otherwise have done, in others it enshrines policy positions which can only be regarded as optional. Is it a universal right that anyone should be free to establish and direct an educational institution, as long as that institution accepts the goals set out in the Covenant's own brief, and reaches a minimum standard? Certainly many liberals might feel this to be 'right', but many socialists have often argued that, for example, private schools are a blight on social development. In the end it is impossible not to see the economic, social and cultural covenant as too obviously the result of compromises and deals between a large number of competing special interest groups, united by no cohesive ideology. All rights documents are ideological. While the civil and political covenant, for better or worse, essentially represents the triumph of a particular Western-based individualistic conception of political rights, this does at least produce a coherent set of attainable goals. The economic, social and cultural covenant might have been expected to represent a similar uniform ideology of at least a moderately egalitarian and social democrat nature, but it shows no sign of this, nor of any alternative general position. (The text of the Preamble and Parts I to IV of the International Covenant on Economic, Social and Cultural Rights is given in the Appendix.)

International Labour Organization (ILO)

The ILO was created in 1919 as part of the post-First World War movement that established the League of Nations, and as such is the senior of all international organizations dedicated to social justice. Its constitution begins 'Whereas universal and lasting peace can be established only if it is based upon social justice . . .', which is similar to statements in documents like the UN's **Universal Declaration of Human Rights**, or the **German Constitution**, to the effect that peace depends on recognition of human rights. The ILO became a specialized agency of the UN in 1946. It has played a vital role in setting standards in all areas involving employment, employment rights, trade unions and workers' rights in general, both at the abstract level of setting goals, and by crafting detailed and technical charters and covenants. How broadly it defines its remit can be seen by the declaration it issued in 1944 reaffirming its fundamental principles, which states in the Preamble:

(a) Labour is not a commodity;

(b) **freedom of expression** and of association are essential to sustained progress;

(c) poverty anywhere constitutes a danger to prosperity everywhere;

(d) the war against want requires . . . (that) representatives of workers and employers, enjoying equal status with those of Governments, join with them in free discussion and democratic decision . . .

Clearly such a programme is deeply embroiled in human rights discussions, not only in the **positive rights** debates involved with documents like the **International Covenant on Economic, Social and Cultural Rights**, but also with the more justiciable types of rights contained in the **International Covenant on Civil and Political Rights**. Most developed countries have been members of the ILO almost from its beginning, and its documents, and even more its research and analysis, have influenced employment and trade union legislation in many countries. There is a whole series of conventions and covenants covering many areas of labour relations. Two of the most important are the Freedom of Association and Protection of the Right to Organize Convention (1948) and the Right to Organize and Collective Bargaining Convention (1949) (see also **freedom of association** and **collective bargaining**), both of which have been ratified by over 100 states. It has also been very active in the areas of sex discrimination and **racial discrimination** (see also **equal opportunities**), thus acting to support very basic rights found in many rights documents and even, partially, in the **Treaty of Rome**. Here the most important measures are probably the Equal Remuneration Convention of 1951 and the Discrimination (Employment and Occupation) Convention of 1958, both similarly ratified by well over 100 states.

Internment

Internment is usually taken to mean **detention** of those either suspected, but not proved, to be guilty of crimes, or thought to have a high probability of being likely to commit crimes even if they are not currently even suspected of having done so. As such, a policy of internment is in flagrant violation of the core human right of **liberty of the person**, which almost all constitutional codes protect. Internment, by its very nature, involves a denial of **due process** and all associated rights, including that to a **fair trial**. Inevitably, internment requires the suspension of the right of **habeas corpus**, because no court could fail to free someone who had been interned even though the state could not prove him guilty of any prior defined offence. Internment has regularly been resorted to, even by liberal democracies during periods of crisis (for example, by the United Kingdom in Northern Ireland

119

between 1971 and 1975), usually, though not only, during wartime. The internment of US citizens of Japanese ancestry during the Second World War is often regarded as the worst part of the Supreme Court's record, because the judges failed to hold it to be unconstitutional, despite it being a clear breach of both the **equal protection** and due process clauses of the **Fourteenth Amendment**. Similarly, decisions by the British courts upholding detention powers, including the notorious Article 18b powers under which both 'enemy aliens' and suspect British sympathizers were detained during the First World War, are frequently cited as the lowest point in the deference of British **public law** to the executive. The practice is still widely used in many countries, such as those operating under states of emergency or experiencing guerrilla conflicts, and in some countries the distinction between **arrest** and detention is far less clear than in the Western liberal democracies.

Interpretation

Any legal document, whether a commercial contract, a parliamentary statute or an article of a constitution, needs to be applied to a specific situation to have effect. The application process is at the heart of the judicial process, and inevitably involves interpreting the meaning of the document. Very few rules can be written with both sufficient clarity and sufficiently broad but precise coverage to be applied in an automatic fashion. Even apparently precise rules possess what legal philosophers have called 'a penumbra of uncertainty' about them. A classic example is a local authority by-law which provides that 'no vehicle may be driven in the park'. Does this include a child's pedal car? If not, does it include a child's car powered by a small electric motor and big enough only to hold one six-year old? If a rule as simple as that by-law cannot be applied without 'interpretation', it is obvious that the judicial enforcement of human rights, which are encapsulated in symbolically powerful but wholly unspecific language, requires very extensive interpretation. The entire text of Article 3 of the **European Convention on Human Rights** simply says 'No one shall be subjected to **torture** or to inhuman or degrading treatment or punishment' (see **degrading punishment**). Not only the words 'torture', 'inhuman' and 'degrading', but even the apparently technical words 'treatment' and 'punishment' can legitimately be the subject of endless debate concerning their interpretation. Is someone compulsorily detained under a Mental Health Act and given electric shock treatment being tortured? Clearly he is not being punished, and is rather undergoing 'treatment'; however, passing electric shocks though someone's brain would, in many contexts, be torture, and even done with good intentions is probably degrading. Yet Article 3 has to be applied to over 30 countries with vastly different legal, moral and political cultures and histories, and so interpretation is crucial.

There are countless books written on interpretative techniques, and innumerable judicial pronouncements in every legal system, from which certain strands emerge. One is the very literal approach, which used to be the official norm among British judges, and is still found occasionally. The judge takes the clearest possible dictionary definition of each word and applies the meanings strictly, and only if the resulting interpretation is manifestly absurd will the rule be further interpreted. The alternative is to take the words as expressing not so much a formal rule as an intention; the legislator must have been trying to achieve something in creating the rule, and as long as this intent can be established, it should be possible to apply the rule sensibly. Such an approach works well with cases that approximate to the imaginary by-law example. One could, perhaps, accept easily enough that the by-law was intended to provide a peaceful and safe play area in the park, and thus as long as the children's play car makes very little noise, travels at a very slow speed and has big bumpers made of very soft rubber it probably is not a 'vehicle' for the purposes of the act. Unfortunately, human rights legislation is seldom like this. Article 3 does not forbid torture to achieve some other end, it forbids torture in itself; there is no other 'intention'. Yet a 'plain meaning' rule will not help either, precisely because torture is so elastic a word, deeply laden with value references which change from culture to culture, and even from person to person. An important historical example of interpretation problems in human rights law comes from the US experience of the incorporation of the **Fourteenth Amendment**, which has focused upon interpreting the substantive meaning of the guarantee of **due process** of law. This problem was partially solved by a judicial fiat which declared that any practice recognized in the US Bill of Rights (see **Bill of Rights (USA)**), which could be seen as inherent to 'any concept of ordered liberty', would be deemed to be incorporated into the idea of due process. Although this still leaves room for argument, for example over whether **jury trial** constitutes such a practice, it does focus the argument and make it somewhat more empirical.

Intention arguments in interpretation about human rights have a special problem, which is the possible 'datedness' of the intention. This has been particularly troublesome with the interpretation of the US Constitution, because the relevant 'intention' refers to whatever can be said to have been in the minds of those who wrote or ratified a document at the end of the 18th century. As awareness of human rights has developed, it would seem appropriate and necessary to raise the expectations of state behaviour, yet this is hard to establish under an intention argument. The Eighth Amendment to the US Constitution, part of the Bill of Rights, forbids **cruel and unusual punishment**, but it could be argued that 18th-century states routinely did things to people, including execution, that much modern opinion would regard as cruel and unusual. Some have asserted that the death penalty is unconstitutional, but the Supreme Court, even at times when it has had a liberal majority, has never felt able to interpret the words 'cruel and unusual' in this way, in part because of a strong current of US judicial thought which says that the 'original position', the position at the time of the Constitution's drafting, must govern interpretation. The most common distinction drawn by commentators between judges is between **strict construction**, sometimes called literal construction or strict interpretation, and 'liberal interpretation', but this distinction itself produces more questions than it answers. The inevitability of interpretation, which is the root cause of judicial **discretion**, is often ignored by politicians who lambaste courts for not giving literal interpretations, usually without realizing how seldom they would like the results were courts routinely to do this. (See also **golden rule**.)

Interrogation

Codes relating to interrogation stem from the core idea founded in most **bills of rights** and constitutions of **due process** and **fair trial**, and details have usually been left to constitutional courts or even legislatures. The idea of fairness in a trial has been seen to necessitate safeguards on activities before the formal trial itself, and consequently there are extensive controls against **torture** or **cruel and unusual punishment**, and control over conditions of **detention**, all of which naturally have a bearing on interrogation. There are three closely related but separable reasons for attempts to control the procedure and atmosphere of police interrogation in the interest of the citizen's due process rights.

Firstly there is an obvious fear that abuses during interrogation may lead to false confessions and the consequent risk of an innocent person being convicted. Secondly, as an extension of that, the **right to silence** is generally upheld to greater or lesser extent in liberal societies, and this is taken to mean that an accused cannot be forced to give the state any information that may help to convict him (see also **Fifth Amendment**). The third point is that the process of interrogation is both frightening and humiliating even for an innocent person who is not subsequently prosecuted, and this infringement on individual liberty must be minimized, particularly in common law countries with an accusatorial system of criminal justice.

Obvious controls over the use of overt brutality, physical or psychological, exist in most systems, and no court in a Western liberal democracy will entertain a confession which is not clearly shown to be truly voluntary, but more general rules on the protection of the right to silence tend to be weaker, and thus the interrogation process itself requires monitoring. Consequently, codes of practice for interrogation involve a variety of procedural safeguards, including tape-recording the interviews, repeated cautions about legal rights (see **caution on arrest**), presence of counsel or other advisers, maximum time lengths and minimum rest breaks, as well as maximum total time in detention before being presented to a magistrate, and so on. Particular combinations are used in different systems, but there is relatively little empirical evidence about the different effects, although the presence of another person apart from the police is generally held to mitigate the oppressiveness of the experience of being arrested and interviewed. The entitlement for anyone under **arrest** to have legal counsel (see **right to counsel**) with him at all stages of the interrogation procedure is now fairly uniform in the Western liberal democracies and, in the United Kingdom, in the case of juveniles the police are actually obliged to have an 'appropriate adult' present during interrogation. In practice the lawyer's chief value may well be as a friendly presence rather than for any specific legal advice tended during the interrogation. Since the passage in the UK of the **Police and Criminal Evidence Act (PACE)** in 1984, all police interrogations have been recorded on audio tapes, and there have been experiments with video taping. Ultimately no interrogation process may be allowed to go on for very long without the police being forced either to release the suspect or charge him, with the secondary rule that interrogation must cease once a charge has been made. The effectiveness of this sort of package has been demonstrated by the relative rarity of criminal convictions made since the passing of PACE being overturned by the British Court of Appeal.

J

Judge-proofing

The term judge-proofing refers to the attempt to write legislation in such a way that the courts have no chance to oversee decisions made under it. It has often been attempted in the United Kingdom, especially by Labour governments because of their inherent suspicion that the courts represent a Conservative element in the constitution. Typically such a piece of legislation, like the Foreign Compensation Act of 1950, which was the subject of a famous case, **Anisminic**, in 1968, will set up administrative tribunals whose decisions are intended to be final, and not liable to appeal, on any ground, to any court. What usually lies behind such attempts is either a suspicion of political bias on the part of the courts, or a more general feeling that administrative convenience should outweigh the time-consuming niceties of a fully judicial style of decision making.

Judge's rules

The judge's rules were the informal rules set out by judges to control police procedure during **interrogation** and **arrest** in the United Kingdom. Originating in 1912 at a meeting of High Court criminal law judges, they were added to in 1918 and a new set was defined in 1964. They had no official statutory force, so someone treated by the police in breach of judge's rules could not, for example, sue for this breach. They covered approximately the area that **due process** covers in other jurisdictions. Cautions had to be given at various stages (see **caution on arrest**), as with the **Miranda warning** in the USA, but their operation depended on an informal agreement between judges. If the police did breach judge's rules in their treatment it might lead to evidence being excluded at trial, but given that the British courts have never operated the fruit of the poisoned tree doctrine (see **probable cause**) very forcefully, even this was not certain. The rules were made irrelevant by the passing of the **Police and Criminal Evidence Act** in 1984.

Judicial review

Judicial review is generally used to mean the power of a court to decide on the constitutionality of legislation or other legal rules, and sometimes executive actions of the state. (It has a special meaning in the United Kingdom, for which see **judicial review (United Kingdom)**.) The first modern political system to incorporate judicial review in this sense was the USA, where the Supreme Court established that it had this right over legislation by the Federal Congress in the landmark case of *Marbury v. Madison* in 1803. It was already accepted that the Federal Supreme Court would necessarily have such a power over the legislation of the separate states. Most **written constitutions** include some power of this sort in the hands of either a court or, as with the French *Conseil Constitutionel*, a special body. To some extent a power like this is necessary if the written constitution includes either or both a separation of powers doctrine or a federal structure, because each implies the possibility of one state body trespassing on the territory of another, with the consequent need for an impartial referee. The scope of the power varies, in part according to the constitution, in part through political factors which influence the extent to which the review body in question is prepared to accept responsibility. So, for example, the constitutional position of the Italian and German Constitutional Courts are not very different, but from the founding of the Federal Republic the **German Constitutional Court** has been very active, whereas the Italian equivalent did not take a major role in politics until relatively recently. Even the absence of a written constitution, or the presence of a constitution which does not appear greatly to limit legislative power, need be of little hindrance to a determined court. The Israeli Supreme Court, equipped with only the minimum of basic laws to interpret, has made a series of far-reaching judgments overturning legislation. The Australian High Court has developed doctrines, largely on the basis of **imputation** from the structure of the constitution, which make up for the absence of a bill of rights, allowing it to protect rights like **freedom of speech**.

Such courts vary in several ways. Firstly, an important institutional factor is whether the judicial review powers are given to the senior court in an ordinary court structure, as with the Supreme Courts of the USA and Canada and the Australian High Court, or are located in a special court solely charged with constitutional **interpretation**, which is the usual model in code law countries. Secondly, there is the question of whether the body can take an actual case before the courts in which a constitutional question arises, or can give what are called 'abstract reviews'. In the latter case other institutions, most usually the parliament, can refer a draft or bill and ask whether or not it would be constitutional if passed. In the former only concrete questions arising in litigation may be referred. All permutations seem possible; the US Supreme Court has only concrete review powers, the German Court has both, as, to a more limited extent, does the Canadian Supreme Court. A power equivalent to judicial review has been given to the **European Court of Justice** over European Union legislation, and one might interpret the role of the **European Court of Human Rights** to include a form of judicial review of signatory states' legislation.

Judicial review (United Kingdom)

In the United Kingdom judicial review has a technical meaning which has little to do with the more usual meaning of the phrase in constitutional law. The normal internationally-recognized meaning of **judicial review** is the process by which a court determines the constitutional validity or otherwise of legislation or executive decrees. No such right adheres in any British court, where the doctrine of parliamentary sovereignty is supreme. Judicial review in the UK refers to a specific process by which administrative acts can be challenged before the courts on the grounds that they are *ultra vires*, or otherwise made illegally or invalidly. The main way to challenge such a decision is by seeking leave from a court to apply for judicial review of an action. This is a **public-law** remedy, and not all instances of unfair or even illegal decisions by an administrative or local government body will be covered by the power. The particular process known as an application for judicial review has existed since 1978, when the process was invented by the courts themselves, though it was shortly thereafter backed by legislation. Most of the doctrines supporting judicial review, and most of the remedies a court can order, already existed however, because it has never been true that the UK completely lacked a body of **administrative law** in the way some commentators used to argue.

Jury trial

Trial by jury is often seen as the single most famous element of the common law protection of human rights, though it is by no means found only in Anglo-American common law jurisdictions, and has no very clear connection to much of what is considered vital about human rights. The right to a trial by jury is deeply rooted in the common law; it is part of the Sixth Amendment to the US Bill of Rights (see **Bill of Rights (USA)**); the Seventh Amendment also guarantees federal juries in most civil cases, which is no longer the rule in all common law jurisdictions. It is a firm part of lay belief in such countries that they are uniquely lucky in having such a system, but the difference between systems is partly definitional. Most jurisdictions rely on lay assessors to help the professional judge or judges in serious cases, though they are not usually called juries and may play a less obviously independent role. The crucial fact about a jury is that it is the judge of fact, not of law; its members are obliged to follow judicial instructions about the applicable law, about what evidence they can consider, and how they should weight it. However, because jury deliberations are secret and cannot be investigated, it is openly accepted by most experienced criminal law judges that their instructions to the jury are frequently ignored, and even more frequently misunderstood. Nevertheless an appeal court can, on rare occasions, overturn a jury decision on the grounds that it is manifestly absurd.

The origin of common law juries lies in the need, with the primitive judicial and police systems of earlier societies, to have trials, often carried out by visiting royal officials with no local knowledge, in some way controlled by local factors. Thus a jury of one's neighbours would understand the folk-law-derived rules of common law as developed in the locality. More to the point, neighbours in small face-to-face societies would be much better judges of truthfulness and character than any nobleman, local or otherwise. With a standardized and largely technical and legislated criminal law, and in the context of modern society, these advantages no longer apply. The main substantive justification for juries has little to do with human rights directly, but with a more general distrust of the state. It is often held that juries simply will not convict people where they feel either that the law itself is unfair, or that it has been applied unfairly, if correctly, to a particular individual. Even if this is true, and even if it provides some residual protection against unpopular laws, its effect would be so partisan as to raise serious questions about the undoubted civil right to **equal protection** of the laws. It can more easily be argued that traditional local standard effects of juries have a place in civil law, but juries are only extensively used in civil law in the USA.

There is nothing sacrosanct about the traditional 12-person juries, and many jury trial jurisdictions do not adhere to that number. The theoretical basis for a jury trial is that an accused is judged by a representative sample of his or her fellow citizens, making an intuitive decision about the truthfulness of witnesses; there is no relevant technical expertise, and it is precisely the ordinary experience of the person in the street that is valuable. There is, of course, absolutely no empirical evidence to prove that a random cross-section of untrained observers is more likely than experienced professionals from the criminal justice system to have this unspecified talent. All that is required of a jury in terms of human rights is that it be impartial. This has been taken in the USA to mean that both prosecution and defence should have the right to challenge potential jurors not only for actual bias, but as representative of potentially biased sections of the public. In consequence the jury selection stage of a major criminal trial can be lengthy, and almost as determinative of the result as the rest of the trial. Unrepresentative juries, particularly on racial or gender bases, can afford a ground for appeal for mistrial, and in capital cases have often been a determining factor. Without any doubt, juries do acquit guilty people for whom they have sympathy. When this occurs simply because the accused individual appears deserving, it represents a merely random fluctuation in the system. There is anecdotal evidence, however, that juries can act systematically when they disapprove of a particular law or the consequences of conviction. It certainly became easier to get murder convictions in the United Kingdom after the death penalty had been abolished, and some believe that it is virtually impossible to get convictions under the Obscene Publications Act because of popular conceptions that the matter has nothing to do with the government. Where a systematic pattern comes to exist, juries may well be regarded as an extra, if rather *ad hoc*, check on the popular legitimacy of certain parts of the law.

Unless the provision of jury trial is taken as a good in itself, it is not clear if human rights codes should show any marked preference for judgment to be given by a random sample of citizens. If those citizens know the accused personally, they will be debarred from hearing the case for fear of bias, and the inability of juries to grasp technical evidence is well known to cause problems in complex trials, particularly those involving fraud. (For a period in modern British legal history such cases were tried before special juries chosen for technical competence.) Where jury trial has been suspended, as in Northern Ireland for terrorist crimes because of the fear of jury intimidation, most people with experience of them have regarded judge-only trials as every bit as fair, and no more likely to convict than an unintimidated lay jury. In fact, trial by a judge sitting alone is more open to appellate control, because in such trials, known in Northern Ireland as 'Diplock Courts', the judge has to give reasons for his decision, whereas a jury's reasonings are lost in the legally-enforced secrecy of jury discussion.

L

Legal aid

Legal aid is the primary British scheme for ensuring that those unable to afford their own lawyers in criminal cases, and in many categories of civil cases, have the services of both solicitors and barristers provided at public expense. All liberal democracies have some version of the scheme. Legal aid is not itself a human right in the normally accepted sense, but the existence of something like it is a necessary logical deduction from more formally acknowledged rights. Essentially any version of a commitment to **due process** of law, or to a **fair trial** as implied by doctrines of **natural justice in English law**, necessitates free provision of legal services to those who cannot afford counsel. This is because of the paramount importance of the accused being able to make their own arguments as efficiently as the prosecution can make their's. Especially in the accusatorial process, but to a large extent also in a continental inquisitorial criminal process, a defendant would be totally vulnerable were he to have to defend himself against charges argued by legal professionals.

It is generally recognized that the need for professional legal advice starts long before the trial, almost certainly at the moment of **arrest**, and thus most legal aid systems provide for free legal counsel in the police station during preliminary **interrogation**. In the USA the **Miranda warning** requires the police expressly to make the point that the suspect is entitled to free legal aid as soon as he is arrested and that he should not say anything to the police in the absence of such counsel. Legal aid systems often provide limited free legal services in civil cases as well. Although this might be seen as a form of welfare provision that a state could legitimately dispense with, there is a very powerful argument, at least in the sort of **public law** cases where constitutional and human rights are being challenged, that free provision of legal services is as much a necessary implication of civil rights as in the criminal process. Throughout the West there is a standard complaint that legal services are so expensive, and the cut-off point at which an applicant for legal aid is deemed rich enough not to be entitled is so low, that people of middle incomes are severely discriminated against. Thus the very provision of legal aid produces a possible rights violation in the sense of discrimination in terms of access to justice. (In October 1997 the new Labour government of the United Kingdom announced plans to address these complaints by introducing a 'no win, no fee' system for civil cases; full legal aid would continue to be available in criminal and human rights cases.) (See also **right to counsel**.)

Level of scrutiny

The level of scrutiny concept is part of the US constitutional **interpretation** of when a statute breaches the guarantee of **equal protection** of the laws in the **Fourteenth Amendment**. In order for a classification of people to be used for policy purposes in statutes, it must be shown that the state has some good reason for making the classification. This is to avoid overt, and even more to avoid subtle, discrimination in breach of basic human rights. For example, a town council might ban parking in the town centre because of overcrowding, but allow certain categories to be exempted. Few would object to exemption for disabled drivers, but it would be quite different if there were exemption for drivers of very expensive cars; in US parlance this second scenario would be an unconstitutional denial of equal protection, while the disabled exception would probably not. The level of scrutiny methodology is a technique for assessing when such distinctions are or are not acceptable. Depending on the basis for the classification, the government may not only have to pass the 'ordinary scrutiny', it may have to pass a 'strict scrutiny', and there exists a less well-defined intermediate version known as 'heightened scrutiny'. A politically uncontroversial classification, perhaps an income classification where welfare legislation is involved, requires the government simply to show that the classification 'reasonably' relates to a 'legitimate' state interest. Where race is involved the strict scrutiny level applies, and almost eradicates the possibility of legitimate use of such a classification; the state would have to show that the classification was 'closely related' to a 'compelling governmental interest'. It has been suggested that nothing short of a major public health crisis or national security issue or something of that kind could now persuade the Supreme Court to find that a racial classification was legitimate. (This idea of **inherently suspect category** goes back to the Court upholding the constitutionality of **internment** for US-Japanese citizens in 1943.) Heightened scrutiny has come to be applied to gender-based classifications, requiring a 'substantial' relation to an 'important' governmental interest. The strict scrutiny test also applies to any classification involving a fundamental protected freedom. Thus if the US Bill of Rights (see **Bill of Rights (USA)**) protected **freedom of movement** (it does not), the example of a parking restriction would probably only be acceptable if overcrowding could be shown to be at crisis levels.

To a large extent these tests are simply formulae to be applied to cases to suit the appropriate judicial system's conception of the importance of the issue and the political sensitivity of the classification. Nothing remotely objective can be made of distinctions between substantial and close connection, nor important or compelling interests. Nevertheless the impact of such classifications, if only through the **chilling effect** of potential litigation, is considerable. Furthermore the mere existence of a hierarchy of scrutinies presents a challenge to pressure groups; the women's movement has tried for 30 years to get gender promoted to the level of strict scrutiny, but, despite winning most of its cases, has not yet achieved this.

Libel

Libel laws exist under a variety of technical names in all jurisdictions and, in common law, libel, along with slander, is only one branch of the general civil tort of defamation. The relevance for human rights is twofold. Some systems actually recognize a right not to be defamed, under the general notion of protecting an individual's 'honour'; the **Universal Declaration of Human Rights** puts such a protection against attacks on 'honour and reputation' along with protections for '**privacy**, family, home or correspondence' in Article 12, suggesting that personal reputation is part of a rather extensive privacy right. The **German Constitution** treats it ambiguously as between a right in itself and a restriction on the right of **freedom of expression**, by making it one of two special limitations on Article 5, where expressive freedom is limited not only by 'provisions of general legislation' but by the need to protect youth and by the 'citizen's right to personal respect'. Consequently **protection of human dignity** is likely to clash with the right to **freedom of speech**, and although it may be argued that no right is unlimited and all rights must be exercised responsibly, this argument may have serious implications for other human rights, particularly in so subjective an area as either personal honour or free expression of truth. Given the restraining power of gagging orders, a strong libel law can effectively prevent any but the most determined, which may mean the richest, newspaper from drawing public attention to a public figure's corruption or other misdeeds. Much depends, of course, on the particular definition of libel in the national law; but most definitions treat the falsity of a published statement as more or less determinative of the guilt of the issuer of the statement, with his or her intent being distinctly secondary. Being more aware of the political importance of freedom of speech than many cultures, the USA has crafted a rather more subtle libel law in this respect. If someone such as a politician or senior general is referred to in a way that proves to be false, he may still not win a libel case unless he can prove that there was a malicious intent, rather than accident or incompetence, lying behind the publication. The principle is that anyone entering the public arena in such a way as to invite, or become a legitimate target for, press interest, must take some risks, and a similar idea lies behind adaptations of the libel law in other countries. In the United Kingdom in the 1993 case of *Derbyshire County Council v. Times Newspapers* the Law Lords held that a local authority could not be libelled, on the grounds that it was imperative in a democracy that elected bodies not be able to use the defamation laws to suppress media inquiry. There have been comparable rulings in Australia. As with so many human rights issues the clash between libel laws, whether or not they enshrine something which is a right in itself, and expression laws can only be solved by careful and largely intuitive use of judicial **discretion**.

Liberty

Liberty and freedom are so closely related that their usage is largely inter-changeable. To the extent that there is any useful distinction, liberty is a more political concept, while freedom connotes a simpler absence of restraint; liberty is usually connected to a desirable or justifiable activity, whereas freedom is neutral. Hence there is freedom of the press; there may be freedom to publish obscene and vilifying lies, but the argument that doing so was an exercise of one's political liberty might sound strange. Political theorists have often contrasted liberty to license, defining the latter as the absolutely uncontrolled exercise of complete freedom, and the former as the legitimate or, at least, purposive use of freedom. The term freedom tends to be used in an undifferentiated way; one is free to do whatever one is not forbidden to do or prevented from doing. Liberty, however, is almost always tied to something (for example, **liberty of the person**, or **civil liberties**), and is set against a background of expected constraint as a specific right. The tension between the two terms reflects the historic tension in political theory at the root of all debates about the individual's right to do what he wants. Few political theories are focused upon freedom in any uncomplicated way, but value it for some reason, often tied to an idea of personal development or the liberating of 'true' human nature. Where a political theory, covertly or overtly, is of this form, liberty is the use of freedom to pursue a good, natural or true aim. Liberty is never thought to be absolute, and consists, effectively, of the freedom which can be allowed.

Liberty (the organization)

Liberty, also known by its full title, the National Council for Civil Liberties (NCCL), is the nearest British equivalent to the **American Civil Liberties Union (ACLU)**. It was founded in 1934 by a freelance journalist, Ronald

Kidd, partly as a result of his concern about the behaviour of the police towards demonstrators during the marches by the unemployed in London during the early 1930s. It rapidly attracted the support of many eminent people on the radical side of British politics, including George Bernard Shaw, who acted as one of their observers during some demonstrations in the mid-1930s, and it has always had a roll call of distinguished political and academic names on its executive council. The focus of Liberty has naturally shifted over the years, concentrating for example on excessive security consciousness by the government in the 1940s, race relations problems in the 1970s and computer invasions of **privacy** in the 1980s. It is, however, prepared to investigate and issue reports on any matter concerning **civil liberties**, and frequently gives evidence to commissions of investigation and parliamentary committees. It is notably aided in its work by good relations with semi-official bodies like the Parliamentary Civil Liberties group. It has itself not infrequently experienced difficulties in its relations with the police and the government, having been regarded by the security services for part of the Cold-War period as a subversive organization. An important part of its work is to study, and try to amend, new legislation with any bearing on civil liberties, and its tendency is to take a much purer libertarian line than any political party could risk; for example, it has always opposed the Prevention of Terrorism Act, even when the Irish Republican Army (IRA) has been most abhorred by British public opinion.

Unlike the ACLU, Liberty cannot be said to be deeply non-partisan. Where problems like the rights of fascist or racist organizations to march or demonstrate arise, Liberty objects to authorities which fail to use their powers, rather than, as with the ACLU, taking **freedom of expression** as all important and helping the bodies in question. It is difficult to assess how effective Liberty has been over time, though it has recently achieved the very unusual status, in the United Kingdom, of being allowed to file an *amicus curiae* brief before the House of Lords.

Liberty of the person

Liberty of the person is a slightly archaic way of referring to physical freedom, as opposed to **freedom of conscience, freedom of speech** or some such liberty that does not require external constraint to remove it. Liberty of the person is the concatenation of a set of freedoms such as freedom from false **arrest**, freedom from unnecessary **pre-trial detention**, **freedom of movement, freedom of assembly** and so on. Its core use is in the context of police **detention**, not only the relatively long-term detention of someone arrested and taken into custody with a view to a criminal charge, but any temporary imposition of physical restraint. Thus the **European Convention on Human Rights** states, in Article 5, that 'Everyone has the right to

liberty and **security of the person**' in the context of defining legitimate powers of arrest. The phrase 'the inviolability of the person' is sometimes used as an alternative, as in Article 2 of the **German Constitution** headed 'Personal freedom'; it tends to connote a ban on physical invasion of the body, as in some types of searches or compulsory taking of blood or tissue samples, which is probably also intended by 'liberty of the person'.

Literal construction (see **strict construction**)

Locke

John Locke (1632–1704) is, without doubt, the founding father of modern civil liberty thought, and had a profound effect on the framers of the American **Declaration of Independence** and the members of the Constitutional Convention, and some have claimed to find the influence of his ideas in the French Revolution. He was associated with the Earl of Shaftesbury in the political upheavals after the restoration of the monarchy in 1660, and went into exile after he fell from power. He lived in the Netherlands from 1683 to 1689, returning with William of Orange when he took the throne in the latter year, then serving as a minor government figure until his death. These private experiences, as well as general reflection on the politics of late 17th-century England, made him, in the context of the day, somewhat of a revolutionary, and his seminal work of political theory, the *Second Treatise on Civil Government* (1690), includes a rudimentary defence of the collective right to revolution.

The essence of his political theory can be simply stated, though the working out of the details is a much more complex philosophical task. Locke argues that, prior to the existence of states, man was endowed with human rights, principally the rights to freedom and **property**. Locke, unlike Thomas Hobbes (1588–1679), whose *Leviathan* (1651) was a critical target in the former's work, did not think that conditions in this pre-social state, known technically as the 'state of nature', were so unbearable that mankind needed to take drastic steps to create political systems and then to avoid their breakdown. He argued that life in ordered society is clearly preferable, so people enter into a contract with a government, making obedience to the government conditional on its protection of their basic rights. Political legitimacy requires the consent of the governed, and lapses if the government damages the very rights of freedom and property it was created to protect. In putting rights before government, and seeing the justification of government precisely in the protection of rights, Locke became a powerful advocate of human rights. The language of the American Declaration of Independence is directly Lockeian: it is declared to be self-evident that men 'are endowed by their Creator with certain inalienable rights; . . . to secure these rights governments are instituted among men, deriving their powers from the consent of the governed'. The reference to 'their Creator', rather than to God, reflects the deistic position typical of Locke's intellectual milieu, as opposed to orthodox Christianity. Among Locke's other important political writings were the *Letters on Toleration* (1689–92), in which he advocated complete religious toleration, except for outright atheists, whom he considered so lacking in a sense of nonearthly powers that they could not be trusted. Clearly its concentration on property marks Locke's work out as limited in its direct 20th-century appeal, though he did in fact have an extensive definition of it which included one's bodily labours. Furthermore, the impossibility of requiring actual consent as the basis of government authority limits the direct applicability of the theory, though again Locke tried to moderate the practical consequences of his writing by a doctrine of 'implied consent'. Nevertheless, Locke's influence has been enormous, and modern imitators, such as Robert **Nozick**, may be thought to add very little to the original design of a rights-limited government.

Locus standi

Locus standi is the Latin term for the legal concept also referred to as 'standing to sue' or just 'standing', covering the rules controlling who may bring a case to a court, or be heard before the court when it is considering litigation brought by others. Although it may seem purely a technical legal concept, there are grounds for thinking it one of the most politically important variables across legal systems, and one with peculiar importance for human rights. The core test, common to most jurisdictions, is that only someone whose own interests are directly affected may sue. So, however concerned some observer of a human rights violation, perhaps a **civil liberties** pressure group, may be, a court may not allow them to bring a case against a government on behalf of victims unwilling or unable to sue themselves. As the victims may be too frightened so to do, or so oppressed that they do not see their treatment as discrimination even though onlookers do, such violations may be beyond the reach of courts which adopt a strict doctrine of *locus standi*. Less dramatically, the scope of a civil rights case may be narrower, and the consequent ruling less powerful, if only the specifically aggrieved person is heard, as counsel for the plaintiff will naturally craft as narrow an argument as possible to increase the chance of his or her client having a specific injustice lifted.

Some legal systems seek to minimize this problem by more generous rules on standing, and US courts commonly allow *amicus* briefs, under which concerned groups or state officials who are not directly party to the conflict may yet address the court. US human rights groups such as the **American Civil Liberties Union (ACLU)** or the **National Association for the Advancement of Colored People (NAACP)** are frequently allowed to present such arguments, ensuring that the whole range of human rights implications of some matter under litigation, say a death penalty appeal or an immigration decision by the Immigration and Naturalization Service, are considered by the court. Such bodies can also, of course, afford far more expensive counsel, and can provide a wealth of research services, in the way that the plaintiff's own counsel, very probably one paid for by the state under some form of **legal aid**, cannot hope to equal. Probably the most extensive of all standing rules are those of the **European Court of Human Rights**, which allows a complaint to be brought against one government by another government on the basis of the first government's treatment of its own citizens, whether or not the citizens themselves are parties to the litigation. The British interpretation of *locus standi*, on the other hand, is one of the most restrictive in the world, though very recently the Law Lords have allowed civil liberty groups to address them on carefully defined issues. One version of the standing rules that is difficult to deal with is where a government policy is not discriminatory, and does not offend a majority of the population, but is seen by some as a breach of constitutional propriety and, in a broad sense, a breach of human rights. There have been cases in the United Kingdom, for example, where trade-union activity threatened the freedom of broadcasting, and individuals sought to take legal action where the government was not prepared to do so. It has been held that the individual has no standing because he is not affected any more than any other citizen, and the essence of standing is a personal hurt. Similarly, the US Supreme Court refused to take any case brought by taxpayer groups opposed to the Vietnam War, on the grounds that merely being a taxpayer did not give enough of a special connection to constitute standing. The easier it is to establish either that one is being hurt by a policy, or that one is entitled to be heard because of someone else's hurt, the more effectively the courts can be used to control arbitrary, oppressive or anti-libertarian activities by states.

M

Magna Carta

The 'Great Charter', granted by King John to the 'free men' of England on 15 June 1215, is widely considered to be the basis of British constitutional liberties. In practice it often receives greater reverence in the USA than in the United Kingdom, where it is hardly ever referred to in courts, and little known in detail to even the educated public. It was born out of the resentment on the part of the country's barons towards royal demands on their money and military service, and in particular to the King's habit of taking hostages to ensure loyalty. Initially King John refused to sign it, but when the barons raised a military rebellion and captured London he was forced to come to terms, and formally adopted and signed the Charter at Runnymede.

The Charter defined the formal relationship between the monarch and the barons, guaranteeing their rights and also formalizing the legal and judicial procedures of the realm. The barons were particularly concerned to curtail what they saw as abuses of feudal land tenure, and to strengthen earlier versions of the right of Parliament to control taxation. Criminal law was modernized and standardized, and additional clauses recognized the rights of important urban centres and reformed currency and trading regulations. The Charter contains the first really firm commitment to the concept of **due process** with the guarantee that: 'No free man shall be arrested or imprisoned or disseised or outlawed or exiled or in any way victimized, neither will we attack him or send anyone to attack him, except by the lawful judgment of his peers or by the law of the land.' Under Henry III, and again at the end of the 13th century, Magna Carta was confirmed and modified by Parliament, and subsequently formed the main theoretical basis for succeeding generations of critics of the royal prerogative. Technically the Charter covered only relations between the monarch and the barons, but later jurists, especially Sir Edward Coke (1552–1634, who instigated the **Petition of Right** of 1628), gave it a much wider coverage, both in terms of whom it covered and as a legal rather than an essentially political document.

Mandamus

Mandamus is one of the traditional common law prerogative writs like *certiorari* and prohibition, and is Latin for 'we command'. It is an order issued by a court, in the United Kingdom by the Divisional Court of the Queen's Bench Division, instructing someone or some organization to carry out some public duty which it is within his or its office to do. It is particularly relevant here in enabling a court to enforce **statutory rights** where some administrative body is failing to perform its functions. Like all such powers its exercise by a court is discretionary; furthermore, in British **public law**, the court will not issue an order of mandamus if there is any other legal remedy available to the applicant.

Martial law

Martial law is distinct from military law, even though the two terms have the same origin. The idea of martial law derives from the medieval system in which there was a body of law administered by the Court of the Martial and Constable, and this military judicial process has developed into two branches: military law, which is the day-to-day legal order for military and naval systems, and martial law. Martial law is an emergency system in which an area is governed directly by occupying military forces, and all breaches of the military's orders are dealt with by special military tribunals, applying whatever penalties the commanding officer of the region thinks fit. It is most frequently used in countries affected by guerrilla conflicts and severe civil unrest. The right of the military to act in this way comes, at least in British law, from the doctrine of the crown's prerogative powers, but it is more of a *de facto* recognition of the sheer power of an occupying army than a legal justification. In practice modern armies have sophisticated legal branches, usually called the Judge Advocate or the Provost Martial's branch, which would normally be in charge of applying and helping define the martial law in operation. There are no generally accepted human rights restrictions on martial law except those that come from the laws of war and international laws on treatment of prisoners, refugees and so forth (see **Geneva conventions**). In exceptional circumstances, such as the threat of invasion, civil war or other major crisis leading to the breakdown of ordinary law and order, martial law can be declared inside the national territory of the military which is to operate it, but it has not happened in the United Kingdom since the 17th century. It is probable that the crown prerogative would not be enough to establish martial law inside the UK nowadays, and that an act of parliament would be necessary. It is one of the features of martial law that not only can the civil courts not interfere while it is in operation, but no acts done under military law can be challenged afterwards as long as they were carried out in good faith, and proportionally to the nature of the crisis.

Minority rights

It might be thought that the majority of human rights theory would be primarily concerned with minority rights, as majorities seldom persecute themselves; in fact, viewing the issue of human rights as a problem of majority treatment of minorities is a modern development. Traditionally, rights were held to be absolutely individualistic, and the state, or other entrenched powers, as potentially antagonistic to anyone, or to everyone bar a few in the élite. It is true that persecution of opinion in breaches of the **freedom of expression**, or discrimination against the believers in a particular faith, are likely to be consequences of the relative rarity of the opinion or faith in question, but this is a matter contingent to the causation of human rights breaches. Most societies have only become widely pluralistic at the ethnic and cultural levels from the middle of the 20th century; therefore recognized minorities in potential cultural conflict with majoritarian states are a recent experience. Where societies were highly pluralist from an earlier point, as with the USA, the tendency was for immigrants to be so eager to acculturate that minority rights as such hardly occurred on the agenda.

One problem with the discussion of minority rights is whether it necessarily requires the acceptance of group rights, which is a step most human rights experts are unwilling to make. If a minority right is no more than the right not to suffer infringements of existing human rights because of one's minority membership, there is no theoretical problem, nor is there anything new to say. Discrimination is a breach of basic human rights, whether it be on the basis of a unique characteristic or one the complainant shares with an identifiable sub-group. However, minority rights tends to mean a claim that a group should have some special status, protection or provision precisely in order to continue to flourish as a group. Thus a claim that there is a human rights entitlement to religiously denominational schools, so that an ethnic group may continue its separate identity, is logically different from the claim that forcing the adherent of a particular religion to attend a school where the precepts of a different religion are taught is a breach of his human rights. Whether or not the recognition of such group rights, and thus of minority rights in this sense, is deemed desirable, the entire tradition of human rights discourse is so wedded to a liberal individualistic conception of mankind that minority rights in this sense are unlikely to make much progress.

Miranda warning

The Miranda warning may be the most famous piece of civil liberty law in Western society—because of the universal appeal of US police dramas on television. When one New York cop turns to another and says 'read him his rights', the card the second officer pulls out and reads from contains the US version of the **caution on arrest**, as instituted by the US Supreme Court in *Miranda v. Arizona* in 1966. The warning must convey each of the following four points, though no specific wording was required by the Court: you have the right to remain silent; anything you say can and will be used against you; you have the right to talk to a lawyer before being questioned and to have him present when you are being questioned; if you cannot afford a lawyer one will be provided for you if you so desire. (See also **right to counsel**, **legal aid**.) The legal basis for this insistence is that the **right to silence** in the **Fifth Amendment** provides a right that is not restricted to the courtroom, but must be protected, because it is literally a right against **self-incrimination** from the very beginning of the investigatory process. Before *Miranda* the courts had used a much looser 'voluntariness' test in which they decided, case-by-case, whether the totality of the experience an accused had gone through made a confession truly voluntary or not. The indifference of many state courts to human rights, particularly where judges, being elected, were sensitive about accusations of 'being soft on crime', had made this very unsatisfactory, and the Miranda warning was meant to make the entire process of protection much more automatic. Although *Miranda* had some effect, a huge number of cases are still dealt with on the basis of supposedly voluntary confessions, and US law has not taken the step of requiring all police interviews under caution to be tape recorded, as introduced in the United Kingdom by the **Police and Criminal Evidence Act in 1984**. Consequently no real check can be carried out on how effectively the police do make the warning, which does not require a frightened suspect to insist on his rights.

Misdemeanour

A misdemeanour was originally a crime at common law generally regarded as less serious than a **felony**, a conviction for which resulted in forfeiture of property to the crown; nevertheless, some misdemeanours, such as riot, could be regarded as serious enough to merit heavy punishment. The somewhat arbitrary distinction was abolished in the United Kingdom in 1967, when both felonies and misdemeanours were replaced with the new distinction of arrestable and non-arrestable offences (see **arrestable offence**). This newer distinction is a more accurate reflection of seriousness of crime, because it was based on the severity of punishment provided. Most US state jurisdictions retain the misdemeanour/felony distinction, though it has for some time accorded more with a seriousness based on punishment doctrine. There can be civil liberty consequences to the distinction, in as much as misdemeanours may be tried at lower levels of courts, or with less of a pre-trial obligation on the prosecution to justify proceeding.

N

National Association for the Advancement of Colored People (NAACP)

The National Association for the Advancement of Colored People was founded in 1909 in New York City to improve the social and economic conditions of black US citizens. The initial spur to creating the NAACP was a riot in 1908, in Springfield, Illinois, which had been the hometown of President Abraham Lincoln (1809–65), where whites had attempted to drive out and even kill black residents, and the organization's first major campaigns were against the still common practice of lynching. Many of the organization's strategies go back to early years, as exemplified by their famous 1915 public boycott of *Birth of a Nation*, a film by D. L. W. Griffith (1875–1948), claiming that it depicted blacks in a degrading way. Perhaps more important was their decade-long fight against voting discrimination, notably the protest over the 'grandfather' clause in the voting laws of certain Southern states, which enfranchised only those whose grandfathers had voted, automatically disenfranchising blacks, whose grandfathers, as slaves, could not vote (see **voting rights**). The NAACP's most famous and most important success was the ***Brown v. Board*** decision of 1954, although its Legal Defense and Education Fund had been fighting previous cases since the late 1930s. After 1963 the NAACP became involved in more direct political action, such as the 'Jobs and Freedom' march on Washington, led by Martin Luther King, Jr (1929–68). Although still very active, with a membership of around half a million, the NAACP has come to be seen as slightly conservative by many black radicals, and is thought to have little support among inner-city black populations, being more attractive to middle class blacks.

National Labor Relations Act (NLRA)

The National Labor Relations Act (NLRA) is a US federal law enacted in 1935, largely at the instigation of President Franklin D. Roosevelt (1882–1945), and often known as the Wagner Act, after its sponsor, Senator Robert F. Wagner (1877–1953). The law governs the labour–management relations of business firms engaged in inter-state commerce, as the federal government does not have jurisdiction to legislate in purely state matters where there is no constitutional involvement. Its aim was to guarantee trade-union rights to workers and protect the legality of strikes, which had often been hotly contested during the earlier days of the great depression, and the Act created the National Labor Relations Board (NLRB) to protect these rights. The Act prevents employers from engaging in unfair labour practices such as coercing employees not to organize or join a union, and from practising discrimination in regard to hiring or dismissal of employees or to any term or condition of employment, in order to encourage or discourage membership in any labour organization. Above all the Act forbids employers to refuse to bargain collectively with the representative chosen by a majority of employees in an enterprise recognized by the NLRB (see **collective bargaining**).

Before the NLRA there had been no federal protection for the development of a union movement, but as a consequence of union activity following the Act, the number of organized workers rose from about 3.5 million in 1935 to about 15 million in 1947. Though later, less pro-union, administrations and congresses amended the Act, particularly with the Taft–Hartley Act in 1947, which ruled out any closed-shop agreement between employers and employees, the basics of US industrial relations law still follow the NLRA process. As such it has had one of the most lasting impacts on civil rights of the entire US New Deal, and is a good example of how legal creation and enforcement of rights can be successful even in a context as unsympathetic to those rights as a society otherwise committed to *laissez-faire* ideals.

Natural justice in English law

Apart from its general importance in legal philosophy, natural justice is a technical term in English common law, with similarities to the concept of **due process** in US legal thinking. US courts use the term 'natural justice', but in a wider sense than in its technical usage in the United Kingdom. Natural justice in the UK refers to the conditions necessary for a judicial or **quasi-judicial** decision to be regarded as fair. These are usually summarized under two requirements: the first is that everyone is entitled to a hearing (*aude alteram partem*); and the second that every judge must be free of bias (*nemo iudex in parte sua*). In themselves the rules might seem quite obvious, and have been described as 'general principles of law common to civilized communities', and recognized as such by international tribunals and many national courts. There has, however, been divergence over the application of these general doctrines by different legal systems. Of the two maxims, the one forbidding a judge to decide a case in which he has an interest is the more straightforward. It has always been interpreted with tremendous rigour in the UK, such that the merest possibility of a judge having a direct interest, however trivial, especially of a financial nature, in the outcome of a case, is enough to disbar him from hearing it. The classic case occurred when, after 10 years of litigation, Lord Cottenham gave a decision in *Dimes v. Grand Junction Canal* (1852). After the decision the losing party discovered that the judge had held a minimal number of shares in the company, and the House of Lords felt required to set aside his decision, even though they insisted that he could not possibly have actually been influenced by the fact. The rule has been extended quite widely, including acquitting people convicted when it was discovered that a member of the jury was related to someone involved in a case.

The rule granting the right to a hearing has been more problematic, especially when the rules of natural justice have been applied to bodies other than actual courts. In these instances it is unclear what specific rights need to be included to ensure an effectively fair, as opposed to a nominally fair, hearing. Should the person concerned be allowed helpers, and if so, can they include professional lawyers? What rights does he have regarding access to documentation and so on? Exactly what must the accused be told of the charges and evidence against him? This is an ever-developing area of law, and the requirements for a fair hearing are steadily extended. Those requirements are: full legal representation, sometimes paid for by the state where an accused is too poor to provide for himself (see **legal aid** and **right to counsel**); a very precise charge; and maximum disclosure of evidence and witnesses by the prosecution. Appeal courts, for example, will throw out a conviction even where the evidence is clear that a crime has been committed by the accused, if the charge inadequately specifies the exact offence.

Over the last 50 years the rules of natural justice have been held to extend to a wider and wider range of institutions. Thus trade unions must observe them before disciplining a member, universities have to follow them in Proctor's courts, and even private organizations like the Football Association, as well as professional regulatory bodies like the BAA (the British Airports Authority), risk having their internal decisions overturned unless guarantees very close to those the courts impose upon themselves are in operation.

Natural rights

Much thinking about human rights and **civil liberties** rests, consciously or otherwise, on the doctrine of natural rights. Such a doctrine has existed since at least the medieval period, and has been philosophically contentious since the utilitarian movement of the 19th century. The core of the doctrine is that all people are entitled to certain basic rights simply by virtue of being human. Philosophical justifications for such a belief vary widely, often based on religious theories, and the doctrine was strongly held by the deist philosophers of the Enlightenment, especially Jean-Jacques Rousseau (1712–72) and Thomas **Paine**, and in documents like the French **Declaration of the Rights of Man and of the Citizen**. The doctrine of natural rights is a sub-set of the general idea that there exist natural laws binding on all humanity in any time and place, and having a status superior to any positive law emanating from any one political system or constitution. Although inherently subjective, there is a large amount of agreement between most listings of supposed natural rights, at least at the most basic level, starting with the **right to life** and rights against **cruel and unusual punishment**. The listings tend to diverge when dealing with rights more remote from physical existence, because they then depend on more complex theories about human nature. Thus a more materialist philosophy will tend to stress **positive rights** to welfare (see **welfare rights**) and perhaps to employment and opportunity (see **choice of occupation** and **right to employment**), while a religious-based theory may take more concern for matters like education, the family, human dignity and development (see **development of the personality, protection of human dignity** and **right to family life**). Ultimately, listings of rights as found in the great human rights documents like the **Universal Declaration of Human Rights** and the **European Convention on Human Rights** reflect the dominant values of the cultures that create them or their recent history, as, for example, with the very strong dignitarian and respect for life basis of the **German Constitution**.

Necessary force

All political systems are obliged to provide for the use of force by their police and military forces in the imposition of law and order, and, according to some definitions, the state differs from all other authoritative agencies precisely because it has the monopoly of the legitimate use of force in society. The imposition of law and order is at the cutting edge of **civil liberties** for two reasons. Firstly, liberties are often established only through action involving semi-legal protest, as states do not naturally welcome the demand for special status made in much civil liberty protection. Although liberal societies may hold peaceful and consensual values *de jure*, these values are often reached after a period of serious conflict, and so the protection of civil liberties requires serious limitations on the state's use of force. Secondly, police actions in imposing order, even where the perpetrators do not share the values of the society, is inherently a violent process. The penal systems of liberal societies do not sanction severe, or even any, physical hurt to even a certain criminal, yet in the process of subduing unrest the police may effectively hurt someone far more than the courts would allow as punishment to those guilty of the disturbance. For example, the death penalty is nowhere authorized for blocking traffic, yet protesters who block highways may conceivably be killed in the process of clearing the streets.

Consequently all legal systems have developed concepts of necessary force, meaning the maximum amount of physical force that can legally be used by state agencies in carrying out their duties. At the highest level such agencies are, everywhere, entitled to kill those they are trying to control in special and clearly identified circumstances, which are usually restricted to those in which only force that may result in death will be sufficient to protect other people's lives. In all other circumstances force much less than deadly may be regarded as disproportionate to the goal of the agencies; a police commander who authorized a baton charge against a group of mothers and children protesting against a school closure would be guilty of using excessive force in most countries, even if nothing worse than a few bruises resulted. In practice courts tend to be exceptionally demanding when investigating the legitimacy of the slightest use of physical force, and the English common law approach is to regard any use of force by anyone as an illegal assault, requiring special conditions to make such assault not liable to criminal prosecution.

Negative rights

Negative rights means the usual type of human right or civil liberty found in traditional rights documents like the US Bill of Rights (see **Bill of Rights (USA)**) or the **European Convention on Human Rights**, which derive from the general political theory of the limited state in a liberal democracy. Such rights, though often phrased in positive language such as **freedom of speech** and **freedom of assembly**, are negative in that they constitute prohibitions on action by the state, or sometimes by private individuals, which might interfere with the prescribed freedoms. The very language, of **liberty** or freedom, points to the basic supposition that a citizen is free to do as he wishes, to worship, publish, meet with others, and so on, and that this freedom may not be curtailed by others' actions. Such a negative right may not be absolute if its exercise clashes with the exercise of an equal-standing right. The right to dignity of the person may, if interpreted to include personal honour, as in the **German Constitution**, imply a restriction to freedom of speech. Some rights are internally complex, so that exercising one aspect may interfere with another's exercise of a different aspect. Thus Greek law recognizes a right not to be subject to undue proselytizing as part of a general right to **religious freedom**.

It is the hallmark of all these negative rights that nothing is guaranteed except the freedom to attempt something. The right to freedom of speech does not imply a duty on anyone to publish what one wants to say. Rights to religious freedom may be taken to mean that a government may not prevent parents sending their children to a denominational school, but it will not usually imply a duty on the part of the government to provide such schools. There are, however, cases where a negative right may imply the duty to provide the means to exercise it. Most modern jurisdictions, for example, recognize a set of rights against **self-incrimination** in the criminal justice system which are widely accepted to imply the **right to counsel**, and thus, in turn, a duty to provide counsel free to those too poor to afford their own lawyer (see also **legal aid**). It is only where there is a procedural requirement before a right can be said to be exercised at all that such a duty of provision applies. Otherwise a duty to provide the means to do something would take the right in question into the category of the purported **positive rights** like **housing rights**.

Nemo iudex in parte sua

Nemo iudex in parte sua is one of the two traditional rules of **natural justice in English law**, and means that no one should ever be a judge in his own case. In practice it refers to the need for absolute impartiality, which can be demonstrated only where it is impossible for a judge to benefit, however remotely, from his decision in a case. Thus the most minor and most indirect financial connection between a judge and either litigant, as for example holding shares in a company even remotely involved with one party to a dispute, would be enough to debar a judge. While there is no real problem in ensuring impartiality with a professional judiciary, the rule becomes much harder to enforce in **quasi-judicial** contexts. So, for example, hearing an appeal from a disciplinary tribunal in a private institution, such as a university, can be complicated because the appellate committee, by virtue of being members of the same body, may be thought to have an interest in upholding the general reputation of the officer facing the disciplinary procedure. For this, among other reasons, there is growing tendency for powers like the British system of judicial review (see **judicial review (United Kingdom)**) to extend their scope over such internal disputes to place them into the external court system.

Nozick

Robert Nozick (1938–) is a modern US political philosopher who, along with John Rawls (1921–) and, to a lesser extent, Ronald **Dworkin** in his **rights jurisprudence**, has tried to revive the sort of argument for human rights developed by John **Locke**. Nozick concentrates on the right to **property** which, along with a more general right to freedom, formed the basis of Locke's theory of political obligation. Nozick argues for seriously reconsidering Locke's starting point, which is that property rights stem from an original pre-political condition; for whatever reason, mankind gains property and has a natural right to it, and so political systems are set up from this original position to protect those rights, and can be legitimate only to the extent that they do so. Yet the history of modern politics is a continual story of property rights being infringed by taxation and other government appropriations to provide welfare and collective goods, without, necessarily, the consent of those who have to give up their property. Locke had already commented, in an age where it did not seem politically unusual to do so, that as government existed to protect property, only those with property should have the vote. Nozick draws attention to the way modern welfare societies, by backing away from such qualifications on democracy, has destroyed the Lockeian foundation for its legitimacy. Nozick develops his theory to call for a 'minimalist' state, which will carry out only those few vital functions which are truly most cost-effective when done by coercive power, leaving everything else, including such apparently natural state functions as policing and fire protection, to private organizations and insurance schemes.

Were Nozick arguing these positions by themselves he would be rightly treated as an extreme libertarian of no particular consequence. It is because he asserts the need for a minimalist state on the grounds of a conception of basic human rights that he is accorded considerable intellectual respect. The problem he raises, along with others who attack the predominantly utilitarian ethos of most modern social thought outside the Marxist camp, is that a real commitment to belief in **natural rights** is necessary if rights are to be seen as very largely dominant over social policy. If rights are not more or less absolute and not to be overturned for policy convenience, there is no more real meaning to, say, **bills of rights**, than to any other temporary listings of socially desirable goals. Yet if rights are absolute and take precedence over social policy, how can we support more than a minimal state? His major work, *Anarchy, State and Utopia* (1974), is a plea for the return to some sort of original position from which truly voluntary states, whose allegiance really does rest on consent, can develop.

O

Ombudsman

The office of ombudsman is originally a feature of Scandinavian legal systems, first created in Sweden in 1809. An ombudsman is someone to whom a citizen may bring complaints against executive or bureaucratic incompetence or injustice, which fall short of actual allegations of illegality. Independent of the government, the ombudsman must investigate such complaints as are legitimately put before him, and recommend some solution to the citizen's complaint. The actual powers of ombudsmen vary widely among the many jurisdictions and sub-state systems in which they have been introduced since the middle of the 20th century. Sometimes they can do no more than report publicly whether or not they believe an injustice has been committed, leaving it to the good faith of the administration, or to political pressures, to effect any remedy. Other ombudsmen may have the power to order a decision to be changed or even to order **compensation** against the offending bureaucracy. In the United Kingdom the Office of the Parliamentary Commissioner for Administration was created as an ombudsman to investigate citizens' complaints against the central state administration. Many other countries have followed suit, including New Zealand in 1962, and partial use of an ombudsman to receive complaints in a particular institution, especially the armed forces, is even more common. European countries often have military ombudsmen precisely because it is an area in which ordinary **public law** cannot easily intrude, but in other cases prefer to trust their often very powerful administrative courts. The British example is one of the more limited versions of the office; specifically, aggrieved citizens have no direct access to the British ombudsman, to whom a complaint can only be put by a member of Parliament. Ombudsmen have also been created for local government, and for the National Health Service. It is unclear whether the ombudsman system achieves very much because, by the nature of the cases it can deal with, injustice falling short of illegality, matters are all too frequently decided upon the wisdom or otherwise of a policy decision, and the ombudsman, like the courts, is ill equipped to deal with such a question.

Ordre public

Ordre public is in one sense only the French translation of the English term **public order**; the French understanding of public order, which is typical of European attitudes in this matter, differs somewhat from the meaning in a common law jurisdiction. Public order in the common law world has the relatively narrow meaning of preventing riot and such crowd or group behaviour as is likely to threaten a breach of the peace or otherwise lead to criminal damage or personal injury. While it has this connotation in Europe, it also has a wider coverage to mean general good and safe public life. In Article 9 of the **European Convention on Human Rights** the right to freedom of thought, conscience and religion is deemed to be limited only where necessary 'in the interests of public safety, for the protection of public order, health or morals . . .' The full delineation in this formula is required because of the several different legal traditions of the member states; had it been restricted to France and other countries whose law is largely derived from French Napoleonic codes, the phrase public order might well have been adequate in itself.

Organization for Security and Co-operation in Europe (OSCE)

The OSCE developed from the Conference on Security and Co-operation in Europe (CSCE), a process which opened with the Helsinki Conference in 1972, and produced the Helsinki Final Accords of 1975 (see **Final Act of the Helsinki Conference**). With reference to human rights this ongoing conference, with regular monitoring meetings every two years, was primarily concerned with what was called, in the CSCE's own terminology, 'basket three', covering human rights and general humanitarian issues. The initial basket three principles agreed to in 1975 were steadily developed and strengthened over the next 15 years as the Cold War abated, culminating effectively with major statements issued at the end of the review meeting in Vienna in 1989. The CSCE process continues, and there were further declarations, notably the Charter of Paris in 1990, but the end of the Cold War and the collapse of the communist regimes of Eastern Europe after 1989 removed most of its effectiveness. Previously the Warsaw Pact nations, in order to gain some degree of acceptance for the USSR's military and political hegemony in Eastern Europe, had been obliged to accept publicly Western-defined human and democratic rights as valid principles, even if they did not act on them. This prompted the formation of various internal pressure groups, such as **Charter 77** in Czechoslovakia, which then drew international public attention to the double standards of the old regimes. As the process developed, a clear shift occurred in the Eastern position. Having initially been unwilling to accept the legitimacy of international concern on human rights, regarding it as unwarranted intrusion in domestic affairs, the Eastern member states began to retaliate against the West by complaining about *their* human rights records. In the event, however, the very fact that the terms of the debate were so thoroughly based upon the liberal-democratic conceptions of rights simply acted further to undermine any legitimacy of the old regimes. Under the leadership of Mikhail Gorbachev, the symbolic support for Eastern European communist regimes by the USSR was reduced, gradually from 1985, and more rapidly from 1988; subsequently the CSCE basket three principles came to be powerful critical weapons which hastened the collapse of the old communist states. After the Vienna follow-up meeting (which lasted from 1986–89), at which basket three issues had far outweighed the other two areas of security and economics, the CSCE principles became very useful standards against which the post-communist regimes could be measured.

P

Paine

Thomas Paine (1737–1809), author of perhaps the most famous line in the poetry of rebellion, 'These are the times that try men's souls' (*The American Crisis*, December 1776), could also be described as the most powerful British writer of human rights literature. Though often assumed to have been an American, he was born in Thetford, Norfolk, and his American nationality was invented by the US Consul to Paris in 1794 to get him out of prison. In fact he had only arrived in the USA months before the War of Independence broke out in 1775, immediately becoming notorious with his first political publication, *Common Sense* (1776), which is held to have inspired the **Declaration of Independence**. During the war he continued to publish revolutionary material, mainly the journal *The American Crisis*. After the war he had a brief political career but returned to Great Britain, where he published his most famous work, *The Rights of Man*, in 1791, mainly as a rebuttal of Edmund Burke's *Reflections on the Revolution in France*, which had been published in the previous year. *The Rights of Man*, containing an outright cry for the abolition of the monarchy, led to his conviction for treason, and he then fled to France, where again he had a brief political career. The publication of his study of deism, *The Age of Reason* (1794), was thought too close to atheism, so he returned to the USA and he lived there in poverty to the end of his life. His work is now relatively neglected, mainly because it never contained a sustained theory of political radicalism or liberalism over and above his passionate hatred of monarchy, while Burke's *Reflections* continue to command respect as a statement of basic conservative principles. Even Paine's reasons for attacking British colonialism were not sufficiently broad-based to be attractive to later generations of anti-colonialists. He remains, nevertheless, a symbolic hero of human rights.

Parental rights

Parental rights occupy a rather ambiguous status in human rights thought, even though in one way or another they are widely accepted. They can, perhaps, be separated into two categories; firstly the right to seek parenthood, and secondly the right of parents, as opposed to the state, to make crucial decisions on behalf of their children. There is, in general, some form of recognition of the first right: the **Universal Declaration of Human Rights**, and all its derivative rights codes, establishes the right of all to 'marry and to found a family' in Article 16 (Clause 1), and, indeed, the family is given a somewhat exalted status there and in other documents (see **right to family life**). Furthermore, the insistence that men and women 'are entitled to equal rights as to marriage, during marriage and at its dissolution' in the same clause would presumably support the rights to be associated with one's children after divorce which form a major part of family law in most developed countries. This sort of right is a fairly orthodox personal right to exercise a general human freedom without undue interference from the state, and is not logically different from, say, the right to **freedom of expression**.

The second area of rights occurs most often in the question of human rights provisions for education. While some rights codes, such as the **International Covenant on Economic, Social and Cultural Rights**, guarantee the positive right to have an education, at least at the elementary level, other codes treat educational choice as a right attaching to parents. Thus the **International Covenant on Civil and Political Rights** demands, in Article 18 (Clause 4), that: 'The States Parties to the present Covenant undertake to have respect for the liberty of parents . . . to ensure the religious and moral education of their children in conformity with their own convictions.' This clause is not, and this is a matter of some interest, replicated in the **European Convention on Human Rights**, though some national constitutions, notably the **German Constitution**, do make similar provisions. In fact states clearly cannot leave crucial decisions on the development of future citizens entirely in the hands of private individuals, nor anywhere do they do so. What is at stake is the sort of condition under which a state will feel itself entitled to intervene. The liberal-democratic consensus has been to leave educational choice in parental hands, subject to the state's right to set standards for all schools, a practice supported by the economic and social covenant; this is actually an ideological choice by liberal democrats, who are not convincing in claiming that education can to any great extent be ideologically neutral. In the USA the issue of parental right to make decisions of this form, particularly where **religious freedom** is involved in educational choice, has been long and hard fought. The US Supreme Court has gone so far as to uphold the rights of parents over the right of the state to insist on a form of secondary education compatible with the rather narrow sectarian beliefs of the Amish people, even though the state argued that this education deprived the children of an equal chance to compete as adults in the modern world.

Parliamentary   Commissioner   for   Administration   (see Ombudsman)

Petition of Right

The Petition of Right, passed by both Houses of Parliament in 1628, was a major step in the constitutional struggle between Parliament and the monarchy, which ultimately led to the English Civil War. It was the first serious effort to produce a formal constitutional restriction on state power since **Magna Carta**, which it in some ways resembles. Its declared aim was to end the use of royal prerogative in favour of the normal course of law, and specifically to prevent the levying of taxes without clear parliamentary assent and to curtail arbitrary **arrest** and imprisonment. In pursuing the second it took note of various ways in which the crown had effectively intimidated people short of formal arrest, for example by billeting soldiers on them (a protection US citizens found sufficiently important much later to put into their Bill of Rights (see **Bill of Rights (USA)**)). It also attempted to restrict another common technique for imposing arbitrary state power, the declaration of **martial law**. As with Magna Carta, the Petition of Right was seen by those who introduced it not as establishing or defining new rights but rather as restoring what they held to be the state of affairs before power had been abused by the current sovereign.

Picket

Picket is both a verb and a noun, and derives from a military usage where a picket was an outlying sentry. To picket means, in a non-military context, to assemble outside some place where a political event or industrial dispute is going on, in an attempt to persuade those going in and out to stop and listen to one's protest, and a picket is one who does this. In the United Kingdom the legacy of bitter industrial relations conflicts in the late 1970s and 1980s is still such that it is hard to give an inoffensive definition. Picketing has a long history in industrial relations relating to the attempt of workers on strike to bring activities in factories to a complete halt by persuading non-striking workers not to 'cross the picket line', that is, not to enter the premises. Similarly pickets have tried to persuade anyone else having business in the premises, whether involved in the strike or not, such as delivery drivers deployed by a completely different firm, not to enter. At their best behaved and most lawful a group of pickets was still a daunting body of impassioned unionists past whom it was at least psychologically hard for a worker who did not share their views to go, and at their worst they exercised clear intimidation, not necessarily non-violently. Policing picket lines was a tremendously difficult and deeply unpopular job, calling for a fine balance between respecting the right to free assembly on the one hand, and the right to unhindered passage along public highways on the other. Where a dispute as bitter as the various coal miners' strikes in the 1980s involved people, including the police themselves, living in close communities, pickets were both very powerful and very oppressive presences. Picketing itself has never been made illegal in most countries, because to do so would not only be by definition very difficult, but also clearly unjustified according to almost any doctrine of **freedom of speech** or **freedom of assembly**. Secondary picketing, currently criminalized in the UK, involves applying the same persuasive techniques to workers and suppliers of industrial enterprises where the management was not in dispute with the original unions, but whose products or services were needed to keep the main target factories working.

Picketing as a tactic has spread to other forms of political protest, and it is common in all countries for political activists to picket places where the influential are to assemble, as in 'picketing Parliament', forcing parliamentary members to pass though crowds shouting out their messages. More nearly equivalent to industrial picketing is the attempt to cut off supplies to some institution with which one is in dispute by assembling a picket-line through which goods have to be transported and attempting to persuade drivers or others having business there not to go in. Not only have places like nuclear power stations been picketed in such a manner, but even universities. (See also **freedom of association**.)

Police and Criminal Evidence Act (PACE)

The Police and Criminal Evidence Act of 1984 was one of the most far-reaching reforms of the British criminal law system ever passed and, despite a plethora of later criminal justice legislation, remains the core of the British system with regard to the rights of accused persons. Until this Act there was very little in the way of legislative protection for those under **arrest** or police investigation. What constraints existed depended on the unofficial **judge's rules**, which originated in 1912 and had most recently been revised in the mid-1960s. PACE imposed a variety of reforms on police procedures, in particular restraints on how long and under what conditions suspects could be detained prior to being charged, as well as imposing severe restrictions on any interviewing after formal charges had been made. The single most important reform was to require all police interviews with suspects to be tape recorded, which enormously reduced the number of cases in which people have later turned out to be convicted on the basis of false confessions, or otherwise altered or 'doctored' statements. By creating the post of Custody Officer in each police station, giving a police officer the clear responsibility to ensure that suspects are granted all the rights included in PACE, the Act made it much harder for collusion to occur between police officers which might result in a suspect's civil rights being evaded—in the way that judge's rules were regularly evaded. Legislation of the same period further restrained the power of the police, notably the transference of prosecution from the police to an independent civilian Crown Prosecution Service, thus bringing the British practice much more in line with both US and, in a different way European, systems. Another independent civilian organization, the Police Complaints Tribunal, replaced the previous system under which citizens' allegations of police mistreatment were handled by police officers themselves. The reforms appear to have been effective: throughout the 1980s and early 1990s there was a series of cases (all pre-dating PACE) brought before the Court of Appeal in which convictions were overturned as unsafe when it was shown that the juries had relied on tainted evidence. (See also **interrogation**.)

Positive rights

Positive rights are a category of putative human rights which require not simply a prohibition on some infringement of a pre-existing liberty, but the actual provision of goods, services or entitlements. Thus the **freedom of speech**, typical of the normal **negative rights** to be found in rights codes, can be guaranteed because it requires only that the government not impose censorship. **Housing rights**, a frequently proposed positive right, actually demands that something be done; the state must allocate social resources in such a way as to make the right effective. There is, understandably, little recognition of positive rights in most human rights documents adopted by individual states, though various UN documents do sometimes include them. Essentially a state cannot, and arguably should not, load substantive policy commitments into a constitution which is meant to be a procedural document. Furthermore, there would be tremendous problems, likely to lead to major political schisms, where, for economic reasons, a state simply could not implement the guarantees of positive rights. For the most part positive rights have been excluded only in rights codes which in themselves were never meant to be justiciable. For example, the Preamble to the 1946 Constitution of the Fourth French Republic sets out that the nation 'guarantees to all, especially children, mothers and elderly workers, the safeguarding of their health, material security, rest and leisure . . .', but it was not until the Fifth Republic that the French accepted that the legal system could enforce the protection of human rights. Although the 1946 Preamble is incorporated into the Constitution of the Fifth Republic, its contents have only ever been used by the *Conseil Constitutionel* to protect negative rights.

Pre-trial detention

Pre-trial detention, termed imprisonment on remand in the United Kingdom, is one of the more contested issues in **civil liberties**. Most human rights codes take as basic the right to **liberty of the person**, and establish that this can only be taken away as punishment for a crime of which one has been convicted with all the protections of **due process**. This necessarily cannot be taken to outlaw the **arrest** of suspects, their **interrogation** and their temporary **detention** before they are brought before a magistrate for some form of pre-trial indictment. The issue is whether or not it is acceptable to continue this arrest-related detention for the whole of the, often lengthy, period before the actual trial. Most criminal justice systems regard such detention as acceptable only to ensure that the person indicted, arraigned, or charged attends his trial, and so the system of bail, developed since the Middle Ages, has been put in place in many jurisdictions by which a financial bond is offered to the court which will be forfeit if the accused flees. Even the possibility of release on bail, or more generally release subject to whatever guarantees the system finds necessary, can be seen as too great an imposition on the liberty of the person if the terms are harsh.

There is a long history of concern that excessive bail can be used as a *de facto* punishment by the state, and it is forbidden not only in the Eighth Amendment of the US Bill of Rights, but also in the much earlier 1689 English Bill of Rights (see **Bill of Rights (USA)** and **Bill of Rights (UK)**). To refuse bail and keep someone in detention before trial is generally acceptable, in the words of the **European Court of Human Rights**, only where the state can show 'relevant and sufficient reasons' of a public-interest kind. In general there are only three kinds of reasons which stand up under analysis: firstly where the accused is likely to abscond; secondly where he is likely to commit other crimes; and thirdly where he is likely to try to intimidate witnesses or otherwise 'pervert the course of justice'. The problem, of course, is that demonstrating any of these is largely subjective and the extent to which liberty of the person is protected in this context depends very largely on the state of trust between the courts and the police. As preventive detention, the imprisonment of someone for what he might do, as opposed to what he has done, is generally thought to be unacceptable, the second of the three reasons is particularly troublesome, and courts everywhere are reluctant to grant its legitimacy. This displeases police every-where, because a significant amount of crime is actually committed by those awaiting trial for other offences.

Jurisdictions vary widely in the way they impose pre-trial detention. It is very difficult to impose in the USA, but notably easier to persuade a British court to order detention. Some jurisdictions go further and allow bail to those convicted but awaiting appeal, but again this is virtually unknown in the UK, where people who win a reduction of sentence on appeal often

157

have to be released immediately having already served longer than their modified sentence.

Presumption of innocence

There is probably no more famous conception in ordinary understanding of human rights than the idea that a person should be assumed to be innocent until proven guilty. It is one of the common mistakes of those from the Anglo-American common law tradition to believe that they alone hold this value and the continental code law systems are inferior for not having it. In fact the 1789 French **Declaration of the Rights of Man and of the Citizen** specifies that 'every man is presumed innocent until declared guilty', something which the US Bill of Rights (see **Bill of Rights (USA)**), also drafted in 1789, omits to mention. When the drafters of the **European Convention on Human Rights** set out in Article 6 (Clause 2) that anyone 'charged with a criminal offence shall be presumed innocent until proved guilty according to law', they did not think they were imposing on a majority of members a value held only in the minority of member states with a common law tradition.

There is a difference between the accusatorial system of the common law world and the inquisitorial system in code law countries when it comes to the presumption of innocence; this concerns how the principle should be protected. In the common law it is a question of the evidence that can be adduced and the **burden of proof**. For example, **self-incrimination**, forbidden by rules like the US **Fifth Amendment**, is partly outlawed on the grounds that as a person cannot be forced to prove his own innocence (which is supposed to be presumed), he has no need to say anything at all. However, the prosecution must prove guilt 'beyond reasonable doubt' in part because, *de facto*, it is not true that the system actually presumes someone charged with a crime is innocent. On the contrary he will not be put up for trial unless there is good reason to think he may be guilty, and **probable cause** (in US usage) has been demonstrated to a magistrate or similar body. Even the burden of proof clause does not always make the presumption of innocence as secure as is widely assumed; possession of some articles, drugs for example, can be taken as presumptive proof of guilt, obliging the accused to establish his innocence.

In the European system there is no 'reasonable doubt' burden of proof requirement because judges there are charged with actually finding out the truth, not, as with the British system of **jury trial**, with choosing the better of two adversarial arguments. In the European context the **European Court of Human Rights** has made it clear that it takes the Article 6 (Clause 2) rule very seriously, and that it requires openness of mind on the part of the trial judges, as well as imposing suitable evidentiary tests.

Privacy

The right to privacy, though in many ways at the heart of much civil libertarian thought, is not well defined, and is nowhere stated precisely in any human rights code. It is perhaps best understood as combining three related desires or needs. The first, and most readily found in civil rights legislation, is the traditional sense of a private physical space the state may not enter except in special cases. The typical protection here is found in restrictions against searches of one's person and possessions, or entry into one's home. All legal codes in developed societies contain some such provisions, even those, like France or the United Kingdom, which do not have formal constitutional **bills of rights** or equivalents. The British saying of 'An Englishman's home is his castle' finds echoes everywhere. Since Napoleonic times, for example, French law has forbidden the police to enter a person's home during the hours of dark except under near emergency conditions. The US Bill of Rights (see **Bill of Rights (USA)**) expressly recognizes this sense of constitutional privacy in the **Fourth Amendment**, with its requirement of **probable cause** before any search warrant may be granted. This has been applied by the Supreme Court to such an extent that a policeman stopping and searching a person on the street and finding the clearest evidence of a crime may not be able to use that evidence if he had no good reason (no probable cause) to suspect the person of the crime in question. This contrasts with the position in the UK where no court would dismiss such evidence, though little remains of the old **Sus Law** which allowed some police forces, especially London's Metropolitan Police, to **stop and search** anyone they regarded as looking suspicious. The French *Conseil Constitutionel* has been able to find enough in their concept of 'French republican traditions' to overrule quite recent French legislation which would allow police extra stop and search powers on the motorways. Even human rights codes like the **German Constitution** may not spell the right out in much detail; Article 13 starts with the very bald statement: 'Privacy of the home is inviolable'.

A second major sense of the right to privacy has become closely intertwined with personal morality, with a strong sense, though little constitutional text backing the sense, that there is a sphere of private activity that the state has no business to regulate. A supreme example is US legal thinking on **abortion**; the famous case of *Roe v. Wade* established, in 1973, a fairly unrestricted right to abortion largely on the basis of a constitutionally-guaranteed right to privacy. This right, however, cannot be found in so many words anywhere in the Constitution, and is usually defined as a 'penumbral right', one that is implied by other more specifically-stated rights, including the search and seizure type rights mentioned above. Similarly, cases before the **European Court of Human Rights** concerning abortion have often been founded on Article 8, which provides that 'Everyone has the right to respect for his private and family life, his home and his correspondence.' In practice the Court has not argued strongly for a right to abortion, and is usually tolerant of the individual states' need for variance on the issue. This is hardly surprising, because Article 8 is itself a very good example of how vague, and in the end how weak, privacy protection tends to be. The second clause of the Article contains one of the widest exception rules, permitting the state to breach this right not only in national security cases, to protect other people's rights, or various other situations one might expect, but 'for the protection of health or morals'.

The third concept of privacy that gets some legal protection at times is best demonstrated in relation to **religious freedom**, which is not only a freedom to practise a religion without hindrance, but can sometimes present itself as a freedom not to be bothered by other people's religious concerns, that is, to have a privacy of belief. This understanding lies behind the very strong US rulings, based on the Supreme Court **interpretation** of the **First Amendment**, against the state in any way at all supporting the presence of religion in educational establishments. Oliver Wendell Holmes (1841–1935), one of the great liberal Supreme Court Justices, once defined freedom as 'the right to be left alone'.

Privacy rights are ultimately autonomy rights, the right to act and to develop in one's own way, but there is also a public concern for privacy, the strong sense that it is improper for other people to pry. This sense of privacy lies behind the recurrent demands for restriction on, for example, tabloid newspapers printing stories about private lives. National jurisdictions vary somewhat on this issue, but any strong curtailment of the media in the interests of privacy runs flatly against the better defined and more entrenched rules on **freedom of speech**.

Privacy of correspondence

Older rights documents, such as the US Bill of Rights (see **Bill of Rights (USA)**), encompass a right to privacy of correspondence in general formulae such as 'The right of the people to be secure in their persons, houses, papers, and effects' (see **Fourth Amendment**). Modern documents, notably the **European Convention on Human Rights**, see it with some precision as a specific and valuable right. So the European Convention, in Article 8 states that 'Everyone has the right to respect for his private and family life, his home and his correspondence.' The placing of the correspondence right in this context of general privacy makes it clear that the right to be protected is not a narrow procedural one. Some forms of communication, primarily between lawyers and doctors and their clients, is 'privileged', in most legal systems simply because the relationships in question cannot function at all unless very great confidentiality is guaranteed. The right to privacy of correspondence, which includes all modern methods of communication, is a right protecting the functioning of the individual in what one jurist has called 'the confident exercise of liberty'. Furthermore, in the context of the European Convention, the phrase 'respect for' has not been given, as might have been the case, a grudging and narrow interpretation, but on the contrary has been used to insist that the state must keep very far back from personal life in its surveillance and regulation.

Probable cause

The phrase 'probable cause' appears in the **Fourth Amendment** of the US Bill of Rights (see **Bill of Rights (USA)**), though it was taken from pre-revolutionary common law language. In the Fourth Amendment it is stated that 'no warrants shall issue but upon probable cause, supported by oath or affirmation'. In the immediate context of the American revolution the concern was that pro-government magistrates had been only too willing to hand out search warrants, especially to Customs and Excise officers, who used them to go on 'fishing expeditions', that is, to search on the off-chance of finding something. Where the state is allowed to act like this the process becomes oppressive even when, or especially when, no evidence is actually found. In a long line of cases the doctrine of probable cause has been developed to restrict the whole **stop and search** area of police behaviour, and has become a vital weapon for the courts to protect, *inter alia*, the right to **privacy**, and to curb police harassment of minorities. At its simplest, the probable cause rule acts to punish the police for breaching the Fourth Amendment rights relatively automatically, because the courts will disallow evidence, however strong, if the police cannot show that they had 'probable cause' to stop and search, or to ask for a 'warrant'. It is a concept largely specific to the USA, because the practice of excluding evidence, often called the doctrine of the fruit of the poisoned tree, has no real counterpart in other jurisdictions.

Procedural due process (see **due process**)

Procedural rights

In a sense, most formally-recognized human rights and **civil liberties** are procedural, at least those (the majority) which can be characterized as **negative rights**; as few, if any, rights can be absolute, a right does not so much prevent a state from doing something as circumscribe the way it can be

161

done. There is no absolute right to **liberty of the person**, but there are restrictive procedures the state must go through before it may detain anyone (see **detention**). In general, a procedural right is one related to **due process** of law or natural justice, the basic rules on how the state must proceed in coming to judgment, even over administrative and welfare matters, on citizens. Typical examples are the **right to counsel**, the rules of **natural justice (in English law)**, rights to **discovery**, and generally any entitlements and restraints that aim to ensure a **fair trial** or correct making of some administrative decision. These are rights of no substantive value in themselves; the right to counsel is not something anyone needs unless he has to appear before a tribunal. Similarly the right of access to the state's evidence against oneself is procedural in the way that, for example, the right to **privacy of correspondence** is not. Privacy of correspondence is a right which will indeed, if adhered to, restrict the state in its efforts to convict someone of a crime, and especially protect the innocent. Even if there is no danger of **arrest** and prosecution, citizens do not want the police reading their private letters, and the right is consequently inherently substantive. Procedural rights have no necessary shape, and so long as fair trials are guaranteed, the details of the procedural rights put in place to ensure the guarantee can legitimately, and in practice do, vary widely.

A substantive right, because it has value in itself, cannot vary in the same way; either the right to free exercise of religion exists or it does not. If two states differ in how that right is protected, it is more likely to mean that it is better protected in one than another, more fully respected, than that purely technical differences in mechanism to achieve the same value are demonstrated. One school of thought seeks to make procedural correctness the whole content of the concept of justice. In this sense any rule or law may be acceptable in a system provided it is applied in a strict and literal sense, is applied equally to all citizens, and does not breach any fundamental principle of **equal protection** of the law or due process of law, to use the language of the US constitution. Even though, philosophically, this may be an impoverished version of the notion of justice, human rights are more easily protected by legal systems to the extent that they do involve primarily procedural rather than substantive values. Because procedural rights are technical rules about how a state may proceed, it is easier to get cross-cultural agreement on their fundamental aspects than with substantive issues of politics and morals.

However, the distinction between procedural and substantive rights can be artificial, as demonstrated by the US experience of racial segregation in education. From 1896 until 1954 the US Supreme Court held that school systems which forced black and white children to go to separate schools were constitutional, on the grounds that the relevant procedural rule in the Fourteenth Amendment required 'equal protection of the laws', but that this was achieved by school districts which could show that the schools were essentially equally provided for, hence the doctrine of 'separate but equal'.

This was ended in 1954 by the ruling in **Brown v. Board** of Education of Topeka that separation was inherently unequal. Discrimination legislation is now subject to a constitutionality test which has set racially-based distinctions as procedurally banned (see **inherently suspect category**).

Property

The right to own property is both one of the most fundamental of human rights, and one of the most controversial. It is also one replete with legal and philosophical difficulties, because they are at the heart of the most fundamental political and ideological divide in Western history over whether property is a natural right, and whether private property is the foundation of modern society or the root of all evil in such society. While most candidates for the status of 'human right' have some form of universal recognition, the same cannot be said for property. No political creed in the modern world actually believes, for example, that **torture** is a positive good, and human rights debate about the right not to be tortured is definitional and about the nature of necessary protections. Most rights can be seen as fairly close to absolute, or at least being legitimately infringed only rarely and for identifiable special reasons, so while the right not to be discriminated against may not be absolute, it is fairly easy to see the outlines of acceptable arguments about legitimate bases for discrimination. Property rights, on the other hand, are always being interfered with, by taxation, by compulsory purchase of land for public use, by environmental and public health restrictions of the use of property, to mention only three of many legitimate policy areas. For these reasons any right to property contained in a **bill of rights** is necessarily hedged by qualifications.

A good example of such a conditional guarantee of property rights is the **European Convention on Human Rights**; it is worth noting that the right is not in the main Convention at all, but in the First Protocol, signed two years later than the Convention itself because drafting a version satisfactory to all members proved to be very difficult. All that the First Protocol guarantees, in Article 1, is that everyone 'is entitled to the peaceful enjoyment of his possessions'. It goes on to say that no one shall be deprived of his possessions 'except in the public interest and subject to the conditions provided for by law'. This does not actually guarantee property rights at all, because the property/possessions distinction is capable of meaning that protection is guaranteed only to what the state actually allows someone to accumulate, rather than suggesting that getting and acquiring property is itself a right. More importantly, the reservation clause effectively means that the only limitation on depriving someone of his property is a matter of procedural rights. To make absolutely sure that government policy is not restrained by any putative property rights, the second clause of the Article repeats that the first clause 'shall not, however, in any way impair the right of a State . . . to control the use of property in accordance with the general interest' and shall not get in the way of tax collection.

Obviously a multinational agreement intended to be signed by countries with governments ranging widely across the left/right spectrum could not set up much more specific a right to property, but the wording adopted in the Convention illustrates that the right to property is so deeply political as to be close to meaningless except in a tightly defined political context. Even constitutional documents drafted in the 18th century, when ideas of economic egalitarianism were exceptionally weak, and works of early political thinkers, such as John **Locke**, explicitly saw protection of property as the purpose of the state, such rights are anything but absolute. The US Constitution does not mention the protection of property in its preamble, and the US Bill of Rights (see **Bill of Rights (USA)**), in the **Fifth Amendment** limits protection to insisting that private property not be taken 'for public use without just compensation'. The nearly contemporaneous French **Declaration of the Rights of Man and of the Citizen** adds more passion, in describing property as 'an inviolable and sacred right', but still allows expropriation, subject to 'just and prior indemnity' where there is a 'public necessity'. It is instructive to note that the 1946 French Constitution, after saying that it 'solemnly reaffirms' the 1789 Declaration, provides in Clause 7 of the Preamble that 'Any property, any enterprise that possesses or acquires the character of a national public service or of a *de facto* monopoly must come under public ownership.' Both of these documents, equally and simultaneously, are regarded by the Constitution of the Fifth Republic as valid constitutional law, and both clauses are used by the ***Conseil Constitutionel*** to interpret the constitutionality of nationalization and privatization legislation. There is no doubt that human rights codes have from time to time been interpreted in extremely proprietorial ways by courts, and the US history of the doctrine of substantive **due process** is a case in point. It is a fear of the left in many political systems, not entirely unjustified, that any entrenched bill of rights will be used in this way, and it probably makes little difference if the constitution in question makes no specific reference to property rights at all.

Proportionality

Proportionality is a concept in continental European **public law** and **administrative law** which some commentators consider should be incorporated into Anglo-American common law; a few suggest that it is already beginning to be assimilated. Although it is easy enough to state in abstract, it is extremely difficult to define how the doctrine of proportionality should be applied. In abstract the doctrine means that an administrative act may be ruled illegal, or more likely *ultra vires*, if its effect on the interests of citizens is disproportionately great compared with the legitimate purpose of the rule or statute in question. The roots of the doctrine lie in much broader and older natural law thinking, especially in the traditional doctrine of the just war, *jus in bello*, under which legitimate military action requires that the means used be proportionate to the legitimating aim of the war. Thus the search and destroy mission, as used during the Vietnam War, for which huge areas within which anything moving could be killed were designated, was seen as a military means disproportionate to the war aim, and risked stripping the entire American military effort of justification. Applied in domestic law, a tribunal might argue that a by-law requiring all young people under the age of 18 to be at home after 10 o'clock at night was a disproportionate interference with **freedom of movement** if it was intended to prevent noisy parties, while accepting that an even more restrictive curfew might be justifiable to prevent the continuation of a series of child murders.

The doctrine of proportionality essentially requires a court to make both a policy analysis and a value judgement at the same time. For a court to decide that a rule is invalid for reasons of proportionality the judges must both decide for themselves the operational question of whether or not some other restriction might achieve the purpose, and also evaluate the relative merits of achieving the purpose and the behaviour being regulated. Such matters are, in the minds of most common law thinkers, pre-eminently for either the executive or parliament, but never for the court. In contrast, the standard British test, known as the **Wednesbury reasonableness** test, insists that only an administrative action so extreme that no reasonable decision-maker could have decided on it can be overturned by the courts. However, because much in European jurisprudence is now influencing the common law through the impact of both the **European Court of Justice** and the **European Court of Human Rights**, it is quite possible that some form of proportionality doctrine will be developed in the United Kingdom. Given the increasing internationalism of common law judgments this would probably mean the appearance of the doctrine in jurisdictions as far away as Australia and Canada.

Protection of human dignity

The centrality of the concept of human dignity to modern human rights theory cannot be over emphasized. The earlier classic human rights codes like the US Bill of Rights (see **Bill of Rights (USA)**) and the French **Declaration of the Rights of Man and of the Citizen** make no reference to the idea, and documents of that era tend to validate human rights, if at all, with a generalized reference to their 'sacred' quality, or to their foundation in natural law. In the second half of the 20th century such appeals have come to be replaced by the primacy of human dignity; this concept is

165

fundamental to the **German Constitution** of 1949. Article 1 (Protection of human dignity), has in its first clause 'The dignity of man is inviolable' and deduces in its second clause that 'The German people *therefore* uphold human rights as inviolable and inalienable and as the basis of every community, of peace and justice in the world' (author's italics). The UN **Universal Declaration of Human Rights** of 1948 makes the same deduction in its first sentence: 'Whereas recognition of the inherent dignity . . . of all members of the human family is the foundation of freedom, justice and peace', noting that the same concept appears in the UN's Charter. (There was no similar reference in the Covenant of the League of Nations signed in 1919.) Nearly all subsequent international human rights charters stress the same dignitarian justification for human rights, in a language of egalitarianism, especially suited to post-colonial international agreements. So, for example, the **African Charter on Human and People's Rights** cites the Charter of the Organization of African Unity in describing dignity as essential to 'the achievement of the legitimate aspirations of the African peoples'.

However, the concept of dignity is not only opaque, but capable of being given meanings that may distort the value-free and libertarian thrust of traditional rights theory, which is largely silent on why human rights are valuable. Thus there is an increasing tendency to distinguish between two approaches to human rights: the more traditionally liberal is often decried as 'merely utilitarian' and contrasted with a supposedly richer, and usually more conservative, approach to which its supporters appropriate the label of 'dignitarian' human rights. This divergence of thought has been particularly evident in the US debate on **religious freedom** rights, where a preponderantly Roman Catholic group of theorists has been active in urging a reversal of US jurisprudence which favours a rigid **separation of church and state** in favour of a definition of religious freedom positively loaded towards the exercise of religion rather than protection from unwelcome religious pressure. This same group decries what have come to be known as contraceptive rights as a utilitarian and non-dignitarian approach to rights. Inevitably, if a theory justifies rights as being valuable because they lead to something else, even if that something else is as broadly consensual as the idea of human dignity, there is a danger of rights becoming the right to do what is approved of, rather than, as originally, the fundamental 'right to be left alone'.

Public law

In general, public law, which in most jurisdictions has a subdivision of **administrative law**, regulates relations between the individual and the state. Although criminal law also involves relations between the individual and the state, it is everywhere treated as a quite separate area of law, even though the distinction can become blurred—for example, the distinction cannot be made simply on the basis that criminal law involves state-enforced penalties, because areas quite clearly in the domain of public law, such as immigration law, often contain penalties like deportation, which can also be the sentences of criminal courts. Similarly, public law cannot be separated from private law in terms of the facts or basis of claims, as it is a feature of English law, regretted by many, that the same personal circumstances may entitle someone to take action both in private law and in public law, and much may depend on which route he chooses. Public law covers matters like challenges to planning decisions, immigration officers' decisions, denial of publicly-provided goods such as housing or welfare benefits, **citizenship**, decisions against corporations by regulatory agencies, and other matters arising out of statute law where the state or an agency, even a largely independent agency, is a party to the matter. Even in this sphere the boundaries of public law can be blurred; for example, a prisoner may challenge an action of a prison governor on the grounds that a common law right freely to communicate with his lawyer has been breached and have this treated as a public law case, while another prisoner may seek damages for an assault by a prison warder and find that this is a matter of private law.

The exact distinction between private and public law differs from jurisdiction to jurisdiction, and may involve, as in France, not only separate bodies of law, but completely different court systems. Where there is no separate court hierarchy, chiefly in common law countries, the extent to which the categorization matters varies considerably. In a sense it matters only where different remedies apply to the different spheres, or where procedural differences may make it easier or harder to establish one's rights according to the classification. As there is a general and increasing tendency to allow all courts to use all remedies, and also to make procedures simpler and fairer, the importance of the distinction may decrease over time, although it may continue to be important in the question of judicial expertise. As most public law issues involve an assessment of the actions of state officials, and can also require a considerable degree of familiarity with technical details of complex statutory schemes, judges with extensive experience of public law cases may be much better at dealing with them than judges whose experience during their legal career has focused on, say, commercial contracts. It is chiefly for this reason that most European jurisdictions have often preferred quite separate administrative law hierarchies, and it may also be the case that judges highly experienced in the ways of the public administration may, unconsciously, be over-sympathetic to administrative difficulties. Distinctions between the common law countries, which have traditionally been thought to have an underdeveloped public law, and many European countries are also beginning to decline under the influence of bodies like the **European Court of Human Rights**, and some believe that a broad international understanding of public law doctrines and techniques is developing everywhere.

Public order

Public order means, at least in the Anglo-American common law world, little more than peace on the streets, in contrast to the rather richer European conception covered by the French legal phrase *ordre public*. Threats to public order, sometimes reduced to the idea of public safety, are standard arguments for curtailing some **civil liberties**, especially the **right of assembly**. They are occasionally produced as justifications for curtailments in **due process**, protection of public order being one of the justifications for **pre-trial detention** recognized by the **European Court of Human Rights**. It is relatively uncontroversial to restrict behaviour otherwise legal in the interests of public order where the behaviour is of itself somewhat aggressive, such as controlling **pickets** or protest marches which are likely to lead to civil disturbances. The argument becomes more sensitive when it is used to justify an infringement on **freedom of speech**, when someone's right to publish or say something, or to show a film, is restricted because it may lead to others reacting with illegal violence. Such an argument, for example, lies behind the justification of criminalizing **blasphemy** in English law; others may react violently to a blasphemous statement, so the statement itself shall be banned. In general, though, the problem is not with the basic argument that government has a duty to preserve public order; after all, few rights are of much value in a riot-torn city. The problem comes in designing machinery to test the state's use of the justification. As the problem tends to become one of operational judgement by police, courts are not usually very efficient instruments for testing public order claims.

Q

Quasi-judicial

Courts are only one of many bodies which carry out the function of applying formal rules to actual situations and then deciding between claims. In any modern state there are literally thousands of administrative tribunals and committees doing, within a restricted sphere, much what the official courts do for the whole of law. Thus a tribunal which decides on disputed welfare entitlements, a committee which dispenses compensation to companies who claim to have lost property abroad as the result of hostile acts of a foreign government, and a local-government officer setting fair rents for private houses all act in a quasi-judicial manner. Similarly, disciplinary bodies within private organizations as, for example, the dean of an Oxford college or a trade union disciplinary committee, act in some ways like a magistrate. In most jurisdictions some powers adhere in the official courts to supervise such quasi-judicial actions, and appeals can be made from within the quasi-judicial hierarchy to the external court systems. The extent to which the courts will or can supervise such activities varies enormously, and they will very seldom hear an appeal on the merits of the case. They are, though, prone to insist on procedural guidelines such as the rules of **natural justice in English law** or the US concept of **due process**. In some countries, notably the United Kingdom, there is occasional irritation with the courts for trespassing on what are seen as administrative matters and imposing inefficient and time-consuming procedures. This has led, in the past, to the attempt to exclude the courts from a supervisory role with some tribunals and decision processes in administrative machinery, often referred to as making legislation judge-proof (see **judge-proofing**). It very seldom works, because courts are assiduous in protecting what they see as their natural prerogative to ensure justice.

Quotas

Setting quotas based on minority status is an obvious way of attempting to make up for past patterns of minority discrimination, and there are two main reasons for applying quotas in selection for jobs and promotion. The first is because there is a fear that selection mechanisms will continue to be biased, whatever the official policy of **equal opportunities** may be; if those in charge of making appointments know they have to select a minimum number of blacks, women, single parents or whatever, they have no room to exercise bias. The second argument is that even an unbiased selection process will not result in many appointments of historically underprivileged groups because they are unlikely to apply in numbers proportionate to their size in the population. Only by appointing a minimum number of candidates from the target group, irrespective of their ranking compared with candidates from the majority population, will enough people from minorities gain the status and privileges historically monopolized by the dominant groups. At its best this argument rests on a strong sociological theory that the real reason for low application rates is the lack of suitable role models for the minorities. It is argued, essentially, that it is worth accepting a period of less than optimum recruitment if that is what it takes to create an employment structure that is not only fair, but seen to be fair. It is this aspect of quotas that has come to make them deeply suspect to many, and led, ultimately, to quotas being ruled more or less unconstitutional in the USA. The problem is obvious: if the state forbids discrimination on, say, racial grounds, and then allows an institution to appoint a person from a minority with lower qualifications than someone from the majority who does not get the place, but would have in the absence of the quota, the majority member has an undeniable argument that he has been discriminated against on an illicit criterion. The better approach would seem to be to ensure full representation of all relevant minorities on selection panels, thus concentrating on abolishing discrimination at the selection process. A related method is to build into selection criteria a way of taking account of the situation of the applicant so that relative achievements can properly be compared. So, for example, in academic appointments nowadays a candidate's publications, always a crucial factor, are assessed taking account of the fact that a woman's career path, if she is a mother, necessarily limits her opportunities of doing research at vital points in her life. (See also **affirmative action, minority rights**.)

R

Race relations acts

The United Kingdom has had three acts to combat **racial discrimination**, the Race Relations Acts of 1965, 1968 and 1976, which show a steady progress away from the sense that either nothing need be done, or that such an act should rely on conciliation mechanisms. All three acts were passed by Labour governments, and they form, with the companion acts aimed at abolishing sex discrimination, passed by the same governments, the 1970 **Equal Pay Act** and the 1975 **Sex Discrimination Act**, the UK's main anti-discrimination efforts. The first Act was far too weak; during its progress through the House of Commons criminal sanctions were dropped for all but the offence of incitement to racial hatred. It was passed by a government which was anxious not to involve the courts, and which hoped that the criminal law would not have to be used at all. Indeed, the government assured the House of Commons when presenting the original bill that they expected no litigation to arise from it. Likewise the Act's institutional support, the Race Relations Board (RRB), and also the Community Relations Commission (CRC) created by the second Act of 1968, were inadequate; although the RRB was entitled to carry out investigations of racial discrimination, it had no **subpoena** powers, and could investigate only where an individual had made a complaint to it. Most important of all, perhaps, individuals could not bring cases directly against discriminators, but had to complain instead to the RRB. The logic behind these two acts was that they were not really intended to attack individual actions of discrimination on behalf of individuals whose rights had been abridged, but were seen as attacking the practice of discrimination generally as a matter of public interest. Lacking any other constitutional protection for their rights, members of racial minorities were therefore prevented, perhaps even discouraged, from pursuing their private interests in the matter.

The 1968 Act did at least widen the area of coverage, by making discrimination illegal in both housing and employment, as the previous Act had only gone as far as to make racially-restrictive covenants in **property** sales unenforceable. Housing discrimination is the single most sociologically-significant form of racial discrimination because of its tendency to create

171

racial ghettos. However, the 1968 Act was still very weak in itself, and the courts proceeded to interpret it very narrowly indeed. In particular they insisted on distinguishing between nationality and race, and allowing discrimination, however overt, on the former criterion. In another set of cases the Lords of Appeal refused to uphold claims of discrimination against clubs affiliated to political parties which refused to allow membership to those of minority races, on the grounds that the Act only forbade discrimination on those offering services to members of the public. The general sense in the courts was effectively that there was a right to discriminate in the common law, and the acts were only meant to limit this basic right. Unless the courts could be brought to see it the other way round, and to see the underlying right as that of not being discriminated against, judicial **interpretation** was likely to be fatal to any legislative approach.

So inadequate were the acts that the 1974–79 Labour government determined to repeal them and effectively start again. The RRB and the CRC were replaced with the Commission for Racial Equality (CRE), and the 1976 Act significantly widened the entire approach. It banned discrimination on the grounds of nationality (to overcome the court rulings) and on grounds of race, colour and ethnic and national origin. Like the Sex Discrimination Act of the previous year, the new Act added a category of 'indirect' discrimination, because it had been very hard to prove that the real reason for discrimination in the past had been racial when the discriminator could claim so easily he was acting for some other reason. In an exact parallel to the Sex Discrimination Act, a complainant under the new Act had to prove three things to establish indirect discrimination. In the context of an actual education case, for example, a private school refused to take a Sikh unless he promised not to wear his turban. The boy's father had to prove firstly that there was a test applied both to Sikhs and others, in this instance of coming to school in uniform; secondly that the test was one which a substantially smaller proportion of Sikhs could comply with than non-Sikhs (in this case, obviously, the proportion able to comply was zero); and thirdly that the actual complainant, his son, could not pass the test. This latter aspect of the law is to ensure that personal cases under the Act actually are cases of personal suffering, not a public interest case, because public interest cases are meant to be dealt with by the CRE. The case is interesting also because the court had to exercise considerable ingenuity in deeming a Sikh to be a member of an ethnic or racial group, as the plaintiff was using the Act to avoid religious discrimination, which is not illegal in the mainland UK, though it is in Northern Ireland. The Act covers most institutions: the professions and trade unions, police, prisons, the military, all local government institutions, education both public and private, employment, and, to overcome the previous court decisions, clubs with more than 25 members, as well as all provision of services to the public. It enabled, for the first time, individuals to bring their cases to county courts and industrial tribunals, as well as relying on the CRE, which in addition has a duty to help them prepare their cases. Though not perfect, the race relations legislation is probably more successful than the comparable sex discrimination statutes.

Racial discrimination

With the possible exception of religion, race has been the most common basis of discrimination practised in modern society. It is extremely difficult to distinguish between racial and ethnic discrimination, and modern sociology essentially makes race a part of ethnicity for analytic purposes, although legal systems have often been cast in purely or predominantly racial, that is skin colour, terms. The British **Race Relations Act** of 1976 is typical of modern anti-discrimination legislation in including ethnicity as part of the definition of race. Interestingly, in mainland United Kingdom, as opposed to Northern Ireland, there is no legal prohibition of religious discrimination, and consequently there have been attempts, sometimes successful, to bring cases of discrimination based entirely on a religious belief under an ethnicity definition. The Act makes it an offence to discriminate racially in several ways, the core aspect being a ban on discrimination in providing any service to any sector of the public.

The problem with legal control on racial discrimination is that although racial tolerance is a prominent value of liberal society, most such societies also hold to a strong belief in freedom of private choice. Thus while few would attempt to defend a state agency discriminating racially, it is less frequently thought appropriate to forbid discrimination by private action, because this transgresses the principle of freedom of choice. Consequently, anti-discrimination measures are both harder to justify and technically more difficult to operate in the private sphere, notably in the housing market, where a myriad of private concerns, including strictly financial ones, have made it difficult to ensure mixing of residential areas. Because so much else, above all educational opportunity, depends on residential patterns, it has become crucial not to allow the seller of a house to refuse to sell to someone whose race or ethnic origin he dislikes. Yet restrictive covenants are a central part of the way land law has developed in most common law countries, and tampering with them is to tamper with the core value attached to the freedom to own **property**.

Even where a state is determined to take action against racial discrimination, there are enormous problems of ensuring compliance with anti-discrimination legislation as, for example, in the area of employment. Frequently it is possible to tackle discriminatory practices only at a macro level, by making the history of hiring in a company count as imputed evidence of discrimination, because proving actual discrimination by any particular selection committee in an individual case is likely to be impossible. Part of the problem in dealing with racial discrimination is that although it may be a theoretically distinguishable phenomenon, it is sociologically mixed. Someone coming from a deprived background in terms of the society's traditional stratus system will probably also be deprived in other ways, and will come from an overall social class which experiences inequality of treatment. Typically, racial discrimination declines only when a proportion of unusually successful members of a group develops the class, income and educational characteristics of the more advantaged. This development makes discrimination against their members much more clearly racial, and therefore identifiable, and also shows it to be less and less justifiable in terms of what may have been mere excuses, but may also have been partially genuine reasons for their past lack of success. There is a severe limitation to the effectiveness of legislated rights protection in this area, but much of the importance of this protection comes from the symbolic value of having society commit itself to the principle of combating discrimination. (See also ***Brown v. Board***, **inherently suspect category**, **National Association for the Advancement of Colored People** and **voting rights**.)

Reasonable time for trial

The requirement that no one should have to wait an unreasonable time between being charged with an offence and the beginning of his trial, though it features in most detailed human rights codes, is partially tempered by the alternative that bail should be allowed if the trial is not to start soon after **arrest**. Where **pre-trial detention** is not used, it is not clear whether the reasonable time requirement is simply one of the many demands of the **due process** right, or a substantively valuable right in itself. Obviously the state could deliberately be very slow to bring to trial someone they had little chance of convicting as a punishment in itself, given the inevitable psychological suffering that would be experienced. However, even relatively liberal states have a serious problem with lengthy delays before trial because of the almost universal overcrowding of the criminal justice system in most advanced countries. There is, in the common law, a rather vague sense that a long-delayed trial is an abuse of justice in itself because of the difficulty of ensuring fairness when evidence, and particular witnesses' recall, will have become unreliable (see also **fair trial**). In practice, trials are delayed as much by defence counsel taking time to prepare cases as they are by the prosecution. It may be that the worst aspect of overcrowding is that it encourages the prosecution to offer plea-bargains to avoid lengthy trials, with the subsequent temptation for the defendant to plead guilty to a lesser charge of which he is nevertheless innocent rather than wait for months and risk conviction on a more serious charge.

Reasoned decisions

As law works by the analysis of formally- and publicly-stated reasons and arguments, **public law**, the branch of law most relevant to discussions of human rights, is crucially dependent on access to the reasoning of decision-makers acting for the state. Only if a court can see, in the decision-maker's own words, what factors he has taken into account, and why he thinks he has the legal authority to do something, can they effectively check on the **arbitrary** or discriminatory use of power which is at the heart of most human rights problems. Consequently a very strong obligation to provide written reasons for any challenged administrative decision has been written into the public law of most states, in both the common law and code law world. Naturally the system has flaws: a really biased administrator can simply lie about his reasons, even if he still has difficulty in finding any plausible reason for his decision. Only with the greatest reluctance will a British court allow, for example, the Home Secretary to exercise a power he clearly has, for example to refuse a citizenship request, without giving reasons for such a decision. An interesting contrast exists here between a **jury trial** and a trial before judges sitting alone, as juries do not give their reasons, and often acquit the clearly guilty, or convict the probably innocent, for reasons of their own, while judges, equally likely to be biased, have to give reasons, and have much less freedom to follow their bias. This was demonstrated notoriously in Northern Ireland when jury trial was abandoned for some terrorist offences. Judges sitting alone frequently convicted suspected terrorists, as a jury would have done, only to have their decisions overturned on appeal because they were unable to give convincing reasoned opinions to compensate for the paucity of evidence. In addition to these arguments, reasoned decisions are the essence of the doctrine of **natural justice in English law** or the US idea of **due process** because, without knowing the case against one, it is impossible adequately to answer it. In the United Kingdom, for example, there has for some time been unease about the mechanism for deciding how long those sentenced to mandatory life imprisonment should actually serve, because the decision is made by civil servants who do not disclose any of their reasons.

Refugees (see **asylum**)

Religious freedom

Religious freedom is one of the most complicated matters in the whole of human rights law and practice, and is not only one of the oldest concerns but is also currently controversial. It comprises an assortment of related rights and entitlements, and can be seen from many perspectives: freedom from discrimination because of one's religion, freedom to practise a religion unhindered, freedom from living in a society that gives preference to any one religion or religion at all, and freedom to enjoy civic respect for one's religion. These civil liberties can impinge on many aspects of society, the most important historically being education, but freedom of religion can also become a rival value to **freedom of speech**, and with regard to discrimination, religion raises problems in employment and wherever provisions of goods or services are concerned.

The right to freedom from discrimination because of one's religion is included, either directly or by implication, in either codes or statutory ways in most countries. Some countries, most notably the USA, have both specific freedom of religion clauses in their constitutions (see **First Amendment**), and complex developed case law on the matter. Others have relatively little formal protection for religious freedom and very little case law, a good example being the United Kingdom, where there is no express prohibition of religiously-based discrimination (although there is in Northern Ireland), but the **Race Relations Act** of 1976 includes a sufficiently wide definition of ethnicity, which is treated as an unacceptable reason for discrimination, to encompass most of what might be concerned with discrimination on the grounds of religion (see **racial discrimination**). Religious freedom in the sense of the state having no religious preference, either for or against religion, or favouring one religion or denomination, is less protected, and it could be argued that many countries with otherwise good human rights records fail in this respect, because established religions are still common in Europe. In practice, however, the establishment of one religion in modern highly-secularized states is less likely to harm other religions than to aid them by ensuring that the state gives at least nominal credence to the importance of religion at all.

Politically, the greatest problem with religious liberty comes in the educational sphere, and at a minimum the state must provide the right to have children educated in a religiously-based school, even if they are unprepared to make any contribution to the costs of such schools. In practice most states either make some financial contribution, or allow religious education to be included in state schools. In France the ***Conseil Constitutionel*** has traditionally given rather more protection to religious schools than would seem to accord with the country's constitutions. More contentious, however, is the situation where states require religion as part of the syllabus, even for children of atheists or for children from other religious backgrounds. The UK still makes minimal religious education compulsory, as do some other European states, notably Italy.

Finally, there is the question of whether freedom of religion requires the state to protect sensibilities, for example against gross and indecent attacks on religions' symbolic figures in the media (see **blasphemy**). Here the stance taken varies considerably, as such protection is directly contrary to the right to freedom of speech. In the UK there is a problem of assessing whether leading decisions on the law of blasphemy can best be seen as protections of religion or restrictions on religious freedom. There are, of course, states in the modern world so committed to one particular religion, particularly and increasingly Islam, where religious freedom as understood elsewhere would not be seen as desirable, and often such states are in breach of the **Universal Declaration of Human Rights** in many areas.

Religious freedom is a right that will always require protection, but is increasingly seen, as in the **German Constitution**, as part of a more general protection of human intellectual and moral autonomy, usually referred to as the right to freedom of conscience. The **European Convention on Human Rights**, in Article 9, would appear to protect religious freedom quite powerfully, but its exact meaning depends on case-by-case interpretation, and many of its implications are still unclear. (See also **separation of church and state**.)

Representation

The right to be represented politically is fundamental to all other **civil liberties** and human rights, because a political system which did not claim legitimacy from the fact that its government was representative of its public would be unlikely to accept any part of the human rights doctrine; the US revolutionary call of 'no taxation without representation' insists that representation is the foundation of the state. Nevertheless, even liberal states deny representation to some categories of citizens, and the most common is the ban on **voting rights** to citizens serving terms of imprisonment; this ban has been challenged recently in several countries, and at the time of writing a significant test case was being fought in Canada. The chief argument made in support of the ban is that because of the nature of the prison system, allowing prisoners to vote could have a distorting impact on the electoral process. A second group of citizens denied the vote is to be found among the mentally ill; the argument here is usually that they should be equated with children who are deemed not to have reached sufficient maturity of understanding or judgement to vote. In many countries there are historical quirks in the withholding of the franchise, as in the United Kingdom where peers of the realm are denied the vote on the grounds that they have a legislative chamber of their own.

These exceptions apart, it is generally deemed necessary that the suffrage be equal and complete for mentally competent adults, although it is often forgotten that in several European countries women did not receive the vote until after the Second World War, and until as late as 1971 and 1984 in the cases of Switzerland and Liechtenstein, respectively. Articles 1 and 2 of the UN Convention on the Political Rights of Women (1952) states that 'Women shall be entitled to vote in all elections . . .' and '. . . shall be eligible for election to all publicly elected bodies, established by national law, on equal terms with men, without any discrimination'. In recent times the most blatant denial of equal suffrage was in the Southern states of the USA, where blacks were regularly denied the vote until the late 1960s, although never overtly on the ground of their race. It is also in the USA that the question of equal voting rights has been raised as a human rights issue because of malproportionment, meaning that those living in unusually large constituencies were in a sense not equally represented compared with fellow citizens in underpopulated areas. Most countries take considerable care to draw up constituency boundaries as equally as possible, using mechanisms as innocent of partisanship as can be achieved.

There is currently little interest in discussion of whether representation can be achieved effectively only by electoral systems, and if so whether only by a geographic as opposed to a functional constituency basis, although elements of European fascist theory did raise unresolved questions on the subject. The only major exceptions to equal geographical representation currently seen as politically acceptable are those special arrangements in federal systems by which component states may be represented in an upper house in a way which is not, and is not intended to be, proportional to population. Here some core sense of representation of units rather than the individual voter is retained, and similar situations necessarily occur in the representation of nation states in international bodies like the European Union. This sense of delegated legitimacy still rests on the equal suffrage inside the member state, or federal component state itself.

Reproductive freedom

The term reproductive freedom involves freedom to decide whether or not to have children, and so it covers the areas of **abortion**, availability of **contraception**, and fertility treatment and attempts to curb the size of families, either by legislation or financial. The only one of these areas which has substantial legal case history is abortion, and no national human rights code contains anything like the right to reproductive freedom, even where abortion has been legitimized. There have, however, been cases where a suggested ban on the supply of contraceptives to under-age school children, to avoid the risk either of pregnancy or sexually-transmitted disease, have been challenged with arguments related to the concept of reproductive freedom.

Typically, freedom in areas of sexual behaviour, including abortion, is defended under a broader and vaguer right to **privacy**. The classic US constitutional case of *Griswold v. Connecticut* (1965) overturned a state law forbidding the sale of contraceptives to unmarried couples on the grounds that it was in breach of a generalized right to privacy which the court deduced from other parts of the Bill of Rights (see **Bill of Rights (USA)**). This same right to privacy was then used in 1973 in *Roe v. Wade* to overturn anti-abortion statutes. *Griswold* demonstrates precisely why campaigners would prefer to see a right to reproductive freedom established directly, as inferred rights from broad concepts like privacy leave too much to judicial **interpretation**. In *Griswold* the main dissent came from Justice Hugo La Fayette Black, a man whose personal values were impeccably liberal, but who could not accept that a right to privacy was implicit in the Constitution, and who felt it dangerous to support specific rights in such a way. Indeed it has been argued ever since *Roe v. Wade* that the legal justification was so slim and tortuous that the right to abortion is very precarious, and could easily be overturned by a future more conservative court. The human rights code in the **German Constitution** is, in many respects, a model of liberal values, but because it contains no right to reproductive freedom, yet has a very strong **right to life** clause, the **German Constitutional Court** has repeatedly struck down legislative attempts to establish abortion rights. Advances in reproductive science and techniques are likely to lead to an increasing number of test cases concerning the rights of an individual to have children against the social desirability of a child being born into particular conditions, for example to a mother well beyond the normal childbearing age, or to a lesbian couple. In many countries the pressure to introduce measures to limit the size of families is likely to increase as the problem of overpopulation worsens, and this too involves serious human rights issues.

Restrictions on death sentence

Since the end of the Second World War nearly all liberal democracies have abolished the death penalty, and it is noteworthy that most of the East European nations which have become democratic since the end of the Cold War have also done so. The USA is the only major democratic society to retain capital punishment, though it is not a sentence available to the courts in all of the separate states; Michigan, for example, abolished capital punishment as early as 1847. There was a brief moratorium on execution in the USA from 1972 because the Supreme Court, in *Furman v. Georgia*, held most of the existing death penalty statutes unconstitutional. They were not able to hold that the death penalty *per se* was a **cruel and unusual punishment**, but the racially-discriminatory incidence of the sentence was enough to allow the court to argue that the existing statutes were a denial of **due process**. Nevertheless, 28 states have subsequently rewritten their capital punishment laws and resumed executions, and decisions of the Supreme

179

Court in the last decade have continued to reduce the legal barriers to execution. None of the major human rights codes outlaws capital punishment as such, because the tide of revulsion against it, from vocal sectors if not from mass public opinion, is a more recent phenomenon than the codes.

The most that courts who have any sort of jurisdiction in the matter have been able to do is to control to some extent the incidence of the death penalty and some ancillary matters. The British Law Lords, in their capacity as the Judicial Committee of the Privy Council, for example, often hear death penalty appeals from those parts of the Commonwealth that still retain the sentence. They have never felt able to pronounce the sentence itself unconstitutional, but have several times struck down death sentences because of undue delay in carrying them out which they have held, in common with the UN Human Rights Committee, to be cruel and unusual. International human rights campaigners have been active in attempting to get the death sentence abolished completely. In 1990 the UN issued an 'Optional Protocol' (the second such) to the **International Covenant on Civil and Political Rights** specifically aimed at encouraging the total abolition of the death penalty, available to be signed by those countries prepared to renounce its use in perpetuity. The signature list is considerably smaller than that for the Covenant itself, and the main Covenant states only that, if the death penalty is retained, it can only be used for the most serious of crimes.

Restrictive covenants (see **race relations acts** and **racial discrimination**)

Restrictive interpretation

A restrictive interpretation of a statute or constitutional document is one that limits a right or entitlement, or the powers of some body or person, to the least that the words of the text can allow. In interpreting social legislation, for example, a judge might give a clause a more or less restrictive interpretation, increasing or decreasing the range of conditions which would qualify for a disability benefit or a rent rebate, thus affecting **statutory rights**. In a **public law** case a judge might restrictively interpret the powers of the Home Secretary to deport those claiming **asylum**, thus enlarging the group of possible asylum seekers. These examples, both from real cases, illustrate that restrictive interpretation is not in itself either liberal or illiberal, conservative or leftwards leaning, but that all depends on the effect of the clause. Thus, like all interpretative techniques, the effect of restriction depends on the original drafting, and is chosen by a judge either from a general methodological preference, or in order to achieve a particular result, with the technique itself being neutral. (See also **interpretation**.)

Retroactivity

It is a basic principle of law that no one can be punished for doing something that was not a crime at the time he carried out the actions in question. This can be generalized to the principle that neither the state nor a private citizen can enforce something as an obligation that had not been established as such in advance of someone incurring that obligation. This principle of the legal nullity of retroactive legislation is usually taken further and said to require the clear public promulgation of the obligation in question. Most codes of human rights either explicitly or by **imputation** ban the retroactive or retrospective effect of criminal law; both the **German Constitution** and the European Convention on Human Rights, for example, contain this rule expressly. Nevertheless, application of the principle is not absolute, and there have been cases in British law in recent decades when quasi-criminal regulations, for example immigration rules, have been applied retroactively.

The principle reflects a general belief that people ought to be able to regulate their life as freely as possible to avoid conflict. Although the popular saying that 'ignorance of the law is no excuse' is technically correct, it neglects to take account of the strong sense that it is culpable ignorance that is no excuse, because if it is impossible for anyone to know the law, their ignorance is a factor to be taken into account. In a similar way judges often argue that certainty in law is a value in its own right, because of the need of the citizen to be able to plan his affairs, and German constitutional doctrine has applied this to require **interpretation** of criminal statutes to be done in such a way as to make the meaning of a law coincide very closely with that which might be given it by an ordinary layperson. Retroactivity is particularly a problem where criminal law, as in the United Kingdom, is to a large extent judge-made. In 1993, for example, the Law Lords changed the English law of rape in upholding the conviction of a man who had raped his wife; previously, if anomalously, the common law had held that rape could not exist in such a situation. The case proceeded on appeal to the **European Court of Human Rights**, on the precise grounds that such a change in the meaning of law after the act amounts to the creation of a retrospective criminal offence. The problem is that judge-made common law contains no mechanism for prospective rulings, so that a strict application of the **European Convention on Human Rights** effectively means that criminal law can be altered only by statute.

Right of petition

Petitions go back far in the history of common law. The right of petition was recognized in **Magna Carta** and specifically guaranteed in the 1689 Bill of Rights (see **Bill of Rights (UK)**). Petitions are simply requests made to any authority, but especially to the monarch, the courts or to parliament, and this right was an important factor in the American revolution and guaranteed in the **First Amendment** to the US Constitution. Indeed, Congress has a settled procedure for accepting petitions, while the British House of Commons long ago adopted the alternative approach that petitions should not be debated, so common had they become. The origin of petition comes from the difficulty of getting access in a recognized way to any court, and the related absence of anything like a normal **public law** machinery for taking the state to court. Hence the only hope of justice on many occasions was to resort to an *ad hoc* request to the sovereign to see that justice was done. As the crown could not be sued, a situation not changed in the United Kingdom until 1947, once the crown came to be an overall legal cover for the state, petitions of right were effectively requests to a government department to waive this protection and allow itself to be taken to court. Nowadays petition in a legal sense is usually just archaic language for some stage of an appeal or routinized approach to the courts, and not the request for an entirely discretionary act of justice that it once was. The practice of sending petitions to the government or parliament is, of course, still part of the methodology of political protest, and any right of petition that might still be seen to be protected would be as part of the generalized right to **freedom of speech**.

Right to counsel

The right to counsel can mean either the right to have any legal representation (the more usual and general meaning), or the right to have legal representation provided where one cannot afford it privately. The basic rules of **natural justice in English law**, of **due process** in the USA, and of the equivalent in code law countries, would nowadays always allow counsel to assist in someone's defence in a criminal trial, and usually in most civil cases, whether before a **public law** tribunal or an ordinary civil court. The **European Convention on Human Rights**, which in this context is more or less identical with the other UN regional and international covenants, guarantees the right in Article 6 (Clause 3c), as part of what it describes as the 'minimum rights' of anyone charged with a criminal offence: 'to defend himself in person or through legal assistance of his own choosing or, if he has not sufficient means to pay for legal assistance, to be given it free when the interests of justice so require'. Most states would now treat 'when the interests of justice so require' as meaning whenever it was requested, but this has not historically always been the case. One of the reasons that it is a right specifically guaranteed in the US Bill of Rights (see **Bill of Rights (USA)**) is precisely because, at common law, the accused did not usually have the right to legal counsel, although this was part of a radically different concept of trial when the accused was also not allowed to give evidence himself. Given the enormous importance of litigation skills in persuading a jury to accept some and reject other evidence, as well as the currently tremendously complex rules of evidence, it would be quite absurd to trust the fairness of a criminal trial to a system in which the state was represented by legal professionals and the accused was not. With the inquisitorial system in operation in continental Europe there might be a case for dispensing with counsel; that the European Convention does not think so makes it all the more obvious why such help is needed in a common law trial, and consequently why some form of **legal aid** system is vital. How widely such a right exists outside of criminal trials is a matter which varies considerably. The trend in natural justice in English law doctrine has been to allow counsel before any tribunal, even one in a private institution like a university or trade union, as long as the tribunal is carrying out what have been described as **quasi-judicial** functions. There are exceptions, and, for example, police officers appearing before disciplinary hearings are not normally allowed actual legal counsel, though they will have some form of representation from police trade-union officials.

Right to employment

The right to employment is capable of several different interpretations, with corresponding differences in its legal nature and degree of justiciability. If taken to mean that everyone has a right to have a job, it is, at best, a **positive right** quite without justiciability, and one neither to be found in, nor plausibly interpreted into, any national or effective international rights document. Indeed, the only exception to this, the granting of a right to guaranteed employment in Article 40 of the last constitution of the USSR, is confined to a lengthy assertion of how the USSR's economic and political system was uniquely able to provide such a right. The most that a generalized right to employment could possibly offer is perhaps best exemplified by Article 23 of the **Universal Declaration of Human Rights**, the first clause of which is worth quoting in full: 'Everyone has the right to work, to free choice of employment, to just and favourable conditions of work *and to protection against unemployment*' (author's italics). The right to work in its full sense can clearly be guaranteed only if, as in this quotation, it is actually part of the combined right to work or to protection against unemployment. Even this is still a largely non-justiciable positive right, akin to the right

183

guaranteed in Article 3 of the Preamble to the Constitution of the Fourth French Republic, now incorporated into the Fifth Republic's Constitution, but never regarded as justiciable in its own terms.

What the right to work does entail is a series of other rights in the application of any employment policy, especially rights against discrimination in the job market on age and sex grounds, which have increasingly been made effective in some countries, such as the USA and Canada, where compulsory retirement ages have been held in breach of constitutional guarantees (see also **age discrimination** and **racial discrimination**). Further than that, the right to employment is largely to be understood in terms of the right to freedom of **choice of occupation**, protected, for example, in the **German Constitution**, and the more widely-protected right against **forced or compulsory labour**.

Right to family life

The right to family life is protected in various rights codes, notably the **European Convention on Human Rights**, by a series of rights, rather than being of itself a direct specified right. There is, for example, the generally recognized right to marry, as well as statements like 'Everyone has the right to respect for his private and family life . . .' (Article 8 of the European Convention). National constitutions detail further aspects of this general legally benevolent approach to family life, and the **German Constitution** states explicitly, in Clause 3 of Article 6, that 'Children may not be separated from their families . . .' and, more generally, in Clause 1, that: 'Marriage and family shall enjoy the special protection of the state'. The core value that family life is taken to have even in the broadest multicultural contexts is exemplified by the UN's **International Covenant on Economic, Social and Cultural Rights**, which declares in Article 10: 'The widest possible protection and assistance should be accorded to the family, which is the natural and fundamental group unit of society, particularly for its establishment and while it is responsible for the care and education of dependent children.' Part of this language is borrowed from the earlier and more widely-supported **Universal Declaration of Human Rights**.

Most rights owe their inclusion in rights codes to the prevailing concerns of the society and period in which they are written, and to the driving philosophy of those who draft them. Given that, it is noteworthy that family life is seen either as not needing special protection, or not worthy of it, in the earlier manifestations of liberal human rights codes. Neither the US Constitution, nor the French **Declaration of the Rights of Man and of the Citizen**, makes any mention of such a right, and even the 1945 French Constitution's Preamble, which covers a wide assortment of socio-economic rights, but which is written in the French tradition of political thought, omits the right. Nowadays the right to family life is most likely to take its protection from some more broadly identified concept like the right to **privacy**.

Right to life

The right to life could be described as the fundamental right of human existence, and is part of the American **Declaration of Independence's** trilogy of the right to 'life, liberty and the pursuit of happiness'. As such, most codes either state the right or, for obvious reasons, take it for granted. Where it is included it is frequently in some version of the US trilogy, as in Article 3 of the **Universal Declaration of Human Rights**, in which 'Everyone has the right to life, liberty and security of person', and the **German Constitution's** Article 2 (Clause 2), where 'Everybody has the right to life and physical integrity', and seems to have a largely rhetorical purpose. Unless the purpose is rhetorical, it would seem odd not to have the right in the first article of any such document. The **European Convention on Human Rights** comes closer to making clear what the actual content of the right, where it has a substantive meaning, actually is, and it is placed in the first substantive article: 'Everyone's right to life shall be protected by law. No one shall be deprived of his life intentionally save in the execution of a sentence of a court . . .' There was, until recently, only one justiciable, negative right, meaning to the right to life, which was to control or ban the use of capital punishment (see **restrictions on death sentence**). Any other meaning of the right to life made it some form of **positive right** exhortation to the state to do everything in its power to banish starvation and ill health.

However, such an analysis is predicated on the assumption that we all know what constitutes a living human. What has made the constitutional right to life politically explosive has been the interpretation by anti-**abortion** movements of the foetus as a living human entitled, as much as its mother, to constitutional protection. As soon as this step is taken, the right to life becomes a matter of intense and insoluble argument. The **German Constitutional Court** is the only court in a major liberal democracy which has accepted the anti-abortion argument that a foetus should be afforded such protection, and it has therefore struck down attempts by the Bundestag to legitimize abortion. The Irish court has expressed similar views and would doubtless take the same action, in the absence of a constitutional amendment allowing abortion.

The other area of modern constitutional concern on the right to life is the debate over claims to the right to die peacefully at a time of one's own choosing. Though suicide itself is seldom treated as an offence any more, assisting suicide, which is what euthanasia often amounts to, is increasingly a problem for courts and legislatures, especially in the USA. Similarly, the right of a person to state in some form, often called a 'living will', that no attempt to resuscitate them should be made under certain conditions, and the right of next of kin to require hospitals to cease artificial methods of keeping alive someone in a coma, all raise problems for the generalized right to life. None of these has been satisfactorily solved, and it seems unlikely that a human right to have life terminated will ever be accepted at the full codification level.

Right to marry

The right to marry and to found a family is protected in so many words by Article 12 of the **European Convention on Human Rights**. The **Universal Declaration of Human Rights**, in Article 16, is even more precise and comprehensive: 'Men and women of full age, without any limitation due to race, nationality or religion, have the right to marry and to found a family.' Interestingly, a justification for this is given, in Clause 3 of the article: 'The family is the natural and fundamental group unit of society and is entitled to protection by society and the State.' Elsewhere the right is given slightly less solid or precise protection, but this concept of the naturalness of the family unit recurs. Article 6 of the **German Constitution**, for example, states: 'Marriage and family shall enjoy the special protection of the state', and goes on to refer to the upbringing of children as both a natural right and duty (see also **right to family life**). While most people will, without hesitation, accept such evaluations, it is in fact relatively rare for rights codes to include what amounts to a sociological theory in support of a protected right. The right to marry is stressed in these documents in large part because restrictions on who can marry whom have often been integral parts of racist laws, as in both the Nazi regime in Germany and during the period of apartheid in South Africa. As such, what is sought is not so much the protection of marriage, which has hardly ever been under threat, but the use of marriage laws to impose other patterns on society.

There are two ways in which marriage as a constitutionally protected right touches on human rights issues: firstly, in many countries marriage practice and legislation is linked to religion, and secondly, social attitudes have altered. In states where a particular religion is established, recognized or privileged, either *de jure* or *de facto*, much of marriage law, and consequently divorce law, remains in the hands of churches and denominations. Thus in Malaysia marriage is entirely a matter for Islamic law, in Israel the laws of religious communities (not, by any means, only Jewish law) govern much of the civil status of marriage, as do the religious institutions of the Orthodox faith in Greece and as did the canon law of Roman Catholicism in Italy and Ireland until quite recently. Such a system of leaving vital matters of human relations to denominational control can obviously cause enormous hardship, and, where a rights code protects marriage, could well be seen as a breach of that protection. Where, as in Ireland and Italy until recently, divorce did not exist, because marriage was recognized only in the terms of Roman Catholicism, it could very well be argued that the European Convention on Human Rights was breached. That argument could not be made in fact, because the Convention's protection was much weaker than it seemed. What Article 12 actually protected was the right to marry 'according to the national laws governing the exercise of this right'. Such an exception looks harmless, apparently deriving from the obvious need to control age of marriage, prevent bigamy and so on. In practice it weakened the right in a way that the much tougher Universal Declaration of Human Rights would not, as it forbade limitations based on religion.

Any right so firmly linked to a substantive belief like the sanctity of the family is inherently at risk because it evokes powerful ideological assumptions, as shown in the other area where marriage rights create constitutional problems. At the time that most modern rights codes were drafted, marriage was still the overwhelmingly predominant mode for adult-life partnerships. Since then heterosexual marriage has begun to decline in popularity, in some Western societies enormously. This necessarily produces demands for legal protection for other forms of partnership, including homosexual partnerships, on terms no less advantageous than traditional marriage. States vary considerably in how much legal support is given to such alternative forms of living partnerships (recognition is most advanced in the Netherlands and the US state of California), but these are treated *ad hoc* in terms of **property** and estate law, or as public law questions of entitlement to welfare and pension rights, or as general family law problems about guardianship and adoption. There is nowhere a generalized constitutional protection for arrangements functionally equivalent to marriage and, in societies where the previous dominant religious conception of marriage has faded, it is hard to see what more ideologically neutral justification could support such a generalized right.

Right to silence

The right to silence is an inexact and often misleading layman's phrase used to cover some aspects of what is more formally described as the privilege against **self-incrimination**. The phrase is mainly used in the United Kingdom, but sometimes elsewhere in the common law world. It refers to privileges long established in common law, and was, until recently, enshrined in England and Wales in the **judge's rules**, until given legislative standing by the 1984 **Police and Criminal Evidence Act**. Essentially, the privilege in question is that of refusing to answer any questions put by police investigating a crime. In itself the privilege would be of little use, because there is no legal way the police could, during an investigation, actually compel a suspect to divulge information. The privilege gets its power from its extension into a courtroom. During a trial the accused cannot be required to go into the witness box, either in his own defence or to answer questions from the prosecution, and the prosecution and the judge are debarred from making any comment to the jury on the accused's refusal to answer questions or offer explanations. The objections from the police are mainly that a suspect can refuse to give any account to them of his whereabouts or actions, and can then at the last minute, in the trial itself, produce an alibi that they are unable to check. Furthermore, by refusing to answer any questions, the suspect can hinder the police's efforts to investigate potential accomplices. The privilege originated in the common law's reaction to judicial **torture** in the middle ages, and to the practices of bodies like the Star Chamber. It is based firmly on the idea that criminal trials in common law countries are accusatorial, not inquisitorial. It is the task of the prosecution to convince a jury beyond reasonable doubt of someone's guilt by evidence they can adduce from their own efforts, and not the task of the court to elicit the truth. Where the latter doctrine applies, in European systems based on an inquisitorial mode, there is no equivalent right to refuse to answer questions. The usual defence of the privilege is that even an innocent person may have good reason to protect his **privacy**. In addition, someone may be innocent of the crime he is accused of, partly because he was involved in committing another crime of which the police are unaware, and to force him to answer a question would directly inculpate him of another crime. The US **Fifth Amendment**, especially as interpreted by the Supreme Court in cases such as *Miranda v. Arizona* (see **Miranda warning**), has made the privilege famous through films and television where suspects have their rights read to them on **arrest**. A similar caution by the police has long been used in the UK, but the Criminal Justice Act (1994) is intended to restrict this privilege considerably, allowing prosecutors considerable power to draw a jury's attention to any exercise of this privilege by the accused, and to invite them to draw damaging conclusions from the accused's behaviour.

Rights jurisprudence

Rights jurisprudence is a phrase used to describe a school of legal philosophy developed since the 1960s, associated generally with political philosophers like Robert **Nozick** and John Rawls (1921–) and, specifically in legal philosophy, with the work of Ronald **Dworkin**. The emphasis on this school is the rejection of positivist legal philosophy as originated by Jeremy **Bentham**, and with most of the arguments of utilitarian philosophy in general. To a large extent the theories are a return to a position associated with John **Locke** and other social contract theorists of the 17th century, who were themselves the originators of the whole tradition of civil liberty and human rights thinking in constitutionalism. The main difference from other schools of legal thought is an insistence that rights are real, and in some senses absolute. Unlike utilitarianism, which can be interpreted as holding that general utility can be an argument to abrogate human rights, those who argue for a rights jurisprudence regard a right, once recognized in a constitution or in some other way, as an absolute; if a person has a right, say to his **property**, nothing can justify taking it away. The basic position can be developed in several different ways, with complex implications, but at heart it rests on a denial of legitimacy of **discretion** in the law, and, in Dworkin's words, that there always is a 'right answer' to a legal dispute. Consequently the whole philosophical thrust is a direct contradiction to legal positivism which had been the dominant school of thought in the common law world from the mid-19th century at least. Whether those who wish to stress the importance of human rights are necessarily helped by adopting a rights jurisprudence is unclear, but the general tenor of thought is certainly more supportive than that of positivism.

Rights of illegitimate children

Given the long historical discrimination against illegitimate children, the writers of modern rights documents have deemed it necessary to add specific protections for them, and where rights codes have not specifically mentioned illegitimacy, there is usually some other protection. Thus the **European Convention on Human Rights**, otherwise silent, has a clause in Article 14 which secures all other rights without discrimination on the basis, *inter alia*, of 'birth or other status'. Often the potential problems of the illegitimate are recognized in some detail. The **International Covenant on Civil and Political Rights**, for example, specifically requires that 'every child shall be registered immediately after birth *and shall have a name*' (author's italics); although this provision is partly intended to prevent the tradition of exposure of unwanted children on birth in certain countries and cultures, it is illegitimate children who are most likely to suffer from this practice. The **Universal Declaration of Human Rights**, in Article 25, which provides for the general provision of basic human needs, singles out motherhood and childhood for 'special care and assistance' and specifically states: 'All children, whether born in or out of wedlock, shall enjoy the same social protection.' Some national codes also take account of the problem. The **German Constitution** is unusually insistent when it actually requires legislation to be passed to provide illegitimate children 'with the same opportunities for their physical and mental development and regarding their place in society as are enjoyed by those born in marriage'. The problems are not, of course, just those of social status. Historically, illegitimate children have had far weaker inheritance rights, if any, and, in the absence of any powerful mechanism to ensure that fathers support all their children, would be likely to have a much less secure economic provision if left in the care of the state or charitable organizations.

S

Security of the person

Security of the person is a phrase occurring in some human rights codes, usually coupled with **liberty of the person**, as in Article 5 of the **European Convention on Human Rights**. It means simply that the state may not inflict physical harm on anyone in any way which would be barred to an ordinary citizen, thereby protecting against undue violence by the police in controlling demonstrations or affecting an **arrest**. Any more intentional or systematic violence would, of course, be covered by the broader bans on any punishment not authorized by **due process** of law. It has a foreign ring to common law ears simply because the common law has always treated the police, or any other agency of the state, as governed by the laws against offences to the person exactly as such laws govern any citizen. It has to be remembered that even the powers of arrest held by a police officer ultimately stem from the common law right of any citizen to use necessary force to prevent a crime or apprehend a criminal. In such a context there is no logical need to give a separate constitutional protection to security of the person.

Sedition

In the United Kingdom and elsewhere in the Commonwealth sedition is a common law crime, treated as part of the law of criminal libel, and has existed in a statutory form from time to time in the USA. It amounts to an attempt to persuade the population to overthrow the government by unlawful means, or more generally to attack the government or the state in ways likely to cause serious problems of national security. So, for example, people have been convicted of sedition even in the post-Second World War period for offences such as delivering pamphlets urging soldiers to refuse to serve in Northern Ireland. Technically, the range of possible seditious acts in the UK would include attacks on the monarchy and the Church of England, and can best be described as a low grade of treason. Dealing with sedition, when it falls short of actual preparation for revolution, necessarily falls foul of any serious commitment to **freedom of speech** and, consequently,

US law has severely restricted the possibility of acts of sedition, under the **clear and present danger** interpretation of the **First Amendment**. The **European Convention on Human Rights**, however, seems to take a more statist view and certainly allows prosecution for spreading disaffection in the armed services, which has always been a key element of sedition.

Self-defence

The 'right' to self-defence is not really a right at all, though some recognition of it exists in most criminal law systems. The need for self-defence is a plea that can be made in defence of a charge of having committed some crime of violence, even, in extreme cases, murder. The idea is a good example of the range of issues covered by the term 'right', and has an odd history in political theory. One major political theorist, Thomas **Hobbes** (1588–1679), included self-defence in the list of **natural rights** he defended in his *Leviathan* (1651), which is particularly remarkable as Hobbes did not otherwise believe that a citizen had any rights at all against the state. According to Hobbes, mankind has all the rights most theorists would list as having existed in the state of nature, that is, before the creation of an organized state, but, in order to create a state powerful enough to protect life, mankind gives up all his rights to the sovereign. The only right he does not surrender is that of self-defence, because it would be logically absurd to argue that one should give up the right to protect one's life if the justification of the state is simply to protect one's life. Hobbes is the apotheosis of rights theory, and the only thinker to give such prominence to the idea of self-defence as a right; not only is it not a right in any usual sense, it is a severely circumscribed defence, and one may not use more than minimum **necessary force**, which must itself be proportional to the end. Thus very little physical violence will be permitted in defence of one's **property**, an understanding that has sometimes been problematic in French law, for example. Even in defending oneself against a potentially deadly attack there are sometimes doctrines, certainly in some US jurisdictions, of a prior duty to flee if possible rather than to stand one's ground and kill to protect one's life. The notion of a form of right to self-defence is limited recognition of inevitable human reaction, and a limiting circumstance to another right, the **right to life**.

Self-incrimination

The right against self-incrimination is basic to ensuring a **fair trial** in the accusatorial system of the common law world, but essentially unknown and irrelevant in a European inquisitorial system. The right is enshrined in various doctrines and dogmas, such as the idea of a **right to silence**, and the importance given to **caution on arrest**. The standard source for the right is the **Fifth Amendment** to the US Constitution. Like all such rights in the United Kingdom it rests only on statute and common law, and the original common law basis set out in the **judge's rules** has been superseded by statute, with the Criminal Justice Act of 1994 making considerable inroads on a previously well-protected right. It is now possible for the prosecution to comment to the jury on an accused's failure to testify and to answer questions. Thus, while there is no actual legal duty to answer a question where the answer may be self-incriminatory, extremely dangerous inferences may be drawn. Even before this change in the law, statutes had largely undone the right in particular contexts, such as some investigations into fraud where it has become an offence not to answer questions put by the Serious Fraud Office. It is a theoretically difficult right, because on the one hand it seems wrong in a sense that a guilty person should go unpunished when an honest answer to a question might prove his guilt, but on the other hand the general approach in criminal law has been to see that the state is so favoured in the general proceedings that, in the interests of overall justice, the state should not get any extra help. In practice, changing the rules may make little difference; the oppressive atmosphere of a police **interrogation** will still intimidate some innocent people, and professional criminals may have little difficulty in getting round the new rules. Although at one time it might have been thought that the right was one little recognized in European systems, the **European Court of Human Rights** has interpreted Article 6 of the **European Convention on Human Rights** to include a rather powerful version of this right. The UK has, in fact, lost a case before the Court for its requirement that certain fraud suspects answer questions under threat of prison if they fail to do so.

Separation of church and state

In many, though by no means all, liberal societies the right to **religious freedom** has been seen as requiring, above all else, a separation between the state and any religious body. While societies since the 18th century have varied in the extent to which religious belief and practice have been supported, tolerated or even opposed by secular powers, an overt and *de jure* identification of the state with one particular faith has been seen as incompatible with religious freedom, or, more properly, the freedom of belief and creed. As in so many other areas, the two leaders on this position have been, since their nearly coincident revolutions, France and the USA. Although neither the 1789 **Declaration of the Rights of Man and of the Citizen** nor the preamble to the Constitution of the French Fourth Republic specifically demands such a state/church separation, the whole tenor of French anti-clericalism, particularly from the Third Republic onwards, combined with the stress placed by these documents on the illegality of discrimination based on religious preference, would make any such combination politically so impossible that a constitutional prohibition is hardly necessary. Where it might matter, in the area of educational policy, statements demanding a secular education system in the preamble, and the definition of the country as a secular state in the Fifth Republic's Constitution, have been enough to make it very hard for any French government to be seen to help organized religion. (However, it must be noted that the **Conseil Constitutionel** has tried to interpret these documents, against parliamentary feeling, to allow limited state financial aid to religious schools.)

The US Bill of Rights (see **Bill of Rights (USA)**), in the first sentence of the **First Amendment**, is very specific, insisting that 'Congress shall make no law respecting an establishment of religion'. This, known as the 'establishment clause' has been interpreted very powerfully by the Supreme Court, requiring an absolute division between the state and any church such that no financial aid, however indirect, may be given to religious institutions, not only educational, but even charitable medical institutions. The clause was debated passionately in the colonies before the passing of the Constitution, and its vehemence stems from the historical experience of many of the original settlers who had fled to America precisely to be able to practise their own brands of Christianity after religious persecution in Great Britain.

The idea of a state specifically licensing one branch of a religion and giving it preference over others, or even a monopoly of legal recognition, is much older than the French and US revolutionary doctrine, and arose from the European wars of religion. Originally the acceptance that the official faith of any society should be that of its ruler was a peace-making idea, a formula on which warring religious-political sects could compromise to end the reformation/counter-reformation conflict of the 16th century. As such, most countries in the post-reformation era had state-authorized religions, and these survive in countries where the resolution sufficiently coincided with internal religious consensus to make them relatively uncontroversial. Thus most Scandinavian countries, as well as the United Kingdom, retain official state churches of a Protestant hue. In Roman Catholic Europe the picture was more mixed, and remains often ambiguous. The Greek state gives special recognition to the Greek Orthodox religion. Where constitutions are recent, and the question has had to be dealt with in the secular world of the 20th century, as in Germany, separation has been accepted as an almost inevitable consequence of religious freedom. This has not necessarily meant the complete ban on financial aid to religious bodies, and indeed the **German Constitution** combines, by incorporating part of the old Weimar constitution, an outright ban on an established church, a guarantee of religious education in schools and state help in collecting a voluntary tax on all members of recognized churches. Although, until recently, the question of establishment of religion would have seemed dated, the rise of fundamentalist faiths to political power has made the issue current again. However, the status of favoured or established religions in a dominantly secular world is rather more complex than in the days of intense religious conflict; although the UK has an established Protestant church, this status is not always opposed by leaders of-non Christian faiths, who see some value in the state's recognition of any religion as opposed to avowed secularism.

Sex discrimination (see *de facto* discrimination)

Sex Discrimination Act

The Sex Discrimination Act of 1975, along with the **Equal Pay Act** of 1970, forms the core of the United Kingdom's legislative provision to reduce sex discrimination, especially in the workplace, and it has a very broad coverage. Initially intended to supplement the Equal Pay Act, it includes all matters of employment omitted by the latter, which was restricted to contractual terms and conditions. Thus it covers problems of unequal chances in recruitment, training and promotion, and working conditions other than actual wage rates, and in addition it covers sex inequality in education, and in the provision of housing, goods, facilities and services. So, for example, cases have arisen under the Act covering education authorities which set higher pass levels for entry into grammar schools for girls than for boys, and even *de facto* **discrimination** in costs of local-authority-provided swimming pools. Both of these cases demonstrate the reason why the Act has rather more power than might originally have been intended.

The Act seeks to prevent both overt and covert sex discrimination. An instance where someone's sex is admitted to be the reason for discrimination, such as a job advert for a secretary saying, in effect, 'only women may apply', would constitute overt sexual discrimination, and be illegal. (Although the Act was primarily intended to help women, it is 'gender neutral' in its legal effect.) The Act also bans discrimination on any ground where the sexes are unequally able to comply with the qualifications; a recruitment policy demanding that all applicants be above a certain height might prove to be illegal were it possible to prove that substantial numbers of women would be disadvantaged, whereas relatively few men would be, by such a test. However, the policy would be illegal only if the person accused of discrimination cannot show it to be justifiable 'irrespective of the sex of the person to whom it is applied'. Hence a physical strength test which far fewer women than men could pass might be acceptable if the employer could show that it really was a vital qualification for the job, which, for example, necessarily involved a considerable amount of lifting of heavy objects. This 'indirect' form of discrimination, included in the Act largely as a result of US experience, has turned out to be by far the more important. In the case of the swimming pool, the local authority, with no intention of disadvantaging either sex, allowed those in receipt of an old-age pension a subsidized entry rate, but as men are not entitled to such a pension until they reach 65, while women can have one at 60, it effectively meant that it was a test which substantially fewer men than women could comply with, and was not necessary for any good reason. This case established, in a very contentious set of divided opinions in the Court of Appeal and the House of Lords, that the Act takes no notice of motive or intention, but sets an external or objective measure.

There are still weaknesses in the operation of the Act, and the **Equal Opportunities Commission** (EOC) is particularly keen to have one element changed. At the moment it is up to the plaintiff to demonstrate that the reason for any unequal treatment is one of discrimination. This **burden of proof** can be very hard to satisfy, especially as the employer or other alleged discriminator is unlikely to be entirely open about his reasons. The EOC (and the European Commission) favour shifting the burden of proof so that the alleged discriminator would have to satisfy a tribunal that he had adequate non-discriminatory reasons for his actions.

Slavery

It might be thought that there was no need in the second half of the 20th century to provide human rights codes specifically for the banning of slavery, but the **Universal Declaration of Human Rights**, and all of its derived rights codes, including the **European Convention on Human Rights**, in Article 4 (Clause 1), contain such a ban. Furthermore, in 1953 the UN issued a protocol amending and updating the League of Nations' Slavery Convention of 1926, and followed it three years later with a full blown Supplementary Convention on the Abolition of Slavery, the Slave Trade, and Institutions and Practices Similar to Slavery. It is the latter part, 'institutions and practices similar to slavery', that cause the modern problem. No state would openly admit even to tolerating slavery as such, and any state which allowed it covertly would be massively indifferent to any UN convention. However, slavery has never been a matter only of the pure legal ownership of a person by another, as made clear by the detailing of what is forbidden in Article 1 of the 1956 Convention. It bans: debt bondage, that is pledging one's services to pay off a debt, unless such a pledge is very tightly limited; serfdom, that is a tenancy in return for living and labouring on the land of another without the right to terminate the agreement; any form of marriage relationship which makes the woman a chattel or in any way deprives her of complete freedom in her marital relations. Clearly there is a wide range of potential sub-slavery conditions, and the problem for any drafter of a rights code is not to step over the boundary by which economic necessity, perhaps to take a job which one hates and for which the remuneration is extremely low, comes to be defined as slavery. The concept must continue to refer to a legal deprivation of freedom, not an *ad hoc* external restraint on choice. The Convention goes into some detail on measures to outlaw mechanisms for enforcing slavery, because making the individual mechanisms, such as branding, criminal offences in their own right, may constitute a more 'policeable' ban than anti-slavery legislation itself.

States' rights

The term states' rights is the claim in any federal system that some area of activity should be left alone by the central or federal government, and that the policy preferred by each separate state should govern in their territory. All federal constitutions have to share out powers and areas of responsibility, some going solely to the federal government, some being left entirely in the hands of the states, and some powers being shared. Inevitably there is an area of vagueness or overlap, and a principal role of a constitutional court is refereeing conflicts on these legal boundaries. From a human rights perspective, the appeal for states' rights is a demand not to have a nation-wide standard or set of rules imposed, and is, in practice, usually an anti-libertarian position. This is because liberal élites are more likely to be able to control a single central source of rights legislation, whether it be a supreme court or a parliament, and their views will be less easily acceptable to groups which may be in a minority nationally but in a majority in particular regions. In the USA, for example, much of the opposition to federally-enforced human rights has traditionally come from Southern states which still tend to be more traditional and conservative than the country as a whole on issues like the death penalty (see **cruel and unusual punishment** and **restrictions on death sentence**), **racial discrimination**, and state involvement in areas of private sexual morality.

There is, inevitably, a problem for a human rights philosophy in any federal system. On the one hand, part of the attraction of **federalism** is to increase democracy and accountability by allowing local preferences and local experiments in law and living. On the other hand, allowing variance on issues of basic rights seems to make some people suffer intrusions in, say, their **privacy**, when this would be protected just a short distance away across a state border. If rights are, in some fundamental sense, **natural rights**, and few advocates of human rights do not think that this is true to some extent, it can be hard to see why a particular region inside the state should not be held to the same standards as other regions voluntarily accept.

Statutory rights

A statutory right is an entitlement which someone has because it has been legislated in an ordinary way by a national parliament, rather than one that is either enshrined in a constitution or human rights convention, or deduced by a court from some fundamental principles. Obviously many rights have both characters, in as much as governments often seek to ensure and formalize rights taken to be fundamental by writing them into formal legislation, but reference to a statutory right need only point to a clause in a specific piece of legislation. Many of the rights people are most conscious of and care about most are in fact purely statutory, such as **welfare rights** or **property** rights. It is characteristic of such rights that they are socially optional; no court would ever try to claim that a citizen had a right to a particular form of welfare, say housing in an emergency, unless it were enshrined in legislation, and different states will define their responsibilities such that some will simply not acknowledge some rights to which another state has given statutory backing. A legal philosopher from a positivist tradition would insist that the only rights that exist are statutory rights, in keeping with **Bentham's** dictum that talk of **natural rights** is 'nonsense upon stilts'.

Stop and search

The powers of police forces to stop suspicious persons in public and search them for evidence of criminal activities is one of the most commonly encountered of **civil liberties** problems. Most modern political systems have some sort of control on this form of police behaviour, though it is always controversial, as are most civil libertarian controls on the police, on the grounds that such restrictions hamper the 'war against crime'. The usual test resembles the US doctrine of **probable cause**, that is, the police officer must have some good prior reason for suspecting that the person he stops has been involved in criminal action, and must not be stopping him purely because he fits a category of those likely to offend. Such is the basic criminal law in the United Kingdom and throughout Western Europe, though it is not a right against intrusion that is usually guaranteed in constitutions or **bills of rights**. Essentially, breaches of such prohibitions on generalized 'stop and search' policies are a form of harassment, and the usual complaint is that the police pick on easily-identified minorities and regularly search them in the hope of straightforward convictions. One reason why it is very hard to protect against such police behaviour is that the 'probable cause', or whatever equivalent test is used, has to be subjective. To specify precisely what reasons would justify a police officer searching someone probably would be an unacceptable restriction on effective policing, but subjective reasons are obviously extremely hard to disprove in a court if a citizen tries to claim damages for an illegal search. Consequently the most effective restraints on the police come where courts are prepared to throw out any case where the evidence was gained without probable cause. (See also **Sus Law**.)

Strict construction

Strict construction refers to a judicial technique of **interpretation**, usually of statutes but also of constitutional documents. A 'strict constructionist' is a judge who goes as far as possible by the literal meaning of the words in the document, rather than giving what is sometimes called a 'purposive' interpretation, or in Europe a 'teleological' interpretation. These latter techniques involve asking what the statute (or constitutional clause) is really trying to do, and interpreting the words along such lines. Strict construction is usually, though not invariably, associated with a restrictive approach to **civil liberties** or other constitutional restraints on government, because it is a technique more likely, in practice, to result in a narrowing of definitions of rights and protections. At times, though, it can produce the opposite effect. Mr Justice Hugo La Fayette Black, usually thought of as a liberal Supreme Court Justice, was noted for his 'strict construction' of the **First Amendment** protection of **freedom of speech**, because he insisted that the clause which says 'Congress shall make no law . . . abridging the freedom of speech or of the press' meant literally what it said: no law, not even one controlling, for example, pornography.

Most constitutional courts have gone through the debate on strict construction at one time or another, and politicians everywhere tend to demand such an approach for fear of judicial involvement in politics. In practice the distinction is over-simplified, and judges alternate between strict and expansionist methodology in order to achieve the results they want. In the USA strict construction is often linked to a related judicial methodology, the 'original position thesis'. The trouble with strict construction is that words simply do not always have a conveniently identifiable strict meaning, and intention has to be taken into account. The trouble with liberal or intentionalist interpretation is that it is easily capable of incorporating anything a judge wants to insist is really teleologically necessary to make sense of the act. (See also **golden rule**.)

Strict interpretation (see **strict construction**)

Subpoena

A subpoena is an order from a court, or from some other institution authorized by statute to issue it, requiring a named person to come before it and give evidence. Ignoring a subpoena puts one in contempt of court for which imprisonment is a possible sentence. In the USA it is also possible to get a court to issue a subpoena to attend a deposition, in which counsel for one party demands the answers to questions which then form a record acceptable in the court. There are two basic forms of subpoena: *subpoena ad testificandum*, which is as described above, and *subpoena duces tecum*, which requires the person served to bring specified documents with him for examination. In the USA subpoenas are regularly used by investigative committees of Congress, as well as by regulatory agencies of the government. The power of subpoena is available not only to the state, as a court will subpoena witnesses and documents on behalf of a plaintiff or defendant where the opposing party is uncooperative.

Substantive due process (see due process)

Suffrage (see representation and voting rights)

Sus Law

The 'Sus Law' in British civil rights parlance referred to what was technically Section 66 of the old Metropolitan Police Act of 1839, one of a set of special statutes enacted for major cities at the time of the creation of the British police forces. Section 66 allowed a police officer to **stop and search** anyone whom he suspected of being in immediate possession of stolen property. The powers were notoriously overused and treated as a legal means to harass anyone the police thought might be guilty of any crime. It contrasted strongly with the **probable cause** test used in US-inspired jurisdictions, given that there was almost no control over when a police officer might plausibly have such a suspicion. Even when the powers were in force, the fact that such powers were limited to specific localities showed the extent to which they were an abrogation of the general common law preference for the **liberty of the person**. The extent of their use in situations when there was little real reason for stopping someone is indicated by the fact that in 1979 only 12% of all stops enforced by the police actually led to an **arrest**. These localized powers were repealed with the passage of the **Police and Criminal Evidence Act** in 1984, which allowed similar, but better-defined and more tightly-regulated, stop and search powers, while other powers for specific purposes like suspicion of carrying a weapon are contained in other legislation. If an arrest does follow a stop and search operation, the courts are likely to acquit if the police cannot now show what would amount to a 'probable cause' for stopping, but there is very little effective remedy where the police do not make an arrest.

Toleration

Although toleration is clearly one of the virtues that goes hand in hand with respect for rights, it is seldom posited as a duty correlative with some right to be tolerated. At most one may find it mentioned in the context of the human personality towards which more clear cut rights can lead. Thus the definition of education in Article 13 of the **International Covenant on Economic, Social and Cultural Rights** justifies the right to education in part on the grounds that it should promote 'understanding, tolerance and friendship'. In fact the duty of tolerance might best be seen as a precursor to the full acceptance of human rights. The problem is that calling for tolerance, or toleration of someone's activities or beliefs, seems to imply that one would have any right whatsoever not to respect their freedom in the relevant area. This point is illustrated by the work of John **Locke**. One of the earliest seminal rights theorists, and a leading influence on the framers of the US Constitution, he advocated human rights, and defended them staunchly in works like the *Second Treatise on Civil Government* (1690), but with regard to **religious freedom** he advocated only tolerance, in his famous *Letters on Toleration* (1689–92), and even this got him into some degree of trouble as being thought too radical. To many thinkers of Locke's period religious conflict was so dangerous that the state was naturally regarded as entitled to legislate about religious observance, not as an institution likely to know better the truths of religion, but because of the political danger of religious pluralism. Indeed, even in the *Letters on Toleration*, Locke advocated that toleration not be extended to atheists because, not believing in God, they could not be trusted to keep their promises. The difference between toleration and the recognition of a right, therefore, is that the former is, in some sense, optional, or at least capable of being 'unaffordable' in some contexts. There is a strand of rights thinking that regards many human rights as luxuries affordable only in stable and affluent societies, although such a theory mistakes the very nature of rights.

Toleration Act

The Toleration Act of 1689 might be seen as one of the first steps towards recognizing basic human rights in Great Britain, as it repealed a series of legislative bars on the freedom of religion established in the wake of the Reformation. By the late 17th century it had become increasingly obvious that not all Protestant aspirations could be held within even a broad Anglican Church, while the Protestant settlement of 1689 (see **Bill of Rights (UK)**), assuaged fears of a Catholic take-over of the English crown. Given these two factors, the establishment moved away from the pursuit of religious uniformity and allowed a limited degree of freedom of worship for the first time in English history. The freedom was limited, and, of course, did not extend to disestablishing the Church of England. Nevertheless most, though not all, branches of the nonconformist faith were allowed to operate their own churches and to ordain ministers, though the churches had to remain permanently unlocked, for fear of unspecified deviant behaviour going on behind closed doors. Some offshoots felt to be too far from the mainstream, such as Unitarians, were still banned. Religious identity remained politically vitally important however, and all non-members of the Anglican Church were barred from holding any public office.

In the USA the state of New Hampshire passed its own version of the Toleration Act in 1819; despite the ban on established churches as far as the federal government was concerned, which was contained in the Bill of Rights (see **Bill of Rights (USA)**), several of the US states continued to favour one faith over others.

Torture

Torture is the deliberate infliction of physical or mental suffering, and is normally thought of as being perpetrated by some agency of the state. The neutrality of this definition is necessitated because there are two rather separate aspects to torture historically, and correspondingly two different theoretical objections to it. In popular fiction torture is most often associated with the idea of hurting someone to make them confess to a crime, or to extract information which the state needs or wants. But torture can also cover the use of pain and suffering as a punishment in itself. The distinction is important because, historically, torture in the first sense has more often been disapproved of than in its second sense. Torture, often referred to as judicial torture, to make a suspect confess to a crime or to gain information about, for example, a suspect's accomplices, though recently used, has, historically, equally frequently been objected to and banned. Under the

Roman Republic torture could only be used on slaves, and even when, under the Empire, it was allowed on citizens, its use was restricted to cases of suspected treason. In fact this limitation to treason, the most heinous of crimes in many penal codes, was usual.

Among the most dramatic of historic uses of torture, by the Inquisition in their attempts to discover and eliminate heresy, gained its legitimacy during the 13th century when the Roman use of torture in treason cases was incorporated into canon law, heresy being seen as a directly equivalent crime. Torture as a legitimate part of canon law was not abolished until a Papal Bull of 1816. Only later, and following this precedent, did most continental European systems adopt torture, and, in adopting it, often expand the range of suspected crimes for which it could be applied. By the early modern era torture was legitimated widely in Europe, though particularly so in the Italian and Germanic states. Torture was not outlawed in these states until various dates during the 18th century: the French abolished it at the Revolution, for example. Torture lingered on as a legitimate weapon of state in some places, being abolished in Naples as late as 1860.

English common law was never comfortable with judicial torture, and although it was practised from time to time, this was almost always under special prerogative writs from the monarch, and, again, only in cases of treason. The well known use of torture under Elizabeth I is an example of both these points. As early as 1628 the English judiciary declared torture illegal when it was proposed to use it on the assassin of the Duke of Buckingham to find the identity of his accomplices. The theoretical argument against torture is a combination of a **due process** argument, the state should not be allowed to manufacture evidence, and a straightforward humanitarian objection to the infliction of pain on possibly innocent people. This is why the concept becomes complex, because humanitarian objections to the infliction of pain on guilty people are much more recent in origin. Many forms of punishment depended primarily on the infliction of pain, as with flogging, were indifferent to the incidental infliction of pain, as with branding, or used pain to add further emphasis to the horror of the punishment for deterrent effects, as with the classically horrifying forms of execution used for some crimes. It is really only in the 20th century that sensitivities have developed to the point where even the punishment of the guilty is regarded as not justifying any avoidable physical or mental suffering, although the beginning of this trend is found in the 18th century with doctrines like the ban on **cruel and unusual punishment** in the US Constitution.

Torture in both senses is banned by a series of international civil rights covenants, such as the UN Convention against Torture and Other Cruel, Inhuman or Degrading Treatment or Punishment (1984, the text of the Preamble and Part I from which is given in the Appendix) and the European Convention for the Prevention of Torture and Inhuman or Degrading Treatment or Punishment (1969).

Treaty of Rome

It was the Treaty of Rome, signed on 25 March 1957, which created the European Economic Community (EEC), now officially titled the Economic Community, and, as such, the most important part of the central pillar of the European Union (EU). Though the Treaty of Maastricht in 1992 substantially revised the Treaty of Rome, the essentials of the EU are still as set out in the 1957 document. Neither Treaty includes a human rights code as such, though some specific rights germane to the original, more narrowly economic, purpose of the Treaty of Rome were included. Thus, for example, a right against sex discrimination in employment is specifically found in Article 119. The Treaty does, however, require that Community law be developed with reference to the common legal traditions of the member states. Quite rapidly human rights became an issue before the Court of Justice of the European Communities, usually referred to as the **European Court of Justice (ECJ)**. The particular problem comes from the fact that the ECJ is dependent on the courts of member states accepting the supremacy of Community law over their own. Courts in several countries, but especially Germany, were quite prepared to accept this supremacy over the ordinary domestic law. The German courts argued however that, as their fundamental duty was to apply their Constitution, to which all domestic law was subject, they would be in breach of their constitutional duty were they to follow any Community law which abridged the human rights clauses in the **German Constitution**. The ECJ has interpreted the Treaty of Rome to allow for this, arguing that the Treaty owes its legal authority to a partial surrender of sovereignty by the member states, but these states could not be thought to have had the legal power, in the first place, to surrender constitutionally-protected rights. Consequently, no act of Community law-making can be valid if it abridges something which is protected as a fundamental right in any of the separate constitutions. The ECJ has gone further and ruled that the **European Convention on Human Rights**, because it is integral to the legal systems of the member states, is also to be seen as incorporated into Community law. The only step the ECJ has not taken is to allow the EU, as such, to sign the Convention, on the grounds that the Treaty of Rome does not allow this form of treaty making.

Treaty rights

An issue on which constitutional theory in liberal democracies varies is the internal legal status of treaties the state makes with other states and with international organizations. Some constitutions, such as the French and Dutch, fully incorporate such treaties so that they are supreme over any domestic legislation, though, necessarily, not over the constitution itself, as this latter would be a logical absurdity. This is probably also the case in US constitutional law. Others, notably the United Kingdom, argue that a treaty is just an agreement between sovereigns, and therefore a treaty signed by the UK can have no impact inside the UK itself unless Parliament separately and specifically legislates for it to do so. The question of treaty rights can have a serious effect on the degree to which human rights are protected in different countries. Most nations are prepared to sign often very high-sounding international accords on human rights, and indeed find it difficult, for reasons of international prestige, not to do so. Where, however, their own constitutional doctrine means that signing such a convention will give their own citizens justiciable rights against the state, they may be much more cautious. Thus the inclusion of **housing rights** pressed for in the international conference Habitat II, the second UN Conference on Human Settlements, which was held in Istanbul, Turkey, in June 1996, was delayed and weakened by the US government for fear it would result in a large number of civil rights cases by the homeless in the USA.

In the UK no treaty has any internal force, and no treaty-based right could be enforced by a British court. In its own way this has been a serious disadvantage to British citizens for several decades, because although the UK is a signatory to the **European Convention on Human Rights**, its doctrine on the status of treaty rights has meant that no one can cite the Convention to their aid in a trial before a British court. One consequence has been that the UK is far more often taken to the **European Court of Human Rights** in Strasbourg by its own citizens for human rights violations, which it regularly loses, than is the case with other member states. The Treaty of Rome and ensuing European Union legislation can have effect in the UK only because of the passage of a special piece of legislation in 1971 empowering British courts to take notice of the Treaty. The legislation could be repealed overnight by Parliament, immediately removing legal effect from any decision of the **European Court of Justice**, something which the anti-European wing of the British Conservative Party regularly calls for. The same political group would be eager to have what direct effect does adhere to the European Convention on Human Rights removed by legislation. Although the UK might then be in breach of its obligations to the European Assembly, no British court could take any notice of this fact. Should the election of a new Labour government in the UK, in 1997, result in the **incorporation** of the European Convention into domestic law, then the UK's distinctiveness over treaty rights would decline.

Tyranny of the majority

The tyranny of the majority is a concept originated by Alexis de Tocqueville (1805–59) in his classic study *Democracy in America* (1835), which is of crucial importance to the study of human rights. His basic premise is that, historically, liberals have feared tyranny because they feared the arbitrary and rapacious power of despots and oligarchies who had no reason to concern themselves with the welfare of the many. There is no guarantee, however, that majorities will be any more concerned with the interests of minorities, and democracy in itself therefore does not take away the problem of tyranny. For this reason, what modern liberals actually aim for is not democracy *per se*, but liberal democracy, a political system within which, while nothing can be done that the majority does not support, it is not true that the majority can do anything it wants. There are two quite distinct bases for fearing the tyranny of the majority. One is a straightforward matter of material interests. A stable long-term identifiable minority, sometimes called a 'permanent' minority, can just as easily be exploited for the economic benefit of the majority as a majority lower class can be exploited in a non-democratic inegalitarian system. Quite separate from this is a more psychologically-based theory which holds that majorities are frightened by, or repelled by, culturally different groups or by unorthodox beliefs or behaviour even by lone and isolated individuals, and that there is a tendency to uniformity in masses, which will not tolerate differences. For either or both of these reasons majority rule is deemed to require restraints to prevent a semi-automatic tendency to crush individuality or to exploit the vulnerable. Much of the civil libertarian approach is focused precisely on establishing these controls over majority rule, and the US Supreme Court is sometimes referred to as a 'counter-majoritarian' institution. However, the theory of tyranny of the majority can also be described as a patronizing and self-serving myth created by a liberal intellectual minority; de Tocqueville was, after all, a French nobleman not entirely free of nostalgia for the *ancien régime*, which was also a subject of his writings.

U

UN declarations and conventions

An important part of the analysis of world problems made by those who constructed the United Nations was that disrespect for human rights, as well as being an evil in itself, had contributed to the breakdown of world society twice in the 20th century. Consequently, respect for human rights was built into the UN Charter itself: 'to reaffirm faith in fundamental human rights . . .' comes second only to the commitment 'to save succeeding generations from the scourge of war . . .' The UN's Economic and Social Council rapidly moved to set up the UN Commission on Human Rights, there is a Division of Human Rights in the UN Secretariat, and other UN bodies, notably the Commission on the Status of Women and the **International Labour Organization (ILO)**, have major human rights concerns. These bodies not only carry out general propaganda and monitoring and research on human rights issues, but have prepared a series of detailed legal instruments with varying degrees of justiciability on many human rights areas. Nevertheless, the Commission on Human Rights has never satisfied many that it can act on real complaints. The most it can do is to carry out fact-finding exercises and publish reports, and even then it dismisses most allegations and complaints, at least partly because it is not institutionalized as a full-time and well-staffed body. Over 50,000 applications for examination of complaints arrive each year, but the Commission and subcommissions only meet for a total of a few weeks in each year. At the same time, political constraints based on the complex and shifting coalitions of UN membership make it pointless for the Commission to get very heavily involved in affairs within most countries.

The prime human rights document of the UN itself is the **Universal Declaration of Human Rights**, adopted in 1948 by the full General Assembly. This document, and its following more legally-binding versions, the **International Covenant on Civil and Political Rights** and the **International Covenant on Economic, Social and Cultural Rights**, have broad general coverage. There is a plethora of other conventions and declarations on more specialized topics, including: the Convention on the Prevention and Punishment of the Crime of **Genocide** (1948); the Declaration on the Protection of All Persons from Being Subjected to **Torture** and Other Cruel, Inhuman or Degrading Treatment or Punishment (1975) and its related Convention against Torture and other Cruel, Inhuman or Degrading Treatment or Punishment (1984); the Convention on the Political Rights of Women (1952); the all-embracing Declaration on the Elimination of All Forms of Intolerance and Discrimination Based on Religion or Belief (1981); and the Convention on the Rights of the Child (1989, the substantive articles of which are given in the Appendix). There is an important distinction between a declaration and a covenant in international law, which has consequences for the production of human rights codes, reflected in the titles of these documents. A Declaration, such as the 1975 Declaration on Protection from Torture, is a statement of principle, in this case a statement contained in a resolution of the General Assembly, but is not binding as such in international law. No specific action is called for from any member state, and indeed the declaration above was adopted by consensus rather than by a vote. To give any degree of effect a declaration has to be reproduced, usually in much more detailed and technical language, in a convention, which is binding only on those member states of the UN which actually sign the convention. The ensuing Convention in 1984 was signed almost immediately by over 50 members, who therefore incurred specific legal obligations, including the duty either to punish anyone guilty of torture found in their territory, even if he is an alien, or to extradite him to another country prepared to punish him.

Universal Declaration of Human Rights

This was the first of the UN pronouncements on human rights, adopted in the same year, 1948, as the UN Charter itself. It became the model for subsequent regional rights codes like the **African Charter on Human and People's Rights** and the **European Convention on Human Rights**, as well as its own more legally-binding UN successor documents, the **International Covenant on Civil and Political Rights** and the **International Covenant on Economic, Social and Cultural Rights**. Sometimes the language of particular sections is reproduced faithfully, but more frequently later or regional versions add to particular freedoms, or specify their content in detail. This in part represents the very widely-shared understanding of human rights, the result of meetings, private and official, by a small group of international and humanitarian law experts over the inter-war and wartime decades. Thus Article 1 of the Universal Declaration and the first sentence of the **American Declaration of the Rights and Duties of Man**, promulgated in the same year, are virtually identical. The Universal Declaration states: 'All human beings are born free and equal in dignity and rights. They are endowed with reason and conscience and should act towards one another in a spirit of brotherhood.' The American Declaration reads: 'All men are born free and equal in dignity and rights, and being endowed by nature with reason and conscience, they should conduct themselves as brothers one to another'. The UN Declaration, unlike its own successors, was not intended to be legally binding, and is not specifically signed by the UN's member states. It is, in its own words, 'a common standard of achievement for all peoples and all nations . . .', so that 'keeping this Declaration constantly in mind, (all) shall strive by teaching and education to promote respect for these rights and freedoms . . .'

The Universal Declaration is not, however, the woolly, verbose and hopelessly utopian document that it might easily have been. It is relatively short, consisting of 30 quite precisely-drafted rights. The first 21 articles cover **negative rights**, that is freedoms which can be guaranteed simply, with no question of policy choice over government expenditure, usually just by the state forbearing to intervene and forbidding private individuals to intervene with free choices, or banning, rather than requiring, actions. The first substantive article, Article 2, is the catch-all ban on discrimination as regards the enjoyment of the subsequently listed rights, akin to the **equal protection** clause in the US **Fourteenth Amendment**, and necessary in any such rights code. The protected rights cover first 'life, **liberty** and **security of person**' and then the more practical considerations. **Slavery** is banned, along with **torture**, **cruel and unusual punishment**, arbitrary **arrest** and **detention**, and the invasion of the **privacy** of family, home or correspondence. **Due process** of law is guaranteed in some detail, including the principles of 'innocent until proved guilty' (see **right to silence**) and no retrospective laws (see **retroactivity**), as are the 'intellectual' freedoms of thought, conscience and religion (see **religious freedom**), and **freedom of speech** and **freedom of association**. Private ownership of **property** is protected, and though the clause has nothing like the strength to be found in some such documents, it was enough to make it impossible for the USSR and some satellites to vote for the Declaration. Basic electoral democracy is required by Article 21. Considerable attention is given, quite naturally in an international model code, to **freedom of movement** in international as well as national terms, including a carefully worded right of **asylum**, which would not protect ordinary criminals. The very right to have a nationality, so clearly a problem shortly after the conclusion of the Second World War, when there were millions of stateless people, is guaranteed in Article 15. The theme of sanctity of the family, developed considerably in some later documents, is dealt with in Article 16, which includes the broad sociological thesis incorporated elsewhere that 'The family is the natural and fundamental group unit of society and is entitled to protection by society and the State' (see also **right to family life**). Articles 22 to 26 are rather more positive in that they make calls on the state for active provision of goods, though they are written in a less demanding tone than many later versions. They include the **right to employment**, or the right to receive unemployment pay, rights to social security, health and education, and to social security (see **welfare rights**). Compared to the earlier rights they are less well drafted, with considerable repetition, and also, curiously, feature some well-established specific rights of a more negative kind, like the right to join a trade union, which would more appropriately have appeared in the earlier part of the list.

Because it was meant to be only a set of standards to aspire to, the Declaration is not always couched in the sort of terms that would be easily justiciable, and there neither is, nor was ever meant to be, any form of enforcement machinery. What is remarkable is that such a document should nevertheless succeed in being substantive enough to mean something, and yet gain the support of 48 out of the then 56 members of the UN. The abstainers were the USSR and its satellites of Czechoslovakia, Poland, Belorussia and Ukraine, along with Yugoslavia, Saudi Arabia and South Africa. (The full text of the Universal Declaration of Human Rights is given in the Appendix.)

Voting rights

The most famous piece of **civil liberties** legislation on voting rights is the US Voting Rights Act of 1965, which was passed because of congressional impatience with the progress of this aspect of the broader **Civil Rights Act** of 1964. The Voting Rights Act banned various forms of voting legislation in the states, such as literacy tests, which were in practice used to keep blacks off the voting register (see *de facto* **discrimination**). It also banned the withholding of the right to vote as a result of failure to pay poll taxes, which had a clear discriminatory effect, and was made fully unconstitutional in the 24th Amendment. Prior to this Act the vast majority of blacks were prevented from voting throughout the traditional deep South of the USA, helping to ensure a racially-biased congressional bloc in Washington. The other major case of **racial discrimination** over voting rights was in South Africa under the open policy of apartheid, where the government denied real participation in electoral political processes to its non-white citizens for as long as possible, refusing to allow them to vote for the majority of seats until the collapse of the policy in the early 1990s. Most countries have historically attempted to restrict the suffrage even after becoming nominally democratic, and the right to vote has been the most keenly fought for of all civil rights. Indeed, it might be argued that it is the primary right without which few other political rights have any value. The classic case of disenfranchisement in systems otherwise committed to democracy is that of disenfranchisement of women. In fact women only got the vote in relatively recent history in some major liberal states; the USA granted female suffrage in 1920, the United Kingdom not fully until 1928, France in 1945 and Switzerland not until 1971.

There are various ways in which *de jure* voting rights can be reduced in impact, the most famous being the practice of gerrymandering, named after Governor Elbridge Gerry of Massachusetts who, in 1811, created abnormally shaped constituencies which looked like salamanders. This is the process by which electoral districts are drawn up so as to mass opposition voters into a few constituencies while the others are devised to provide the party doing the gerrymandering with a large number of slim majorities. Even when no overt intention to discriminate lay behind an original electoral map, failure to update it can seriously deprive voters of equal political power when population changes make some constituencies much more densely populated than other declining constituencies. Such a pattern of demographic change in the USA led to an increasing dominance of conservative congressmen from thinly-populated rural constituencies, who delayed the process of electoral re-districting for decades, until the US Supreme Court held, in *Baker v. Carr* (1962), such a failure to act to be a violation of **equal protection** rights, in effect saying it was a denial of the fundamental principle of 'one person, one vote'. This principle in itself has not always been seen as an integral part of the right to vote; until 1947 the UK had a complex suffrage which allowed some people to vote in more than one constituency, as well as having some non-geographical constituencies to represent graduates of the older universities. In any political system the process for regular re-districting is a sensitive one which political parties watch with great care, and almost invariably with some allegations of bias. (See also **representation**.)

W

Warrant

A warrant is an authority issued by a court for a specific action, which would otherwise be illegal; under common law, and to a large extent under civil law too, the state as such has no inherent power to act in a way a private person cannot. The most common warrants are for the purposes of either search or **arrest**, and they may also be used to allow actions such as telephone tapping. In civil jurisdiction, warrants may be issued to authorize the entry on to premises for the purposes of the seizure or repossession of goods. Warrants must be specific as to time, place and person (the US **Fourth Amendment** specifically prohibits the issue of general warrants) and the state must demonstrate **probable cause** in support of its request; it must give adequate reasons for believing that the specified documents, for example, are to be found in the specified place and are reasonably necessary to establish guilt of a specified person. The idea of state action authorized only by warrant is fundamental to **civil liberties**, but the rigour of the court's scrutiny of the terms requested is dependent on general political and sociological patterns.

Warren, Earl

Earl Warren (1891–1974) was the Chief Justice of the US Supreme Court from 1953 to 1969, a period always referred to as the 'Warren Court', during which the foundation was laid for most of the civil-libertarian doctrines of US constitutional law as it developed in the post-war world. It was no accident that what is usually regarded as the single most important case this century, the overruling of **racial discrimination** in education in **Brown v. Board** of Education of Topeka came shortly after his appointment, in 1954. The **American and Civil Liberties Union (ACLU)** and **National Association for the Advancement of Colored People (NAACP)** had been trying for years to get the Court to make such a decision, but it took Warren's political skills as well as his deeply-felt liberalism to bring it about. Warren was primarily a politician, although he had entered politics as his

214

state's attorney-general, who came to prominence as a liberal Republican Governor of California, and was believed to have been appointed Chief Justice in return for supporting President Dwight D. Eisenhower's presidential campaign. Eisenhower (1890–1969) had not expected him to become so active a liberal jurist, and is reputed to have claimed later that the appointment was the biggest mistake of his presidency. From a legal point of view his work had a number of shortcomings, and many landmark decisions of the Warren Court are so inadequately reasoned constitutionally that they are always open to attack. His legacy is that of a leader of the Supreme Court who helped to shape vital constitutional doctrine not only on equal rights, but on **criminal civil liberties**, in decisions like the drafting in 1966 of the **Miranda warning**, detailing the rights of police suspects, and also on politically far-reaching decisions enforcing reapportionment of electoral boundaries (see **voting rights**).

Wednesbury unreasonableness

The 1948 case of *Associated Picture Houses v. Wednesbury Corporation* has been hailed as the occasion when English **public law** broke through from a long period of subservience to the state administration. The case gave its name to a fundamental definition of when courts will intervene to protect a member of the public from **arbitrary** exercise of administrative discretion, known as Wednesbury unreasonableness. When the Wednesbury Corporation, exercising a statutory power to license Sunday cinema opening, imposed a condition that children under 15 should not be admitted, the cinema owner asked for a declaration that the decision was inapplicable as it was unreasonable. The owner lost his case, but his action prompted a discussion by the presiding judge, Lord Greene (1883–1952), which has ever since been the standard test of unreasonableness in discretionary decision-making (see **discretion**), setting out the limits of when a court may intervene. The unreasonableness test has two forms: under the first a decision-maker must 'direct himself properly in the law', that is, his expressed understanding of the law must be correct; he must consider everything that is relevant; he must not consider any matter that is irrelevant. Providing he passes these tests, the decision-maker will not be overruled just because the court thinks he is wrong; even if the court would not come to the same conclusion, they will defer to the statutory discretion. This places tremendous importance on the decision-maker's publicly-stated reasons, which is why **reasoned decisions** are so vital to a properly working public law system. The second form of the test is where the court accepts that even within this framework a decision-maker might do something so absurd that it was, as it were, substantively unreasonable, the very oddness of the decision constituting evidence that he had acted unreasonably. This form is dangerously subjective and is not used very frequently; when it has been used the cases have usually attracted serious criticism for being politically biased.

Welfare rights

Welfare rights come into the general category of **positive rights**; there are rights which require the state to do something (such as a right to unemployment pay), and are not normally included in any human rights code with a justiciable force. There are also rights in positive law, under which the state must abide by its own statutory obligations to supply a certain benefit; these rights are justiciable, but also entirely contingent as there is nothing to require the state to provide the right in question, nor to provide it in any particular form or quantity. In common parlance much of 'rights talk' in fact refers to such matters, and is not truly about human rights at all, and the common assertion 'I know my rights', apart from usually being empirically false, generally refers to some vague conception of entitlements that the claimant thinks he has to welfare. The real connection between human rights properly so conceived and welfare rights comes in terms of questions about the application and design of welfare programmes which may entail protections against discrimination, which do fall within the ambit of guaranteed rights. Thus failure to provide retirement pensions on the same terms to both men and women would, in general, be a breach of human rights because the relevant rights codes, say the US Constitution, or with this specific example the **Treaty of Rome**, forbid sex discrimination in this context (see also **age discrimination**). The right protected here is the right to have a pension if pensions are to be granted at all, not the right to have a pension in itself, and only a much broader argument about necessary implications of accepted rights could turn a welfare claim into a human right in its full sense. It might possibly be argued that a rights code which grants, for example, the **right to family life**, as the **German Constitution** might be said to in Article 6, must also be seen to guarantee, where necessary, some form of welfare entitlement to single mothers. It is very unlikely that any constitutional court would be prepared, however, to order the state to institute such a scheme. (It could be argued that the **German Constitutional Court** has done something roughly equivalent, when in order to protect the **right to life** it not only struck down legislation intended to allow **abortion**, but demanded that the Bundestag initiate legislation making it a criminal offence for doctors to facilitate abortion. The analogy, however, is a weak one because the right to life is, in the special sense used here, a **negative right**.)

Written constitutions

As there is no such thing as an unwritten constitution, the term written constitution is used for countries such as the USA, Germany, France, Australia,

Canada and so on where there exists a single coherent document, framed by a specific group of people at a particular time and ratified in some way or other by the citizens it controls or their representatives. By contrast, in countries like the United Kingdom, New Zealand or Israel, the rules governing the distribution of powers and responsibilities in the state consist of a mass of separate documents; some are ordinary legislation, some judicial opinions, some textbooks by leading constitutional writers, some internal civil service rules of procedure. Even the famous conventions which are held to form the constitution in a country like the UK do not exist in some intuitive vacuum, and are only known and transmittable in written form. Even with a so-called written constitution, the full truth of any article in the constitution is unlikely to be discoverable by referring only to the original constitutional document and those amendments formally added to it by the amending process over time, chiefly because the words in the constitution are too vague, are over simple, or, if taken literally, anachronistic. Constitutions are subject to **interpretation**, and even written constitutions accrue traditions: for example, the special scope of presidential power under the French Fifth Constitution now includes aspects of economic policy-making, because under presidents after de Gaulle the rest of the political élite allowed such a drift of power into presidential hands, although the text of the Constitution was never amended to add economic policy to areas reserved to the Presidency. Furthermore, the French *Conseil Constitutionel* regards itself as entitled to look at a large range of material, including ordinary parliamentary statutes of previous republics to derive the fundamental principles of the French 'republican tradition'.

Political structures arise as *ad hoc* arrangements are consolidated into common practice, and to a large extent formal written constitutions reflect pre-existing understandings and patterns. In some situations, like the emergency conditions of the birth of Israel, there is no time to formalize these at the beginning of the regime, and no felt need to do so afterwards. Where there is no clear agreement on issues, constitutions usually gloss over the problem, leaving it for later generations to develop understandings, and it is relatively rare for countries to bother writing these later workings out into their constitutional text. Nevertheless, written constitutions do function differently from those traditionally regarded as unwritten, as the mere existence of a formal document can act as a restraint in a way that conventions cannot, and constitutions of the formal kind, because they have been expressly ratified, can take on a symbolic force in politics. Although constitutions are more properly seen as reflecting rather than forming political forces, the question of the importance of a formal, and necessarily 'written', bill of rights (see **bills of rights**) is quite separate. It is a common mistake to suppose that a written constitution is weakened by the **entrenchment** of a bill of rights outside it.

APPENDIX

This Appendix consists of texts, and extracts from texts, of the constitutional and human rights documents which are of most relevance to the subject material covered in the alphabetical entries which appear in the earlier part of this book.

List of Documents

Magna Carta, 1215

The following is the full text of Magna Carta, in translation from the original Latin.

John, by the grace of God, king of England, lord of Ireland, duke of Normandy and Aquitaine, and count of Anjou, to the archbishops, bishops, abbots, earls, barons, justiciars, foresters, sheriffs, stewards, servants, and to all his bailiffs and faithful subjects, greeting. Know that we, out of reverence for God and for the salvation of our soul and those of all our ancestors and heirs, for the honour of God and the exaltation of holy church, and for the reform of our realm, on the advice of our venerable fathers, Stephen, archbishop of Canterbury, primate of all England and cardinal of the holy Roman church, Henry archbishop of Dublin, William of London, Peter of Winchester, Jocelyn of Bath and Glastonbury, Hugh of Lincoln, Walter of Worcester, William of Coventry and Benedict of Rochester, bishops, of master Pandulf, subdeacon and member of the household of the lord pope, of brother Aymeric, master of the order of Knights Templar in England, and of the noble men William Marshal earl of Pembroke, William earl of Salisbury, William earl of Warenne, William earl of Arundel, Alan of Galloway constable of Scotland, Warin fitz Gerold, Peter fitz Herbert, Hubert de Burgh seneschal of Poitou, Hugh de Neville, Matthew fitz Herbert, Thomas Basset, Alan Basset, Philip de Aubeney, Robert of Ropsley, John Marshal, John fitz Hugh, and others, our faithful subjects:

1   In the first place have granted to God, and by this our present charter confirmed for us and our heirs for ever that the English church shall be free, and shall have its rights undiminished and its liberties unimpaired; and it is our will that it be thus observed; which is evident from the fact that, before the quarrel between us and our barons began, we willingly and spontaneously granted and by our charter confirmed the freedom of elections which is reckoned most important and very essential to the English church, and obtained confirmation of it from the lord pope Innocent III; the which we will observe and we wish our heirs to observe it in good faith for ever. We have also granted to all free men of our kingdom, for ourselves and our heirs for ever, all the liberties written below, to be had and held by them and their heirs of us and our heirs.

2   If any of our earls or barons or others holding of us in chief by knight service dies, and at his death his heir be of full age and owe relief he shall have his inheritance on payment of the old relief, namely the heir or heirs of an earl £100 for a whole earl's barony, the heir or heirs of a baron £100 for a whole barony, the heir or heirs of a knight 100s, at most, for a whole knight's fee; and he who owes less shall give less according to the ancient usage of fiefs.

3   If, however, the heir of any such be under age and a ward, he shall have his inheritance when he comes of age without paying relief and without making fine.

4   The guardian of the land of such an heir who is under age shall take from the land of the heir no more than reasonable revenues, reasonable customary dues and reasonable services, and that without destruction and waste of men or goods; and if we commit the wardship of the land of any such to a sheriff, or to any other who is answerable to us for its revenues, and he destroys or wastes what he has wardship of, we will take compensation from him and the land shall be committed to two lawful and discreet men of that fief, who shall be answerable for the revenues to us or to him to whom we have assigned them; and if we give or sell to anyone the wardship of any such land and he causes destruction or waste therein, he shall lose that wardship, and it shall be transferred to two lawful and discreet men of that fief, who shall similarly be answerable to us as is aforesaid.

5   Moreover, so long as he has the wardship of the land, the guardian shall keep in repair the houses, parks, preserves, ponds, mills and other things pertaining to the land out of the revenues from it; and he shall restore to the heir when he comes of age his land fully stocked with ploughs and the means of husbandry according to what the season of husbandry requires and the revenues of the land can reasonably bear.

6   Heirs shall be married without disparagement, yet so that before the marriage is contracted those nearest in blood to the heir shall have notice.

7   A widow shall have her marriage portion and inheritance forthwith and without difficulty after the death of her husband; nor shall she pay anything to have her dower or her marriage portion or the inheritance which she and her husband held on the day of her husband's death; and she may remain in her husband's house for forty days after his death, within which time her dower shall be assigned to her.

8   No widow shall be forced to marry so long as she wishes to live without a husband, provided that she gives security not to marry without our consent if she holds of us, or without the consent of her lord of whom she holds, if she holds of another.

9   Neither we nor our bailiffs will seize for any debt any land or rent, so long as the chattels of the debtor are sufficient to repay the debt; nor will those who have gone surety for the debtor be distrained so long as the principal debtor is himself able to pay the debt; and if the principal debtor fails to pay the debt, having nothing wherewith to pay it, then shall the sureties answer for the debt; and they shall, if they wish, have the lands and rents of the debtor until they are reimbursed for the debt which they have paid for him, unless the principal debtor can show that he has discharged his obligation in the matter to the said sureties.

10 If anyone who has borrowed from the Jews any sum, great or small, dies before it is repaid, the debt shall not bear interest as long as the heir is under age, of whomsoever he holds; and if the debt falls into our hands, we will not take anything except the principal mentioned in the bond.

11 And if anyone dies indebted to the Jews, his wife shall have her dower and pay nothing of that debt; and if the dead man leaves children who are under age, they shall be provided with necessaries befitting the holding of the deceased; and the debt shall be paid out of the residue, reserving, however, service due to lords of the land; debts owing to others than Jews shall be dealt with in like manner.

12 No scutage or aid shall be imposed in our kingdom unless by common counsel of our kingdom, except for ransoming our person, for making our eldest son a knight, and for once marrying our eldest daughter; and for these only a reasonable aid shall be levied. Be it done in like manner concerning aids from the city of London.

13 And the city of London shall have all its ancient liberties and free customs as well by land as by water. Furthermore, we will and grant that all other cities, boroughs, towns, and ports shall have all their liberties and free customs.

14 And to obtain the common counsel of the kingdom about the assessing of an aid (except in the three cases aforesaid) or of a scutage, we will cause to be summoned the archbishops, bishops, abbots, earls and greater barons, individually by our letters—and, in addition, we will cause to be summoned generally through our sheriffs and bailiffs all those holding of us in chief—for a fixed date, namely, after the expiry of at least forty days, and to a fixed place; and in all letters of such summons we will specify the reason for the summons. And when the summons has thus been made, the business shall proceed on the day appointed, according to the counsel of those present, though not all have come who were summoned.

15 We will not in future grant any one the right to take an aid from his free men, except for ransoming his person, for making his eldest son a knight and for once marrying his eldest daughter, and for these only a reasonable aid shall be levied.

16 No one shall be compelled to do greater service for a knight's fee or for any other free holding than is due from it.

17 Common pleas shall not follow our court, but shall be held in some fixed place.

18 Recognitions of novel disseisin, or mort d'ancestor, and of darrein presentment, shall not be held elsewhere than in the counties to which they relate, and in this manner—we, or, if we should be out of the

realm, our chief justiciar, will send two justices through each county four times a year, who, with four knights of each county chosen by the county, shall hold the said assizes in the county and on the day and in the place of meeting of the county court.

19 And if the said assizes cannot all be held on the day of the county court, there shall stay behind as many of the knights and freeholders who were present at the county court on that day as are necessary for the sufficient making of judgments, according to the amount of business to be done.

20 A free man shall not be amerced for a trivial offence except in accordance with the degree of the offence, and for a grave offence he shall be amerced in accordance with its gravity, yet saving his way of living; and a merchant in the same way, saving his stock-in-trade; and a villein shall be amerced in the same way, saving his means of livelihood—if they have fallen into our mercy: and none of the aforesaid amercements shall be imposed except by the oath of good men of the neighbourhood.

21 Earls and barons shall not be amerced except by their peers, and only in accordance with the degree of the offence.

22 No clerk shall be amerced in respect of his lay holding except after the manner of the others aforesaid and not according to the amount of his ecclesiastical benefice.

23 No vill or individual shall be compelled to make bridges at river banks, except those who from of old are legally bound to do so.

24 No sheriff, constable, coroners, or others of our bailiffs, shall hold pleas of our crown.

25 All counties, hundreds, wapentakes and trithings shall be at the old rents without any additional payment, except our demesne manors.

26 If anyone holding a lay fief of us dies and our sheriff or bailiff shows our letters patent of summons for a debt that the deceased owed us, it shall be lawful for our sheriff or bailiff to attach and make a list of chattels of the deceased found upon the lay fief to the value of that debt under the supervision of law-worthy men, provided that none of the chattels shall be removed until the debt which is manifest has been paid to us in full; and the residue shall be left to the executors for carrying out the will of the deceased. And if nothing is owing to us from him, all the chattels shall accrue to the deceased, saving to his wife and children their reasonable shares.

27 If any free man dies without leaving a will, his chattels shall be distributed by his nearest kinsfolk and friends under the supervision of the church, saving to every one the debts which the deceased owed him.

28 No constable or other bailiff of ours shall take anyone's corn or other chattels unless he pays on the spot in cash for them or can delay payment by arrangement with the seller.

29   No constable shall compel any knight to give money instead of castle-guard if he is willing to do the guard himself or through another good man, if for some good reason he cannot do it himself; and if we lead or send him on military service, he shall be excused guard in proportion to the time that because of us he has been on service.

30   No sheriff, or bailiff of ours, or anyone else shall take the horses or carts of any free man for transport work save with the agreement of that free man.

31   Neither we nor our bailiffs will take, for castles or other works of ours, timber which is not ours, except with the agreement of him whose timber it is.

32   We will not hold for more than a year and a day the lands of those convicted of felony, and then the lands shall be handed over to the lords of the fiefs.

33   Henceforth all fish-weirs shall be cleared completely from the Thames and the Medway and throughout all England, except along the sea coast.

34   The writ called Praecipe shall not in future be issued to anyone in respect of any holding whereby a free man may lose his court.

35   Let there be one measure for wine throughout our kingdom, and one measure for ale, and one measure for corn, namely 'the London quarter'; and one width for cloths whether dyed, russet or halberget, namely two ells within the selvedges. Let it be the same with weights as with measures.

36   Nothing shall be given or taken in future for the writ of inquisition of life or limbs: instead it shall be granted free of charge and not refused.

37   If anyone holds of us by fee-farm, by socage, or by burgage, and holds land of another by knight service, we will not, by reason of that fee-farm, socage, or burgage, have the wardship of his heir or of land of his that is of the fief of the other; nor will we have custody of the fee-farm, socage, or burgage, unless such fee-farm owes knight service. We will not have custody of anyone's heir or land which he holds of another by knight service by reason of any petty serjeanty which he holds of us by the service of rendering to us knives or arrows or the like.

38   No bailiff shall in future put anyone to trial upon his own bare word, without reliable witnesses produced for this purpose.

39   No free man shall be arrested or imprisoned or disseised or outlawed or exiled or in any way victimized, neither will we attack him or send anyone to attack him, except by the lawful judgment of his peers or by the law of the land.

40   To no one will we sell, to no one will we refuse or delay right or justice.

41   All merchants shall be able to go out of and come into England safely and securely and stay and travel throughout England, as well by land

as by water, for buying and selling by the ancient and right customs free from all evil tolls, except in time of war and if they are of the land that is at war with us. And if such are found in our land at the beginning of a war, they shall be attached, without injury to their persons or goods, until we, or our chief justiciar, know how merchants of our land are treated who were found in the land at war with us when war broke out; and if ours are safe there, the others shall be safe in our land.

42 It shall be lawful in future for anyone, without prejudicing the allegiance due to us, to leave our kingdom and return safely and securely by land and water, save, in the public interest, for a short period in time of war—except for those imprisoned or outlawed in accordance with the law of the kingdom and natives of a land that is at war with us and merchants (who shall be treated as aforesaid).

43 If anyone who holds of some escheat such as the honour of Wallingford, Nottingham, Boulogne, Lancaster, or of other escheats which are in our hands and are baronies dies, his heir shall give no other relief and do no other service to us than he would have done to the baron if that barony had been in the baron's hands; and we will hold it in the same manner in which the baron held it.

44 Men who live outside the forest need not henceforth come before our justices of the forest upon a general summons, unless they are impleaded or are sureties for any person or persons who are attached for forest offences.

45 We will not make justices, constables, sheriffs or bailiffs save of such as know the law of the kingdom and mean to observe it well.

46 All barons who have founded abbeys for which they have charters of the kings of England or ancient tenure shall have the custody of them during vacancies, as they ought to have.

47 All forests that have been made forest in our time shall be immediately disafforested; and so be it done with river-banks that have been made preserves by us in our time.

48 All evil customs connected with forests and warrens, foresters and warreners, sheriffs and their officials, river-banks and their wardens shall immediately be inquired into in each county by twelve sworn knights of the same county who are to be chosen by good men of the same county, and within forty days of the completion of the inquiry shall be utterly abolished by them so as never to be restored, provided that we, or our justiciar if we are not in England, know of it first.

49 We will immediately return all hostages and charters given to us by Englishmen, as security for peace or faithful service.

50 We will remove completely from office the relations of Gerard de Athée so that in future they shall have no office in England, namely

Engelard de Cigogné, Peter and Guy and Andrew de Chanceaux, Guy de Cigogné, Geoffrey de Martigny and his brothers, Philip Marc and his brothers and his nephew Geoffrey, and all their following.

51 As soon as peace is restored, we will remove from the kingdom all foreign knights, cross-bowmen, serjeants, and mercenaries, who have come with horses and arms to the detriment of the kingdom.

52 If anyone has been disseised of or kept out of his lands, castles, franchises or his right by us without the legal judgment of his peers, we will immediately restore them to him: and if a dispute arises over this, then let it be decided by the judgment of the twenty-five barons who are mentioned below in the clause for securing the peace: for all the things, however, which anyone has been disseised or kept out of without the lawful judgment of his peers by king Henry, our father, or by king Richard, our brother, which we have in our hand or are held by others, to whom we are bound to warrant them, we will have the usual period of respite of crusaders, excepting those things about which a plea was started or an inquest made by our command before we took the cross; when however we return from our pilgrimage, or if by any chance we do not go on it, we will at once do full justice therein.

53 We will have the same respite, and in the same manner, in the doing of justice in the matter of the disafforesting or retaining of the forests which Henry our father or Richard our brother afforested, and in the matter of the wardship of lands which are of the fief of another, wardships of which sort we have hitherto had by reason of a fief which anyone held of us by knight service, and in the matter of abbeys founded on the fief of another, not on a fief of our own, in which the lord of the fief claims he has a right; and when we have returned, or if we do not set out on our pilgrimage, we will at once do full justice to those who complain of these things.

54 No one shall be arrested or imprisoned upon the appeal of a woman for the death of anyone except her husband.

55 All fines made with us unjustly and against the law of the land, and all amercements imposed unjustly and against the law of the land, shall be entirely remitted, or else let them be settled by the judgment of the twenty-five barons who are mentioned below in the clause for securing the peace, or by the judgment of the majority of the same, along with the aforesaid Stephen, archbishop of Canterbury, if he can be present, and such others as he may wish to associate with himself for this purpose, and if he cannot be present the business shall nevertheless proceed without him, provided that if any one or more of the aforesaid twenty-five barons are in a like suit, they shall be removed from the judgment of the case in question, and others chosen, sworn and put in their place by the rest of the same twenty-five for this case only.

56 If we have disseised or kept out Welshmen from lands or liberties or other things without the legal judgment of their peers in England or in Wales, they shall be immediately restored to them; and if a dispute arises over this, then let it be decided in the March by the judgment of their peers—for holdings in England according to the law of England, for holdings in Wales according to the law of Wales, and for holdings in the March according to the law of the March. Welshmen shall do the same to us and ours.

57 For all the things, however, which any Welshman was disseised of or kept out of without the lawful judgment of his peers by king Henry, our father, or king Richard, our brother, which we have in our hand or which are held by others, to whom we are bound to warrant them, we will have the usual period of respite of crusaders, excepting those things about which a plea was started or an inquest made by our command before we took the cross; when however we return, or if by any chance we do not set out on our pilgrimage, we will at once do full justice to them in accordance with the laws of the Welsh and the foresaid regions.

58 We will give back at once the son of Llywelyn and all the hostages from Wales and the charters that were handed over to us as security for peace.

59 We will act toward Alexander, king of the Scots, concerning the return of his sisters and hostages and concerning his franchises and his right in the same manner in which we act towards our other barons of England, unless it ought to be otherwise by the charters which we have from William his father, formerly king of the Scots, and this shall be determined by the judgment of his peers in our court.

60 All these aforesaid customs and liberties which we have granted to be observed in our kingdom as far as it pertains to us towards our men, all of our kingdom, clerks as well as laymen, shall observe as far as it pertains to them towards their men.

61 Since, moreover, for God and the betterment of our kingdom and for the better allaying of the discord that has arisen between us and our barons we have granted all these things aforesaid, wishing them to enjoy the use of them unimpaired and unshaken for ever, we give and grant them the under-written security, namely, that the barons shall choose any twenty-five barons of the kingdom they wish, who must with all their might observe, hold and cause to be observed, the peace and liberties which we have granted and confirmed to them by this present charters of ours, so that if we, or our justiciar, or our bailiffs or any one of our servants offend in any way against anyone or transgress any of the articles of the peace or the security and the offence be notified to four of the aforesaid twenty-five barons, those four barons shall come

to us, or to our justiciar if we are out of the kingdom, and, laying the transgression before us, shall petition us to have that transgression corrected without delay. And if we do not correct the transgression, or if we are out of the kingdom, if our justiciar does not correct it, within forty days, reckoning from the time it was brought to our notice or to that of our justiciar if we were out of the kingdom, the aforesaid four barons shall refer that case to the rest of the twenty-five barons and those twenty-five barons together with the community of the whole land shall distrain and distress us in every way they can, namely, by seizing castles, lands, possessions, and in such other ways as they can, saving our person and the persons of our queen and our children, until, in their opinion, amends have been made; and when amends have been made, they shall obey us as they did before. And let anyone in the land who wishes take an oath to obey the orders of the said twenty-five barons for the execution of all the aforesaid matters, and with them to distress us as much as he can, and we publicly and freely give anyone leave to take the oath who wishes to take it and we will never prohibit anyone from taking it. Indeed, all those in the land who are unwilling of themselves and of their own accord to take an oath to the twenty-five barons to help them to distrain and distress us, we will make them take the oath as aforesaid at our command. And if any of the twenty-five barons dies or leaves the country or is in any other way prevented from carrying out the things aforesaid, the rest of the aforesaid twenty-five barons shall choose as they think fit another one in his place, and he shall take the oath like the rest. In all matters the execution of which is committed to these twenty-five barons, if it should happen that these twenty-five are present yet disagree among themselves about anything, or if some of those summoned will not or cannot be present, that shall be held as fixed and established which the majority of those present ordained or commanded, exactly as if all the twenty-five had consented to it; and the said twenty-five shall swear that they will faithfully observe all the things aforesaid and will do all they can to get them observed. And we will procure nothing from anyone, either personally or through anyone else, whereby any of these concessions and liberties might be revoked or diminished; and if any such thing is procured, let it be void and null, and we will never use it either personally or through another.

62   And we have fully remitted and pardoned to everyone all the ill-will, indignation and rancour that have arisen between us and our men, clergy and laity, from the time of the quarrel. Furthermore, we have fully remitted to all, clergy and laity, and as far as pertains to us have completely forgiven, all trespasses occasioned by the same quarrel between Easter in the sixteenth year of our reign and the restoration of peace. And, besides, we have caused to be made for them letters testimonial patent of the lord Stephen archbishop of Canterbury, of the

lord Henry archbishop of Dublin and of the aforementioned bishops and of master Pandulf about this security and the aforementioned concessions.

63 Wherefore we wish and firmly enjoin that the English church shall be free, and that the men in our kingdom shall have and hold all the aforesaid liberties, rights and concessions well and peacefully, freely and quietly, fully and completely, for themselves and their heirs from us and our heirs, in all matters and in all places for ever, as is aforesaid. An oath, moreover, has been taken, as well on our part as on the part of the barons, that all these things aforesaid shall be observed in good faith and without evil disposition. Witness the above-mentioned and many others. Given by our hand in the meadow which is called Runnymede between Windsor and Staines on the fifteenth day of June, in the seventeenth year of our reign.

Bill of Rights (United Kingdom), 1689 (An Act Declaring the Rights and Liberties of the Subject and Settling the Succession of the Crown)

The text appearing below is that of the Bill of Rights up to that point beyond which it is concerned with the succession to the crown.

Whereas the Lords Spiritual and Temporal and Commons assembled at Westminster, lawfully, fully and freely representing all the estates of the people of this realm, did upon the thirteenth day of February in the year of our Lord one thousand six hundred eighty-eight present unto their Majesties, then called and known by the names and style of William and Mary, prince and princess of Orange, being present in their proper persons, a certain declaration in writing made by the said Lords and Commons in the words following, viz:

Whereas the late King James the Second, by the assistance of divers evil counsellors, judges and ministers employed by him, did endeavour to subvert and extirpate the Protestant religion and the laws and liberties of this kingdom;

By assuming and exercising a power of dispensing with and suspending of laws and the execution of laws without consent of Parliament;

By committing and prosecuting divers worthy prelates for humbly petitioning to be excused from concurring to the said assumed power;

By issuing and causing to be executed a commission under the great seal for erecting a court called the Court of Commissioners for Ecclesiastical Causes;

By levying money for and to the use of the Crown by pretence of prerogative for other time and in other manner than the same was granted by Parliament;

By raising and keeping a standing army within this kingdom in time of peace without consent of Parliament, and quartering soldiers contrary to law;

By causing several good subjects being Protestants to be disarmed at the same time when papists were both armed and employed contrary to law;

By violating the freedom of election of members to serve in parliament;

By prosecutions in the Court of King's Bench for matters and causes cognizable only in parliament, and by divers other arbitrary and illegal courses;

And whereas of late years partial corrupt and unqualified persons have been returned and served on juries in trials, and particularly divers jurors in trials for high treason which were not freeholders;

And excessive bail hath been required of persons committed in criminal cases to elude the benefit of the laws made for the liberty of the subjects;

And excessive fines have been imposed;

And illegal and cruel punishments inflicted;

And several grants and promises made of fines and forfeitures before any conviction or judgment against the persons upon whom the same were to be levied;

All which are utterly and directly contrary to the known laws and statutes and freedom of this realm;

And whereas the said late King James the Second having abdicated the government and the throne being thereby vacant, his Highness the prince of Orange (whom it hath pleased Almighty God to make the glorious instrument of delivering this kingdom from popery and arbitrary power) did (by the advice of the Lords Spiritual and Temporal and divers principal persons of the Commons) cause letters to be written to the Lords Spiritual and Temporal being Protestants, and other letters to the several counties, cities, universities, boroughs and cinque ports, for the choosing of such persons to represent them as were of right to be sent to Parliament, to meet and sit at Westminster upon the two and twentieth day of January in this year one thousand six hundred eighty and eight, in order to such an establishment as that their religion, laws and liberties might not again be in danger of being subverted, upon which letters elections having been accordingly made;

And thereupon the said Lords Spiritual and Temporal and Commons, pursuant to their respective letters and elections, being now assembled in a full and free representative of this nation, taking into their most serious consideration the best means for attaining the ends aforesaid, do in the first place (as their ancestors in like case have usually done) for the vindicating and asserting their ancient rights and liberties declare

That the pretended power of suspending of laws or the execution of laws by regal authority without consent of Parliament is illegal;

That the pretended power of dispensing with laws or the execution of laws by regal authority, as it hath been assumed and exercised of late, is illegal;

That the commission for erecting the late Court of Commissioners for Ecclesiastical Causes, and all other commissions and courts of like nature, are illegal and pernicious;

That levying money for or to the use of the Crown by pretence of prerogative, without grant of Parliament, for longer time, or in other manner than the same is or shall be granted, is illegal;

That it is the right of the subjects to petition the king, and all commitments and prosecutions for such petitioning are illegal;

That the raising or keeping a standing army within the kingdom in time of peace, unless it be with consent of Parliament, is against law;

That the subjects which are Protestants may have arms for their defence suitable to their conditions and as allowed by law;

That election of members of Parliament ought to be free;

That the freedom of speech and debates or proceedings in Parliament ought not to be impeached or questioned in any court or place out of Parliament;

That excessive bail ought not to be required, nor excessive fines imposed, nor cruel and unusual punishments inflicted;

That jurors ought to be duly impanelled and returned, and jurors which pass upon men in trials for high treason ought to be freeholders;

That all grants and promises of fines and forfeitures of particular persons before conviction are illegal and void;

And that for redress of all grievances, and for the amending, strengthening and preserving of the laws, Parliaments ought to be held frequently.

And they do claim, demand and insist upon all and singular the premises as their undoubted rights and liberties, and that no declarations, judgments, doings or proceedings to the prejudice of the people in any of the said premises ought in any wise to be drawn hereafter into consequence or example; to which demand of their rights they are particularly encouraged by the declaration of his Highness the prince of Orange as being the only means for obtaining a full redress and remedy therein. Having therefore an entire confidence that his said Highness the prince of Orange will perfect the deliverance so far advanced by him, and will still preserve them from the violation of their rights which they have here asserted, and from all other attempts upon their religion, rights and liberties, the said Lords Spiritual and Temporal and Commons assembled at Westminster do resolve that William and Mary, prince and princess of Orange, be and be declared king and queen of England, France and Ireland and the dominions thereunto belonging, . . .

Bill of Rights (USA), 1791

The Ten Original Amendments to the Constitution of the USA were ratified on 15 December 1791, less than three years after the adoption of the seven Articles of the Constitution itself. They are collectively usually referred to as the US Bill of Rights.

Amendment I

Congress shall make no law respecting an establishment of religion, or prohibiting the free exercise thereof; or abridging the freedom of speech or of the Press; or the right of the people peaceably to assemble and to petition the Government for a redress of grievances.

Amendment II

A well-regulated militia being necessary to the security of a free State, the right of the people to keep and bear arms shall not be infringed.

Amendment III

No soldier shall, in time of peace, be quartered in any house without the consent of the owner, nor in time of war, but in a manner to be prescribed by law.

Amendment IV

The right of the people to be secure in their persons, houses, papers, and effects, against unreasonable searches and seizures, shall not be violated, and no warrants shall issue but upon probable cause, supported by oath or affirmation, and particularly describing the place to be searched, and the persons or things to be seized.

Amendment V

No person shall be held to answer for a capital or otherwise infamous crime unless on a presentment or indictment of a Grand Jury, except in cases arising in the land or naval forces, or in the militia, when in actual service, in time of war or public danger; nor shall any person be subject for the same offence to be twice put in jeopardy of life or limb; nor shall be compelled in any criminal case to be a witness against himself, nor be deprived of life, liberty, or property, without due process of law; nor shall private property be taken for public use without just compensation.

Amendment VI

In all criminal prosecutions, the accused shall enjoy the right to a speedy and public trial, by an impartial jury of the State and district wherein the crime shall have been committed, which districts shall have been previously ascertained by law, and to be informed of the nature and cause of the accusation; to be confronted with the witnesses against him; to have compulsory process for obtaining witnesses in his favour, and to have the assistance of counsel for his defence.

Amendment VII

In suits at common law, where the value in controversy shall exceed 20 dollars, the right of trial by jury shall be preserved, and no fact tried by a jury shall be otherwise re-examined in any court of the United States than according to the rules of the common law.

Amendment VIII

Excessive bail shall not be required, nor excessive fines imposed, nor cruel and unusual punishments inflicted.

Amendment IX

The enumeration in the Constitution of certain rights shall not be construed to deny or disparage others retained by the people.

Amendment X

The powers not delegated to the United States by the Constitution, nor prohibited by it to the States, are reserved to the States respectively, or to the people.

Declaration of the Rights of Man and of the Citizen of 26 August 1789

The attachment of the French people to the rights and principles of national sovereignty established in the Declaration of the Rights of Man and of the Citizen are reaffirmed in the Preamble to the Constitution of the French Fifth Republic, 1958.

The representatives of the French people, formed into a National Assembly, considering that ignorance, disregard or contempt of the rights of man are the sole causes of public misfortunes and of the corruption of governments, have resolved to set forth in a solemn declaration the natural, inalienable and sacred rights of man, in order that this declaration, continually before all members of the body politic, may be a perpetual reminder of their rights and duties; in order that the acts of the legislative power and those of the executive power, since they may constantly be compared with the aim of every political institution, may thereby be more respected; in order that the demands of the citizens, founded henceforth on simple and incontestable principles, may always be directed towards the maintenance of the Constitution and the happiness of all.—Accordingly, the National Assembly recognizes and proclaims, in the presence and under the auspices of the Supreme Being, the following rights of man and of the citizen.

Article 1

Men are born and remain free and equal in rights. Social distinctions may be based only upon considerations of general usefulness.

Article 2

The aim of every political association is the preservation of the natural and inalienable rights of man. These rights are liberty, property, security and resistance to oppression.

Article 3

The source of all sovereignty resides essentially in the nation; no body, no individual may exercise authority not emanating expressly therefrom.

Article 4

Liberty consists of the power to do whatever is not injurious to others; thus, the exercise of the natural rights of every man has for its limits only those that assure other members of society the enjoyment of those same rights. These limits may be determined only by law.

Article 5

The law has the right to forbid only those actions which are injurious to society. Whatever is not forbidden by law may not be prevented, and no one may be constrained to do what it does not command.

Article 6

The law is the expression of the general will. All citizens have the right to participate personally, or through their representatives, in its formation. The law must be the same for all, whether it protects or punishes. All citizens, being equal before it, are equally admissible to all high offices, public positions and employments, according to their capacities and without other distinction than that of their virtues and talents.

Article 7

No man may be accused, arrested or detained, except in the cases determined by law and according to the procedures which it has prescribed. Those who solicit, expedite, execute, or cause to be executed arbitrary orders must be punished; but any citizen summoned or apprehended in pursuance of the law must obey immediately; he renders himself culpable by resistance.

Article 8

The law is to establish only penalties that are absolutely and obviously necessary; and no one may be punished except by virtue of a law established and promulgated prior to the offence and legally applied.

Article 9

Since every man is presumed innocent until declared guilty, if arrest be deemed indispensable, all unnecessary severity for securing the suspect must be severely repressed by law.

Article 10

No one is to be importuned because of his opinions, even religious ones, provided their manifestation does not disturb the public order established by law.

Article 11

Free communication of ideas and opinions is one of the most precious of the rights of man. Consequently, every citizen may speak, write and print freely; yet he may have to answer for the abuse of that liberty in the cases determined by law.

Article 12

The guarantee of the rights of man and of the citizen necessitates a public force; this force is, therefore, instituted for the advantage of all and not for the particular use of those to whom it is entrusted.

Article 13

For the maintenance of the public force and for the expenses of administration, a common tax is indispensable; it must be assessed equally among all citizens in proportion to their means.

Article 14

All citizens have the right to ascertain, by themselves or through their representatives, the necessity of the public tax, to consent to it freely, to supervise its use and to determine its amount, assessment basis, collection and duration.

Article 15

Society has the right to require of every public official an accounting of his administration.

Article 16

Any society in which the guarantee of rights is not assured, or the separation of powers not determined, has no constitution at all.

Article 17

Since property is an inviolable and sacred right, no one may be deprived thereof unless a legally established public necessity obviously requires it, and on condition of just and prior indemnity.

Observations on the Declaration of Rights from Thomas Paine, *Rights of Man*, 1791

In Rights of Man *Paine reproduces the Declaration of the Rights of Man and of the Citizen, and follows this with his own commentary upon it.*

The three first articles comprehend in general terms, the whole of a Declaration of Rights: All the succeeding articles either originate from them, or follow as elucidations. The 4th, 5th, and 6th, define more particularly what is only generally expressed in the 1st, 2d and 3d.

The 7th, 8th, 9th, 10th, and 11th articles, are declaratory of principles upon which laws shall be constructed, conformable to rights already declared. But it is questioned by some very good people in France, as well as in other countries, whether the 10th article sufficiently guarantees the right it is intended to accord with: besides which, it takes off from the divine dignity of religion, and weakens its operative force upon the mind, to make it a subject of human laws. It then presents itself to Man, like light intercepted by a cloudy medium, in which the source of it is obscured from his sight, and he sees nothing to reverence in the dusky ray.

The remaining articles, beginning with the twelfth, are substantially contained in the principles of the preceding articles; but, in the particular situation which France then was, having to undo what was wrong, as well as to set up what was right, it was proper to be more particular than what in another condition of things would be necessary.

While the Declaration of Rights was before the National Assembly, some of its members remarked, that if a Declaration of Rights was published, it should be accompanied by a Declaration of Duties. The observation discovered a mind that reflected, and it only erred by not reflecting far enough. A Declaration of Rights is, by reciprocity, a Declaration of Duties also. Whatever is my right as a man, is also the right of another; and it becomes my duty to guarantee, as well as to possess.

The three first articles are the basis of Liberty, as well individual as national; nor can any country be called free, whose government does not take its beginning from the principles they contain, and continue to preserve them pure; and the whole of the Declaration of Rights is of more value to the world, and will do more good, than all the laws and statutes that have yet been promulgated.

In the declaration exordium which prefaces the Declaration of Rights, we see the solemn and majestic spectacle of a Nation opening its commission, under the auspices of its Creator, to establish a Government; a scene so new, and so transcendantly unequalled by any-thing in the European world, that the name of a Revolution is diminutive of its character, and it rises into a Regeneration of man. What are the present Governments of Europe, but a scene of iniquity and oppression? What is that of England? Do not its own inhabitants say, It is a market where every man has his price, and where corruption is common traffic, at the expence of a deluded people? No wonder, then, that the French Revolution is traduced. Had it confined itself merely to the destruction of flagrant despotism, perhaps Mr Burke and some others had been silent. Their cry now is, 'It is gone too far:' that is, it has gone too far for them. It stares corruption in the face, and the venal tribe are all alarmed. Their fear discovers itself in their outrage, and they are but publishing the groans of a wounded vice. But from such opposition, the French Revolution, instead of suffering, receives an homage. The more it is struck, the more sparks it will emit; and the fear is, it will not be struck enough. It has nothing to dread from attacks: Truth has given it an establishment; and Time will record it with a name as lasting as his own.

Having now traced the progress of the French Revolution through most of its principal stages, from its commencement, to the taking of the Bastille, and its establishment by the Declaration of Rights, I will close the subject with the energetic apostrophe of M. de la Fayette—May this great monument

236

raised to Liberty, serve as a lesson to the oppressor, and an example to the oppressed!

Preamble to the Constitution of the French Fourth Republic, 1946

Along with the Declaration of the Rights of Man and of the Citizen (see above), the principles established in the Preamble to the Constitution of the French Fourth Republic are reaffirmed in the Preamble to the Constitution of the French Fifth Republic, 1958.

On the morrow of the victory gained by the free peoples over the regimes which attempted to enslave and degrade the human person, the French people proclaim anew that every human being, without distinction of race, religion or creed, possesses inalienable and sacred rights. They solemnly reaffirm the rights and freedoms of man and of the citizen as set forth in the Declaration of Rights of 1789, and the fundamental principles recognized by the laws of the Republic.

In addition, they proclaim as particularly necessary in our time, the following political, economic and social principles:

The law guarantees to women equal rights with men, in all spheres.

Any person persecuted because of his activity in furtherance of freedom has the right of asylum in the territories of the Republic.

It is the duty of all to work and the right of all to obtain employment. No one shall be allowed to suffer wrong in his work or employment because of his origin, opinions or beliefs.

Everyone may protect his rights and interests by trade-union action and belong to the union of his choice.

The right to strike is recognized within the framework of the laws that govern it.

Every worker participates, through his delegates, in the collective determination of working conditions as well as in the management of enterprises.

Any property, any enterprise that possesses or acquires the character of a national public service or of a *de facto* monopoly must come under public ownership.

The nation guarantees to the individual and the family the conditions necesssary for their development.

It guarantees to all, especially children, mothers and elderly workers, the safeguarding of their health, material security, rest and leisure. Every human being who is unable to work because of his age, his physical or mental condition, or because of the economic situation, is entitled to obtain from the community the appropriate means of existence.

The nation proclaims the solidarity and equality of all the French people with respect to the burdens resulting from national disasters.

The nation guarantees the equal access of children and adults to education, vocational training and culture. The establishment of free and secular public education at all levels is a duty of the State.

The French Republic, faithful to its traditions, conforms to the rules of public international law. It will undertake no war for conquest and will never employ its forces against the liberty of any people.

On condition of reciprocity, France accepts the limitations of its sovereignty which are necessary for the organization and the defence of peace.

France, together with the peoples of the overseas territories, forms a Union founded upon equality of rights and duties, without distinction of race or religion.

The French Union is composed of nations and peoples who place in common or co-ordinate their resources and efforts to develop their respective civilizations, further their well-being and ensure their security.

Faithful to its traditional mission, France is intent on leading the peoples for whom it has assumed responsibility, to a state of freedom in which they govern themselves and conduct their own affairs democratically; rejecting any form of colonial rule based upon arbitrary power, it guarantees to all equal access to the public service, and the individual or collective exercise of the rights and liberties proclaimed or confirmed above.

Basic Law for the Federal Republic of Germany, 1949

The German Basic Law, or Grundgesetz, was ratified in 1949, and has subsequently functioned as the country's constitution: with only minor amendment, it became the constitution of the entire German nation in October 1990, following the accession of the five newly re-established eastern Länder and East Berlin to the Federal Republic of Germany. Chapter 1, which appears below, contains extensive human rights provisions.

Preamble

Conscious of their responsibility before God and humankind,

Animated by the resolve to serve world peace as an equal part of a united Europe,

The German people have adopted, by virtue of their constituent power, this Basic Law.

Chapter 1: Basic Rights

Article 1 (Protection of human dignity)

1   The dignity of man is inviolable. To respect and protect it shall be the duty of all public authority.

2 The German people therefore uphold human rights as inviolable and inalienable and as the basis of every community, of peace and justice in the world.

3 The following basic rights shall bind the legislature, the executive and the judiciary as directly enforceable law.

Article 2 (Personal freedom)

1 Everybody has the right to self-fulfilment in so far as they do not violate the rights of others or offend against the constitutional order or morality.

2 Everybody has the right to life and physical integrity. Personal freedom is inviolable. These rights may not be encroached upon save pursuant to a law.

Article 3 (Equality before the law)

1 All people are equal before the law.

2 Men and women have equal rights. The state shall seek to ensure equal treatment of men and women and to remove existing disadvantages.

3 Nobody shall be prejudiced or favoured because of their sex, birth, race, language, national or social origin, faith, religion or political opinions. No one may be discriminated against on account of their disability.

Article 4 (Freedom of faith, conscience and creed)

1 Freedom of faith and conscience as well as freedom of creed, religious or ideological, are inviolable.

2 The undisturbed practice of religion shall be guaranteed.

3 Nobody may be forced against their conscience into military service involving armed combat. Details shall be the subject of a federal law.

Article 5 (Freedom of expression)

1 Everybody has the right freely to express and disseminate their opinions orally, in writing or visually and to obtain information from generally accessible sources without hindrance. Freedom of the press and freedom of reporting through audiovisual media shall be guaranteed. There shall be no censorship.

2 These rights are subject to limitations embodied in the provisions of general legislation, statutory provisions for the protection of young persons and the citizen's right to personal respect.

3 Art and scholarship, research and teaching shall be free. Freedom of teaching shall not absolve anybody from loyalty to the constitution.

Article 6 (Marriage and family, children born outside marriage)

1 Marriage and family shall enjoy the special protection of the state.

2 The care and upbringing of children are a natural right of parents and a duty primarily incumbent on them. It is the responsibility of the community to ensure that they perform this duty.

3 Children may not be separated from their families against the will of their parents or guardians save in accordance with a law in cases where they fail in their duty or there is a danger of the children being seriously neglected for other reasons.

4 Every mother is entitled to the protection and care of the community.

5 Children born outside marriage shall be provided by law with the same opportunities for their physical and mental development and regarding their place in society as are enjoyed by those born in marriage.

Article 7 (School education)

1 The entire school system shall be under the supervision of the state.

2 Parents and guardians have the right to decide whether children receive religious instruction.

3 Religious instruction shall form part of the curriculum in state schools except non-denominational schools. Without prejudice to the state's right of supervision, religious instruction shall be given in accordance with the doctrine of the religious community concerned. Teachers may not be obliged to give religious instruction against their will.

4 The right to establish private schools shall be guaranteed. Private schools as alternatives to state schools shall require the approval of the state and be subject to Land legislation. Such approval shall be given where private schools are not inferior to state schools in terms of their educational aims, their facilities and the training of their teaching staff and where it does not encourage segregation of pupils according to the means of their parents. Approval shall be withheld where the economic and legal status of the teaching staff is not adequately secured.

5 A private elementary school shall be approved only where the education authority finds that it meets a special educational need or where, at the request of parents or guardians, it is to be established as a non-denominational, denominational or alternative school and no state elementary school of that type exists locally.

6 Preparatory schools shall remain abolished.

Article 8 (Freedom of assembly)

1 All Germans have the right to assemble peacefully and unarmed without prior notification or permission.

2 In the case of outdoor assemblies this right may be restricted by or pursuant to a law.

Article 9 (Freedom of association)

1 All Germans have the right to form associations, partnerships and corporations.

2 Associations whose aims or activities contravene criminal law or are directed against the constitutional order or the notion of international understanding shall be banned.

3   The right to form associations in order to safeguard and improve working and economic conditions shall be guaranteed to every individual and all occupations and professions. Agreements restricting or intended to hamper the exercise of this right shall be null and void; measures to this end shall be illegal. Measures taken pursuant to article 12a, paragraphs 2 and 3 of article 35, paragraph 4 of article 87a, or article 91 may not be directed against industrial disputes engaged in by associations within the meaning of the first sentence of this paragraph in order to safeguard and improve working and economic conditions.

Article 10 (Privacy of correspondence, posts and telecommunications)

1   Privacy of correspondence, posts and telecommunications is inviolable.

2   Restrictions may only be ordered pursuant to a law. Where a restriction serves to protect the free democratic basic order or the existence or security of the Federation or a Land the law may stipulate that the person affected shall not be informed of such restriction and that recourse to the courts shall be replaced by a review of the case by bodies and subsidiary bodies appointed by parliament.

Article 11 (Freedom of movement)

1   All Germans have the right to move freely throughout the federal territory.

2   This right may be restricted only by or pursuant to a law and only where a person does not have a sufficient livelihood and his or her freedom of movement would be a considerable burden on the community or where such restriction is necessary to avert an imminent danger to the existence or the free democratic basic order of the Federation or a Land, or to prevent an epidemic, a natural disaster, grave accident or criminal act, or to protect young persons from serious neglect.

Article 12 (Free choice of occupation or profession, prohibition of forced labour)

1   All Germans have the right freely to choose their occupation or profession, their place of work, study or training. The practice of an occupation or profession may be regulated by or pursuant to a law.

2   Nobody may be forced to do work of a particular kind except as part of a traditional compulsory community service that applies generally and equally to all.

3   Forced labour may only be imposed on people deprived of their liberty by court sentence.

Article 12a (Compulsory military or alternative service)

1   Men who have reached the age of eighteen may be required to serve in the Armed Forces, the Federal Border Guard or a civil defence organization.

2   Anybody who refuses military service involving armed combat on grounds of conscience may be assigned to alternative service. The period of

alternative service shall not exceed that of military service. Details shall be the subject of a law which shall not impair the freedom to decide in accordance with the dictates of conscience and must also provide for the possibility of alternative service not connected with units of the Armed Forces or the Federal Border Guard.

3   People liable to compulsory military service who are not assigned to service pursuant to paragraph 1 or 2 of this article may, if the country is in a state of defence, be assigned by or pursuant to a law to employment involving civilian service for defence purposes, including protection of the civilian population; they may not be assigned to public employment except to carry out police or other responsibilities of public administration as can only be discharged by public servants. People may be assigned to employment of the kind referred to in the first sentence of this paragraph with the Armed Forces, including the supplying and servicing of the latter, or with public administrative authorities; assignments to employment connected with supplying and servicing the civilian population shall not be permissible except in order to meet their vital requirements or to ensure their safety.

4   Where, if the country is in a state of defence, civilian service requirements in the civilian health system or in the stationary military hospital organization cannot be met on a voluntary basis women between eighteen and fifty-five years of age may be assigned to such service by or pursuant to a law. They may on no account be assigned to military service involving armed combat.

5   Prior to a state of defence, assignments under paragraph 3 of this article may only be made where the requirements of paragraph 1 of article 80a are satisfied. Attendance at training courses in preparation for any service in accordance with paragraph 3 of this article which demands special knowledge or skills may be required by or pursuant to a law. To this extent the first sentence of this paragraph shall not apply.

6   Where a state of defence exists and manpower requirements for the purposes referred to in the second sentence of paragraph 3 of this article cannot be met on a voluntary basis the right of German citizens to give up their occupation, profession or employment may be restricted by or pursuant to a law in order to meet those requirements. The first sentence of paragraph 5 of this article shall apply mutatis mutandis prior to a state of defence.

Article 13 (Privacy of the home)

1   Privacy of the home is inviolable.

2   Searches may be ordered only by a judge or, if there is a danger in delay, by other authorities as provided for by law and may be carried out only in the manner prescribed by the law.

3   Intrusions and restrictions shall otherwise only be permissible to avert danger to the public or to the life of an individual or, pursuant to a law, an acute threat to public safety and order, in particular to relieve a housing shortage, to prevent an epidemic or to protect young persons at risk.

Article 14 (Property, inheritance, expropriation)

1   Property and the right of inheritance shall be guaranteed. Their substance and limits shall be determined by law.

2   Property entails obligations. Its use should also serve the public interest.

3   Expropriation shall only be permissible in the public interest. It may only be ordered by or pursuant to a law which determines the nature and extent of compensation. Compensation shall reflect a fair balance between the public interest and the interests of those affected. In case of dispute regarding the amount of compensation recourse may be had to the ordinary courts.

Article 15 (Public ownership)

Land, natural resources and means of production may be transferred to public ownership or other forms of public enterprise by a law which determines the nature and extent of compensation. In respect of compensation the third and fourth sentences of paragraph 3 of article 14 shall apply mutatis mutandis.

Article 16 (Nationality, extradition)

1   Nobody may be deprived of their German citizenship. Loss of citizenship may only occur pursuant to a law, and against the will of those affected only if they do not thereby become stateless.

2   No German may be extradited to another country.

Article 16a (Asylum)

1   Anybody persecuted on political grounds has the right of asylum.

2   Paragraph 1 may not be invoked by anybody who enters the country from a member state of the European Communities or another third country where the application of the Convention relating to the Status of Refugees and the Convention for the Protection of Human Rights and Fundamental Freedoms is assured. Countries outside the European Communities which fulfil the conditions of the first sentence of this paragraph shall be specified by legislation requiring the consent of the Bundesrat. In cases covered by the first sentence measures terminating a person's sojourn may be carried out irrespective of any remedy sought by that person.

3   Legislation requiring the consent of the Bundesrat may be introduced to specify countries where the legal situation, the application of the law and the general political circumstances justify the assumption that neither political persecution nor inhumane or degrading punishment or treatment

takes place there. It shall be presumed that a foreigner from such a country is not subject to persecution on political grounds so long as the person concerned does not present facts supporting the supposition that, contrary to that presumption, he or she is subject to political persecution.

4 The implementation of measures terminating a person's sojourn shall, in the cases referred to in paragraph 3 and in other cases that are manifestly ill-founded or considered to be manifestly ill-founded, be suspended by the court only where serious doubt exists as to the legality of the measure; the scope of the investigation may be restricted and objections submitted after the prescribed time-limit may be disregarded. Details shall be the subject of a law.

5 Paragraphs 1 to 4 do not conflict with international agreements of member states of the European Communities among themselves and with third countries which, with due regard for the obligations arising from the Convention relating to the Status of Refugees and the Convention for the Protection of Human Rights and Fundamental Freedoms, whose application must be assured in the contracting states, establish jurisdiction for the consideration of applications for asylum including the mutual recognition of decisions on asylum.

Article 17 (Right of petition)

Everybody has the right individually or jointly with others to address written requests or complaints to the appropriate authorities and to parliament.

Article 17a (Restriction of certain basic rights by legislation on defence and alternative service)

1 Legislation on military and alternative service may restrict during their period of service the basic right of members of the Armed Forces and of the alternative services freely to express and disseminate their opinions orally, in writing or visually (first half-sentence of paragraph 1 of article 5), the freedom of assembly (article 8), and the right of petition (article 17) in so far as this right permits the submission of requests or complaints jointly with others.

2 Legislation serving defence purposes including protection of the civilian population may provide for restriction of the basic rights of freedom of movements (article 11) and privacy of the home (article 13).

Article 18 (Forfeiture of basic rights)

Those who abuse their freedom of expression, in particular freedom of the press (paragraph 1 of article 5), freedom of teaching (paragraph 3 of article 5), freedom of assembly (article 8), freedom of association (article 9), privacy of correspondence, posts and telecommunications (article 10), property (article 14), or the right of asylum (article 16a) in order to undermine the free democratic basic order shall forfeit these basic rights. Such forfeiture and its extent shall be determined by the Federal Constitutional Court.

Article 19 (Restriction of basic rights)

1   In so far as a basic right may, under this Basic Law, be restricted by or pursuant to a law the law shall apply generally and not merely to one case. Furthermore, the law shall specify the basic right and relevant article.

2   In no case may the essence of a basic right be encroached upon.

3   The basic rights shall also apply to domestic legal persons to the extent that the nature of such rights permits.

4   Where rights are violated by public authority the person affected shall have recourse to law. In so far as no other jurisdiction has been established such recourse shall be to the ordinary courts. The second sentence of paragraph 2 of article 10 shall not be affected by the provisions of this paragraph.

Canadian Charter of Rights and Freedoms, 1982

Part I of the Constitution Act of 1982, which consists of 34 sections, constitutes the Canadian Charter of Rights and Freedoms.

Whereas Canada is founded upon principles that recognize the supremacy of God and the rule of law:

Guarantee of Rights and Freedoms

1   The Canadian Charter of Rights and Freedoms guarantees the rights and freedoms set out in it subject only to such reasonable limits prescribed by law as can be demonstrably justified in a free and democratic society.

Fundamental Freedoms

2   Everyone has the following fundamental freedoms:

a   freedom of conscience and religion;

b   freedom of thought, belief, opinion and expression, including freedom of the press and other media of communication;

c   freedom of peaceful assembly; and

d   freedom of association.

Democratic Rights

3   Every citizen of Canada has the right to vote in an election of members of the House of Commons or of a legislative assembly and to be qualified for membership therein.

4 (1)   No House of Commons and no legislative assembly shall continue for longer than five years from the date fixed for the return of the writs of a general election of its members.

(2)   In time of real or apprehended war, invasion or insurrection, a House of Commons may be continued by Parliament and a legislative

assembly may be continued by the legislature beyond five years if such continuation is not opposed by the votes of more than one-third of the members of the House of Commons or the legislative assembly, as the case may be.

5   There shall be a sitting of Parliament and of each legislature at least once every twelve months.

Mobility Rights

6 (1)   Every citizen of Canada has the right to enter, remain in and leave Canada.

(2)   Every citizen of Canada and every person who has the status of a permanent resident of Canada has the right

   a   to move to and take up residence in any province; and

   b   to pursue the gaining of a livelihood in any province.

(3)   The rights specified in subsection (2) are subject to

   a   any laws or practices of general application in force in a province other than those that discriminate among persons primarily on the basis of province of present or previous residence; and

   b   any laws providing for reasonable residency requirements as a qualification for the receipt of publicly-provided social services.

(4)   Subsections (2) and (3) do not preclude any law, program or activity that has as its object the amelioration in a province of conditions of individuals in that province who are socially or economically disadvantaged if the rate of employment in that province is below the rate of employment in Canada.

Legal Rights

7   Everyone has the right to life, liberty and security of the person and the right not to be deprived thereof except in accordance with the principles of fundamental justice.

8   Everyone has the right to be secure against unreasonable search or seizure.

9   Everyone has the right not to be arbitrarily detained or imprisoned.

10   Everyone has the right on arrest or detention

   a   to be informed promptly of the reasons therefor;

   b   to retain and instruct counsel without delay and to be informed of that right; and

   c   to have the validity of the detention determined by way of *habeas corpus* and to be released if the detention is not lawful.

11   Any person charged with an offence has the right

   a   to be informed without unreasonable delay of the specific offence;

   b   to be tried within a reasonable time;

c not to be compelled to be a witness in proceedings against that person in respect of the offence;

d to be presumed innocent until proven guilty according to law in a fair and public hearing by an independent and impartial tribunal;

e not to be denied reasonable bail without just cause;

f except in the case of an offence under military law tried before a military tribunal, to the benefit of trial by jury where the maximum punishment for the offence is imprisonment for five years or a more severe punishment;

g not to be found guilty on account of any act or omission unless, at the time of the act or omission, it constituted an offence under Canadian or international law or was criminal according to the general principles of law recognized by the community of nations;

h if finally acquitted of the offence, not to be tried for it again and, if finally found guilty and punished for the offence, not to be tried or punished for it again; and

i if found guilty of the offence and if the punishment for the offence has been varied between the time of commission and the time of sentencing, to the benefit of the lesser punishment.

12 Everyone has the right not to be subjected to any cruel and unusual treatment or punishment.

13 A witness who testifies in any proceedings has the right not to have any incriminating evidence so given used to incriminate that witness in any other proceedings, except in a prosecution for perjury or for the giving of contradictory evidence.

14 A party or witness in any proceedings who does not understand or speak the language in which the proceedings are conducted or who is deaf has the right to the assistance of an interpreter.

Equality Rights

15 (1) Every individual is equal before and under the law and has the right to the equal protection and equal benefit of the law without discrimination and, in particular, without discrimination based on race, national or ethnic origin, colour, religion, sex, age or mental or physical disability.

(2) Subsection (1) does not preclude any law, program or activity that has as its object the amelioration of conditions of disadvantaged individuals or groups including those that are disadvantaged because of race, national or ethnic origin, colour, religion, sex, age or mental or physical disability.

Official Languages of Canada

16 (1) English and French are the official languages of Canada and have equality of status and equal rights and privileges as to their use in all institutions of the Parliament and government of Canada.

(2) English and French are the official languages of New Brunswick and have equality of status and equal rights and privileges as to their use in all institutions of the legislature and government of New Brunswick.

(3) Nothing in this Charter limits the authority of Parliament or a legislature to advance the equality of status or use of English and French.

17 (1) Everyone has the right to use English or French in any debates and other proceedings of Parliament.

(2) Everyone has the right to use English or French in any debates and other proceedings of the legislature of New Brunswick.

18 (1) The statutes, records and journals of Parliament shall be printed and published in English and French and both language versions are equally authoritative.

(2) The statutes, records and journals of the legislature of New Brunswick shall be printed and published in English and French and both language versions are equally authoritative.

19 (1) Either English or French may be used by any person in, or in any pleading in or process issuing from, any court established by Parliament.

(2) Either English or French may be used by any person in, or in any pleading in or process issuing from, any court of New Brunswick.

20 (1) Any member of the public in Canada has the right to communicate with, and to receive available services from, any head or central office of an institution of the Parliament or government of Canada in English or French, and has the same right with respect to any other office of any such institution where

a there is a significant demand for communications with and services from that office in such language; or

b due to the nature of the office, it is reasonable that communications with and services from that office be available in both English and French.

(2) Any member of the public in New Brunswick has the right to communicate with, and to receive available services from, any office of an institution of the legislature or government of New Brunswick in English or French.

21 Nothing in sections 16 to 20 abrogates or derogates from any right, privilege or obligation with respect to the English and French languages, or either of them, that exists or is continued by virtue of any other provision of the Constitution of Canada.

22 Nothing in sections 16 to 20 abrogates or derogates from any legal or customary right or privilege acquired or enjoyed either before or after

the coming into force of this Charter with respect to any language that is not English or French.

Minority Language Educational Rights

23 (1)   Citizens of Canada

    a   whose first language learned and still understood is that of the English or French linguistic minority population of the province in which they reside, or

    b   who have received their primary school instruction in Canada in English or French and reside in a province where the language in which they received that instruction is the language of the English or French linguistic minority population of the province, have the right to have their children receive primary and secondary school instruction in that language in that province.

  (2)   Citizens of Canada of whom any child has received or is receiving primary or secondary school instruction in English or French in Canada, have the right to have all their children receive primary and secondary school instruction in the same language.

  (3)   The right of citizens of Canada under subsections (1) and (2) to have their children receive primary and secondary school instruction in the language of the English or French linguistic minority population of a province

    a   applies wherever in the province the number of children of citizens who have such a right is sufficient to warrant the provision to them out of public funds of minority language instruction; and

    b   includes, where the number of those children so warrants, the right to have them receive that instruction in minority language educational facilities provided out of public funds.

Enforcement

24 (1)   Anyone whose rights or freedoms, as guaranteed by this Charter, have been infringed or denied may apply to a court of competent jurisdiction to obtain such remedy as the court considers appropriate and just in the circumstances.

  (2)   Where, in proceedings under subsection (1), a court concludes that evidence was obtained in a manner that infringed or denied any rights or freedoms guaranteed by this Charter, the evidence shall be excluded if it is established that, having regard to all the circumstances, the admission of it in the proceedings would bring the administration of justice into disrepute.

General

25   The guarantee of this Charter of certain rights and freedoms shall not be construed so as to abrogate or derogate from any aboriginal treaty

or other rights or freedoms that pertain to the aboriginal peoples of Canada including

a   any rights or freedoms that have been recognized by the Royal Proclamation of October 7, 1763; and

b   any rights or freedoms that may be acquired by the aboriginal peoples of Canada by way of land claims settlement.

26   The guarantee in this Charter of certain rights and freedoms shall not be construed as denying the existence of any other rights or freedoms that exist in Canada.

27   This Charter shall be interpreted in a manner consistent with the preservation and enhancement of the multicultural heritage of Canadians.

28   Notwithstanding anything in this Charter, the rights and freedoms referred to in it are guaranteed equally to male and female persons.

29   Nothing in this Charter abrogates or derogates from any rights or privileges guaranteed by or under the Constitution of Canada in respect of denominational, separate or dissentient schools.

30   A reference in this Charter to a province or to the legislative assembly or legislature of a province shall be deemed to include a reference to the Yukon Territory and the Northwest Territories, or the appropriate legislative authority thereof, as the case may be.

31   Nothing in this Charter extends the legislative powers of any body or authority.

Application of Charter

32 (1)   This Charter applies

a   to the Parliament and government of Canada in respect of all matters within the authority of Parliament including all matters relating to the Yukon Territory and Northwest Territories; and

b   to the legislature and government of each province in respect of all matters within the authority of the legislature of each province.

(2)   Notwithstanding subsection (1), section 15 shall not have effect until three years after this section comes into force.

33 (1)   Parliament or the legislature of a province may expressly declare in an Act of Parliament or of the legislature, as the case may be, that the Act or a provision thereof shall operate notwithstanding a provision included in section 2 or sections 7 to 15 of this Charter.

(2)   An Act or a provision of an Act in respect of which a declaration made under this section is in effect shall have such operation as it would have but for the provision of this Charter referred to in the declaration.

(3)   A declaration made under subsection (1) shall cease to have effect five years after it comes into force or on such earlier date as may be specified in the declaration.

(4)   Parliament or the legislature of a province may re-enact a declaration made under subsection (1).

(5)   Subsection (3) applies in respect of a re-enactment made under subsection (4).

Citation

34   This Part may be cited as the Canadian Charter of Rights and Freedoms.

Universal Declaration of Human Rights, 1948

The Universal Declaration of Human Rights was adopted and proclaimed by the General Assembly of the United Nations on 10 December 1948.

Preamble

Whereas recognition of the inherent dignity and of the equal and inalienable rights of all members of the human family is the foundation of freedom, justice and peace in the world;

Whereas disregard and contempt for human rights have resulted in barbarous acts which have outraged the conscience of mankind, and the advent of a world in which human beings shall enjoy freedom of speech and belief and freedom from fear and want has been proclaimed as the highest aspiration of the common people,

Whereas it is essential, if man is not to be compelled to have recourse, as a last resort, to rebellion against tyranny and oppression, that human rights should be protected by the rule of law,

Whereas it is essential to promote the development of friendly relations between nations,

Whereas the peoples of the United Nations have in the Charter reaffirmed their faith in fundamental human rights, in the dignity and worth of the human person and in the equal rights of men and women and have determined to promote social progress and better standards of life in larger freedom,

Whereas Member States have pledged themselves to achieve, in co-operation with the United Nations, the promotion of universal respect for and observance of human rights and fundamental freedoms,

Whereas a common understanding of these rights and freedoms is of the greatest importance for the full realization of this pledge,

Now, therefore,

The General Assembly

Proclaims this Universal Declaration of Human Rights as a common standard of achievement for all peoples and all nations, to the end that every individual and every organ of society, keeping this Declaration constantly in mind, shall strive by teaching and education to promote respect for these rights and freedoms and by progressive measures, national and international, to secure their universal and effective recognition and observance, both among the peoples of Member States themselves and among the peoples of territories under their jurisdiction.

Article 1

All human beings are born free and equal in dignity and rights. They are endowed with reason and conscience and should act towards one another in a spirit of brotherhood.

Article 2

Everyone is entitled to all the rights and freedoms set forth in this Declaration, without distinction of any kind, such as race, colour, sex, language, religion, political or other opinion, national or social origin, property, birth or other status.

Furthermore, no distinction shall be made on the basis of the political, jurisdictional or international status of the country or territory to which a person belongs, whether it be independent, trust, non-self-governing or under any other limitation of sovereignty.

Article 3

Everyone has the right to life, liberty and security of person.

Article 4

No one shall be held in slavery or servitude; slavery and the slave trade shall be prohibited in all their forms.

Article 5

No one shall be subjected to torture or to cruel, inhuman or degrading treatment or punishment.

Article 6

Everyone has the right to recognition everywhere as a person before the law.

Article 7

All are equal before the law and are entitled without any discrimination to equal protection of the law. All are entitled to equal protection against any discrimination in violation of this Declaration and against any incitement to such discrimination.

Article 8

Everyone has the right to an effective remedy by the competent national tribunals for acts violating the fundamental rights granted him by the constitution or by law.

Article 9

No one shall be subjected to arbitrary arrest, detention or exile.

Article 10

Everyone is entitled in full equality to a fair and public hearing by an independent and impartial tribunal, in a determination of his rights and obligations and of any criminal charge against him.

Article 11

1 Everyone charged with a penal offence has the right to be presumed innocent until proved guilty according to law in a public trial at which he has had all the guarantees necessary for his defence.

2 No one shall be held guilty of any penal offence on account of any act or omission which did not constitute a penal offence, under national or international law, at the time when it was committed. Nor shall a heavier penalty be imposed than the one that was applicable at the time the penal offence was committed.

Article 12

No one shall be subjected to arbitrary interference with his privacy, family, home or correspondence, nor to attacks upon his honour and reputation. Everyone has the right to the protection of the law against such interference or attacks.

Article 13

1 Everyone has the right to freedom of movement and residence within the borders of each state.

2 Everyone has the right to leave any country, including his own, and to return to his country.

Article 14

1 Everyone has the right to seek and to enjoy in other countries asylum from persecution.

2 This right may not be invoked in the case of prosecutions genuinely arising from non-political crimes or from acts contrary to the purposes and principles of the United Nations.

Article 15

1 Everyone has the right to a nationality.

2 No one shall be arbitrarily deprived of his nationality nor denied the right to change his nationality.

Article 16

1 Men and women of full age, without any limitation due to race, nationality or religion, have the right to marry and to found a family. They are entitled to equal rights as to marriage, during marriage and at its dissolution.

2   Marriage shall be entered into only with the free and full consent of the intending spouses.

3   The family is the natural and fundamental group unit of society and is entitled to protection by society and the State.

Article 17

1   Everyone has the right to own property alone as well as in association with others.

2   No one shall be arbitrarily deprived of his property.

Article 18

Everyone has the right to freedom of thought, conscience and religion; this right includes freedom to change his religion or belief, and freedom, either alone or in community with others and in public or private, to manifest his religion or belief in teaching, practice, worship and observance.

Article 19

Everyone has the right to freedom of opinion and expression; this right includes freedom to hold opinions without interference and to seek, receive and impart information and ideas through any media and regardless of frontiers.

Article 20

1   Everyone has the right to freedom of peaceful assembly and association.

2   No one may be compelled to belong to an association.

Article 21

1   Everyone has the right to take part in the government of his country, directly or through freely chosen representatives.

2   Everyone has the right of equal access to public service in his country.

3   The will of the people shall be the basis of the authority of government; this will shall be expressed in periodic and genuine elections which shall be by universal and equal suffrage and shall be held by secret vote or by equivalent free voting procedures.

Article 22

Everyone, as a member of society, has the right to social security and is entitled to realization, through national effort and international co-operation and in accordance with the organization and resources of each State, of the economic, social and cultural rights indispensable for his dignity and the free development of his personality.

Article 23

1   Everyone has the right to work, to free choice of employment, to just and favourable conditions of work and to protection against unemployment.

2   Everyone, without any discrimination, has the right to equal pay for equal work.

3   Everyone who works has the right to just and favourable remuneration ensuring for himself and his family an existence worthy of human dignity, and supplemented, if necessary, by other means of social protection.

4   Everyone has the right to form and to join trade unions for the protection of his interests.

Article 24

Everyone has the right to rest and leisure, including reasonable limitation of working hours and periodic holidays with pay.

Article 25

1   Everyone has the right to a standard of living adequate for the health and well-being of himself and of his family, including food, clothing, housing and medical care and necessary social services, and the right to security in the event of unemployment, sickness, disability, widowhood, old age or other lack of livelihood in circumstances beyond his control.

2   Motherhood and childhood are entitled to special care and assistance. All children, whether born in or out of wedlock, shall enjoy the same social protection.

Article 26

1   Everyone has the right to education. Education shall be free, at least in the elementary and fundamental stages. Elementary education shall be compulsory. Technical and professional education shall be made generally available and higher education shall be equally accessible to all on the basis of merit.

2   Education shall be directed to the full development of the human personality and to the strengthening of respect for human rights and fundamental freedoms. It shall promote understanding, tolerance and friendship among all nations, racial or religious groups, and shall further the activities of the United Nations for the maintenance of peace.

3   Parents have a prior right to choose the kind of education that shall be given to their children.

Article 27

1   Everyone has the right freely to participate in the cultural life of the community, to enjoy the arts and to share in scientific advancement and its benefits.

2   Everyone has the right to the protection of the moral and material interests resulting from any scientific, literary or artistic production of which he is the author.

Article 28

Everyone is entitled to a social and international order in which the rights and freedoms set forth in this Declaration can be fully realized.

Article 29

1 Everyone has duties to the community in which alone the free and full development of his personality is possible.

2 In the exercise of his rights and freedoms, everyone shall be subject only to such limitations as are determined by law solely for the purpose of securing due recognition and respect for the rights and freedoms of others and of meeting the just requirements of morality, public order and the general welfare in a democratic society.

3 These rights and freedoms may in no case be exercised contrary to the purposes and principles of the United Nations.

Article 30

Nothing in this Declaration may be interpreted as implying for any State, group or person any right to engage in any activity or to perform any act aimed at the destruction of any of the rights and freedoms set forth herein.

International Covenant on Civil and Political Rights, 1966

The International Covenant on Civil and Political Rights, adopted by the General Assembly of the United Nations on 16 December 1966, expands upon the rights and freedoms enshrined in the Universal Declaration of Human Rights (see above). The substantive articles are numbered 1 to 27, and comprise Parts I to III, which are reprinted below. Its counterpart in the economic, social and cultural sphere is the International Covenant on Economic, Social and Cultural Rights (see below).

Preamble

The States Parties to the present Covenant,

Considering that, in accordance with the principles proclaimed in the Charter of the United Nations, recognition of the inherent dignity and of the equal and inalienable rights of all members of the human family is the foundation of freedom, justice and peace in the world,

Recognizing that these rights derive from the inherent dignity of the human person,

Recognizing that, in accordance with the Universal Declaration of Human Rights, the ideal of free human beings enjoying civil and political freedom and freedom from fear and want can only be achieved if conditions are created whereby everyone may enjoy his civil and political rights, as well as his economic, social and cultural rights,

Considering the obligation of States under the Charter of the United Nations to promote universal respect for, and observance of, human rights and freedoms,

Realizing that the individual, having duties to other individuals and to the community to which he belongs, is under a responsibility to strive for the promotion and observance of the rights recognized in the present Covenant,

Agree upon the following articles:

Part I

Article 1

1 All peoples have the right of self-determination. By virtue of that right they freely determine their political status and freely pursue their economic, social and cultural development.

2 All peoples may, for their own ends, freely dispose of their natural wealth and resources without prejudice to any obligations arising out of international economic co-operation, based upon the principle of mutual benefit, and international law. In no case may a people be deprived of its own means of subsistence.

3 The States Parties to the present Covenant, including those having responsibility for the administration of Non-Self-Governing and Trust Territories, shall promote the realization of the right of self-determination, and shall respect that right, in conformity with the provisions of the Charter of the United Nations.

Part II

Article 2

1 Each State Party to the present Covenant undertakes to respect and to ensure to all individuals within its territory and subject to its jurisdiction the rights recognized in the present Covenant, without distinction of any kind, such as race, colour, sex, language, religion, political or other opinion, national or social origin, property, birth or other status.

2 Where not already provided for by existing legislative or other measures, each State Party to the present Covenant undertakes to take the necessary steps, in accordance with its constitutional processes and with the provisions of the present Covenant, to adopt such legislative or other measures as may be necessary to give effect to the rights recognized in the present Covenant.

3 Each State Party to the present Covenant undertakes:

a To ensure that any person whose rights or freedoms as herein recognized are violated shall have an effective remedy, notwithstanding that the violation has been committed by persons acting in an official capacity;

b To ensure that any person claiming such a remedy shall have his right thereto determined by competent judicial, administrative or legislative authorities, or by any other competent authority provided for by the legal system of the State, and to develop the possibilities of judicial remedy;

257

c To ensure that the competent authorities shall enforce such remedies when granted.

Article 3

The States Parties to the present Covenant undertake to ensure the equal right of men and women to the enjoyment of all civil and political rights set forth in the present Covenant.

Article 4

1 In time of public emergency which threatens the life of the nation and the existence of which is officially proclaimed, the States Parties to the present Covenant may take measures derogating from their obligations under the present Covenant to the extent strictly required by the exigencies of the situation, provided that such measures are not inconsistent with their other obligations under international law and do not involve discrimination solely on the ground of race, colour, sex, language, religion or social origin.

2 No derogation from articles 6, 7, 8 (paragraphs 1 and 2), 11, 15, 16 and 18 may be made under this provision.

3 Any State Party to the present Covenant availing itself of the right of derogation shall immediately inform the other States Parties to the present Covenant, through the intermediary of the Secretary-General of the United Nations, of the provisions from which it has derogated and of the reasons by which it was actuated. A further communication shall be made, through the same intermediary, on the date on which it terminates such derogation.

Article 5

1 Nothing in the present Covenant may be interpreted as implying for any State, group or person any right to engage in any activity or perform any act aimed at the destruction of any of the rights and freedoms recognized herein or at their limitation to a greater extent than is provided for in the present Covenant.

2 There shall be no restriction upon or derogation from any of the fundamental human rights recognized or existing in any State Party to the present Covenant pursuant to law, conventions, regulations or custom on the pretext that the present Covenant does not recognize such rights or that it recognizes them to a lesser extent.

Part III

Article 6

1 Every human being has the inherent right to life. This right shall be protected by law. No one shall be arbitrarily deprived of his life.

2 In countries which have not abolished the death penalty, sentence of death may be imposed only for the most serious crimes in accordance

with the law in force at the time of the commission of the crime and not contrary to the provisions of the present Covenant and to the Convention on the Prevention and Punishment of the Crime of Genocide. This penalty can only be carried out pursuant to a final judgment rendered by a competent court.

3   When deprivation of life constitutes the crime of genocide, it is understood that nothing in this article shall authorize any State Party to the present Covenant to derogate in any way from any obligation assumed under the provisions of the Convention on the Prevention and Punishment of the Crime of Genocide.

4   Anyone sentenced to death shall have the right to seek pardon or commutation of the sentence. Amnesty, pardon or commutation of the sentence of death may be granted in all cases.

5   Sentence of death shall not be imposed for crimes committed by persons below eighteen years of age and shall not be carried out on pregnant women.

6   Nothing in this article shall be invoked to delay or to prevent the abolition of capital punishment by any State Party to the present Covenant.

Article 7

No one shall be subjected to torture or to cruel, inhuman or degrading treatment or punishment. In particular, no one shall be subjected without his free consent to medical or scientific experimentation.

Article 8

1   No one shall be held in slavery; slavery and the slave-trade in all their forms shall be prohibited.

2   No one shall be held in servitude.

3   a No one shall be required to perform forced or compulsory labour;

   b Paragraph 3a shall not be held to preclude, in countries where imprisonment with hard labour may be imposed as a punishment for a crime, the performance of hard labour in pursuance of a sentence to such punishment by a competent court;

   c For the purpose of this paragraph the term 'forced or compulsory labour' shall not include:

   i Any work or service, not referred to in subparagraph b, normally required of a person who is under detention in consequence of a lawful order of a court, or of a person during conditional release from such detention;

   ii Any service of a military character and, in countries where conscientious objection is recognized, any national service required by law of conscientious objectors;

iii Any service exacted in cases of emergency or calamity threatening the life or well-being of the community;

iv Any work or service which forms part of normal civil obligations.

Article 9

1 Everyone has the right to liberty and security of person. No one shall be subjected to arbitrary arrest or detention. No one shall be deprived of his liberty except on such grounds and in accordance with such procedure as are established by law.

2 Anyone who is arrested shall be informed, at the time of arrest, of the reasons for his arrest and shall be promptly informed of any charges against him.

3 Anyone arrested or detained on a criminal charge shall be brought promptly before a judge or other officer authorized by law to exercise judicial power and shall be entitled to trial within a reasonable time or to release. It shall not be the general rule that persons awaiting trial shall be detained in custody, but release may be subject to guarantees to appear for trial, at any other stage of the judicial proceedings, and, should occasion arise, for execution of the judgment.

4 Anyone who is deprived of his liberty by arrest or detention shall be entitled to take proceedings before a court, in order that that court may decide without delay on the lawfulness of his detention and order his release if the detention is not lawful.

5 Anyone who has been the victim of unlawful arrest or detention shall have an enforceable right to compensation.

Article 10

1 All persons deprived of their liberty shall be treated with humanity and with respect for the inherent dignity of the human person.

   a Accused persons shall, save in exceptional circumstances, be segregated from convicted persons and shall be subject to separate treatment appropriate to their status as unconvicted persons;

   b Accused juvenile persons shall be separated from adults and brought as speedily as possible for adjudication.

2 The penitentiary system shall comprise treatment of prisoners the essential aim of which shall be their reformation and social rehabilitation. Juvenile offenders shall be segregated from adults and be accorded treatment appropriate to their age and legal status.

Article 11

No one shall be imprisoned merely on the ground of inability to fulfil a contractual obligation.

Article 12

1 Everyone lawfully within the territory of a State shall, within that territory, have the right to liberty of movement and freedom to choose his residence.

2 Everyone shall be free to leave any country, including his own.

3 The above-mentioned rights shall not be subject to any restrictions except those which are provided by law, are necessary to protect national security, public order (ordre public), public health or morals or the rights and freedoms of others, and are consistent with the other rights recognized in the present Covenant.

4 No one shall be arbitrarily deprived of the right to enter his own country.

Article 13

An alien lawfully in the territory of a State Party to the present Covenant may be expelled therefrom only in pursuance of a decision reached in accordance with law and shall, except where compelling reasons of national security otherwise require, be allowed to submit the reasons against his expulsion and to have his case reviewed by, and be represented for the purpose before, the competent authority or a person or persons especially designated by the competent authority.

Article 14

1 All persons shall be equal before the courts and tribunals. In the determination of any criminal charge against him, or of his rights and obligations in a suit at law, everyone shall be entitled to a fair and public hearing by a competent, independent and impartial tribunal established by law. The press and the public may be excluded from all or part of a trial for reasons of morals, public order (ordre public) or national security in a democratic society, or when the interest of the private lives of the parties so requires, or to the extent strictly necessary in the opinion of the court in special circumstances where publicity would prejudice the interests of justice; but any judgment rendered in a criminal case or in a suit at law shall be made public except where the interest of juvenile persons otherwise requires or the proceedings concern matrimonial disputes or the guardianship of children.

2 Everyone charged with a criminal offence shall have the right to be presumed innocent until proved guilty according to law.

3 In the determination of any criminal charge against him, everyone shall be entitled to the following minimum guarantees, in full equality:

   a To be informed promptly and in detail in a language which he understands of the nature and cause of the charge against him;

   b To have adequate time and facilities for the preparation of his defence and to communicate with counsel of his own choosing;

   c To be tried without undue delay;

    d To be tried in his presence, and to defend himself in person or through legal assistance of his own choosing; to be informed, if he does not have legal assistance, of this right; and to have legal assistance assigned to him, in any case where the interests of justice so require, and without payment by him in any such case if he does not have sufficient means to pay for it;

    e To examine, or have examined, the witnesses against him and to obtain the attendance and examination of witnesses on his behalf under the same conditions as witnesses against him;

    f To have the free assistance of an interpreter if he cannot understand or speak the language used in court;

    g Not to be compelled to testify against himself or to confess guilt.

4 In the case of juvenile persons, the procedure shall be such as will take account of their age and the desirability of promoting their rehabilitation.

5 Everyone convicted of a crime shall have the right to his conviction and sentence being reviewed by a higher tribunal according to law.

6 When a person has by a final decision been convicted of a criminal offence and when subsequently his conviction has been reversed or he has been pardoned on the ground that a new or newly discovered fact shows conclusively that there has been a miscarriage of justice, the person who has suffered punishment as a result of such conviction shall be compensated according to law, unless it is proved that the non-disclosure of the unknown fact in time is wholly or partly attributable to him.

7 No one shall be liable to be tried or punished again for an offence for which he has already been finally convicted or acquitted in accordance with the law and penal procedure of each country.

Article 15

1 No one shall be held guilty of any criminal offence on account of any act or omission which did not constitute a criminal offence, under national or international law, at the time when it was committed. Nor shall a heavier penalty be imposed than the one that was applicable at the time when the criminal offence was committed. If, subsequent to the commission of the offence, provision is made by law for the imposition of the lighter penalty, the offender shall benefit thereby.

2 Nothing in this article shall prejudice the trial and punishment of any person for any act or omission which, at the time when it was committed, was criminal according to the general principles of law recognized by the community of nations.

Article 16

Everyone shall have the right to recognition everywhere as a person before the law.

Article 17

1   No one shall be subjected to arbitrary or unlawful interference with his privacy, family, home, or correspondence, nor to unlawful attacks on his honour and reputation.

2   Everyone has the right to the protection of the law against such interference or attacks.

Article 18

1   Everyone shall have the right to freedom of thought, conscience and religion. This right shall include freedom to have or to adopt a religion or belief of his choice, and freedom, either individually or in community with others and in public or private, to manifest his religion or belief in worship, observance, practice and teaching.

2   No one shall be subject to coercion which would impair his freedom to have or to adopt a religion or belief of his choice.

3   Freedom to manifest one's religion or beliefs may be subject only to such limitations as are prescribed by law and are necessary to protect public safety, order, health, or morals or the fundamental rights and freedoms of others.

4   The States Parties to the present Covenant undertake to have respect for the liberty of parents and, when applicable, legal guardians to ensure the religious and moral education of their children in conformity with their own convictions.

Article 19

1   Everyone shall have the right to hold opinions without interference.

2   Everyone shall have the right to freedom of expression; this right shall include freedom to seek, receive and impart information and ideas of all kinds, regardless of frontiers, either orally, in writing or in print, in the form of art, or through any other media of his choice.

3   The exercise of the rights provided for in paragraph 2 of this article carries with it special duties and responsibilities. It may therefore be subject to certain restrictions, but these shall only be such as are provided by law and are necessary:

    a For respect of the rights or reputations of others;

    b For the protection of national security or of public order (ordre public), or of public health or morals.

Article 20

1   Any propaganda for war shall be prohibited by law.

2   Any advocacy of national, racial or religious hatred that constitutes incitement to discrimination, hostility or violence shall be prohibited by law.

Article 21

The right of peaceful assembly shall be recognized. No restrictions may be placed on the exercise of this right other than those imposed in conformity with the law and which are necessary in a democratic society in the interests of national security or public safety, public order (ordre public), the protection of public health or morals or the protection of the rights and freedoms of others.

Article 22

1   Everyone shall have the right to freedom of association with others, including the right to form and join trade unions for the protection of his interests.

2   No restrictions may be placed on the exercise of this right other than those which are prescribed by law and which are necessary in a democratic society in the interests of national security or public safety, public order (ordre public), the protection of public health or morals or the protection of the rights and freedoms of others. This article shall not prevent the imposition of lawful restrictions on members of the armed forces and of the police in their exercise of this right.

3   Nothing in this article shall authorize States Parties to the International Labour Organisation Convention of 1948 concerning Freedom of Association and Protection of the Right to Organize to take legislative measures which would prejudice, the guarantees provided for in that Convention.

Article 23

1   The family is the natural and fundamental group unit of society and is entitled to protection by society and the State.

2   The right of men and women of marriageable age to marry and to found a family shall be recognized.

3   No marriage shall be entered into without the free and full consent of the intending spouses.

4   States Parties to the present Covenant shall take appropriate steps to ensure equality of rights and responsibilities of spouses as to marriage, during marriage and at its dissolution. In the case of dissolution, provision shall be made for the necessary protection of any children.

Article 24

1   Every child shall have, without any discrimination as to race, colour, sex, language, religion, national or social origin, property or birth, the right to such measures of protection as are required by his status as a minor, on the part of his family, society and the State.

2   Every child shall be registered immediately after birth and shall have a name.

3   Every child has the right to acquire a nationality.

Article 25

Every citizen shall have the right and the opportunity, without any of the distinctions mentioned in article 2 and without unreasonable restrictions:

a   To take part in the conduct of public affairs, directly or through freely chosen representatives;

b   To vote and to be elected at genuine periodic elections which shall be by universal and equal suffrage and shall be held by secret ballot, guaranteeing the free expression of the will of the electors;

c   To have access, on general terms of equality, to public service in his country.

Article 26

All persons are equal before the law and are entitled without any discrimination to the equal protection of the law. In this respect, the law shall prohibit any discrimination and guarantee to all persons equal and effective protection against discrimination on any ground such as race, colour, sex, language, religion, political or other opinion, national or social origin, property, birth or other status.

Article 27

In those States in which ethnic, religious or linguistic minorities exist, persons belonging to such minorities shall not be denied the right, in community with the other members of their group, to enjoy their own culture, to profess and practise their own religion, or to use their own language.

International Covenant on Economic, Social and Cultural Rights, 1966

The International Covenant on Economic, Social and Cultural Rights, adopted by the General Assembly of the United Nations on 16 December 1966, expands upon the rights and freedoms enshrined in the Universal Declaration of Human Rights (see above). The substantive articles are numbered 1 to 25, and comprise Parts I to IV, which are reprinted below. Its counterpart in the civil and political sphere is the International Covenant on Civil and Political Rights (see above).

Preamble

The States Parties to the present Covenant,

Considering that, in accordance with the principles proclaimed in the Charter of the United Nations, recognition of the inherent dignity and of the equal and inalienable rights of all members of the human family is the foundation of freedom, justice and peace in the world,

Recognizing that these rights derive from the inherent dignity of the human person,

Recognizing that, in accordance with the Universal Declaration of Human Rights, the ideal of free human beings enjoying freedom from fear and want can only be achieved if conditions are created whereby everyone may enjoy his economic, social and cultural rights, as well as his civil and political rights,

Considering the obligation of States under the Charter of the United Nations to promote universal respect for, and observance of, human rights and freedoms,

Realizing that the individual, having duties to other individuals and to the community to which he belongs, is under a responsibility to strive for the promotion and observance of the rights recognized in the present Covenant,

Agree upon the following articles:

Part I

Article 1

1 All peoples have the right of self-determination. By virtue of that right they freely determine their political status and freely pursue their economic, social and cultural development.

2 All peoples may, for their own ends, freely dispose of their natural wealth and resources without prejudice to any obligations arising out of international economic co-operation, based upon the principle of mutual benefit, and international law. In no case may a people be deprived of its own means of subsistence.

3 The States Parties to the present Covenant, including those having responsibility for the administration of Non-Self-Governing and Trust Territories, shall promote the realization of the right of self-determination, and shall respect that right, in conformity with the provisions of the Charter of the United Nations.

Part II

Article 2

1 Each State Party to the present Covenant undertakes to take steps, individually and through international assistance and co-operation, especially economic and technical, to the maximum of its available resources, with a view to achieving progressively the full realization of the rights recognized in the present Covenant by all appropriate means, including particularly the adoption of legislative measures.

2 The States Parties to the present Covenant undertake to guarantee that the rights enunciated in the present Covenant will be exercised without discrimination of any kind as to race, colour, sex, language, religion, political and other opinion, national or social origin, property, birth or other status.

3 Developing countries, with due regard to human rights and their national economy, may determine to what extent they would guarantee the economic rights recognized in the present Covenant to non-nationals.

Article 3

The States Parties to the present Covenant undertake to ensure the equal right of men and women to the enjoyment of all economic, social and cultural rights set forth in the present Covenant.

Article 4

The States Parties to the present Covenant recognize that, in the enjoyment of those rights provided by the State in conformity with the present Covenant, the State may subject such rights only to such limitations as are determined by law only in so far as this may be compatible with the nature of these rights and solely for the purpose of promoting the general welfare in democratic society.

Article 5

1   Nothing in the present Covenant may be interpreted as implying for any State, group or person any right to engage in any activity or to perform any act aimed at the destruction of any of the rights or freedoms recognized herein, or at their limitation to a greater extent than is provided for in the present Covenant.

2   No restriction upon or derogation from any of the fundamental human rights recognized or existing in any country in virtue of law, conventions, regulations or custom shall be admitted on the pretext that the present Covenant does not recognize such rights or that it recognizes them to a lesser extent.

Part III

Article 6

1   The State Parties to the present Covenant recognize the right to work, which includes the right of everyone to the opportunity to gain his living by work which he freely chooses or accepts, and will take appropriate steps to safeguard this right.

2   The steps to be taken by a State Party to the present Covenant to achieve the full realization of this right shall include technical and vocational guidance and training programmes, policies and techniques to achieve steady economic, social and cultural development and full and productive employment under conditions safeguarding fundamental political and economic freedoms to the individual.

Article 7

The States Parties to the present Covenant recognize the right of everyone to the enjoyment of just and favourable conditions of work, which ensure, in particular:

a   Remuneration which provides all workers, as a minimum, with:

i   Fair wages and equal remuneration for work of equal value without distinction of any kind, in particular women being guaranteed conditions of work not inferior to those enjoyed by men, with equal pay for equal work;

ii A decent living for themselves and their families in accordance with the provisions of the present Covenant;

b Safe and healthy working conditions;

c Equal opportunity for everyone to be promoted in his employment to an appropriate higher level, subject to no considerations other than those of seniority and competence;

d Rest, leisure and reasonable limitation of working hours and periodic holidays with pay, as well as remuneration for public holidays.

Article 8

1 The States Parties to the present Covenant undertake to ensure:

a The right of everyone to form trade unions and join the trade union of his choice, subject only to the rules of the organization concerned, for the promotion and protection of his economic and social interests. No restrictions may be placed on the exercise of this right other than those prescribed by law and which are necessary in a democratic society in the interests of national security or public order or for the protection of the rights and freedoms of others;

b The right of trade unions to establish national federations or confederations and the right of the latter to form or join international trade-union organizations;

c The right of trade unions to function freely subject to no limitations other than those prescribed by law and which are necessary in a democratic society in the interests of national security or public order or for the protection of the rights and freedoms of others;

d The right to strike, provided that it is exercised in conformity with the laws of the particular country.

2 This article shall not prevent the imposition of lawful restrictions on the exercise of these rights by members of the armed forces or of the police or of the administration of the State.

3 Nothing in this article shall authorize States Parties to the International Labour Organisation Convention of 1948 concerning Freedom of Association and Protection of the Right to Organize to take legislative measures which would prejudice, or apply the law in such a manner as would prejudice, the guarantees provided for in that Convention.

Article 9

The States Parties to the present Covenant recognize the right of everyone to social security, including social insurance.

Article 10

The States Parties to the present Covenant recognize that:

1 The widest possible protection and assistance should be accorded to the family, which is the natural and fundamental group unit of society, particularly for its establishment and while it is responsible for the care and education of dependent children. Marriage must be entered into with the free consent of the intending spouses.

2 Special protection should be accorded to mothers during a reasonable period before and after childbirth. During such period working mothers should be accorded paid leave or leave with adequate social security benefits.

3 Special measures of protection and assistance should be taken on behalf of all children and young persons without any discrimination for reasons of parentage or other conditions. Children and young persons without any discrimination for reasons of parentage or other conditions. Children and young persons should be protected from economic and social exploitation. Their employment in work harmful to their morals or health or dangerous to life or likely to hamper their normal development should be punishable by law. States should also set age limits below which the paid employment of child labour should be prohibited and punishable by law.

Article 11

1 The States Parties to the present Covenant recognize the right of everyone to an adequate standard of living for himself and his family, including adequate food, clothing and housing, and to the continuous improvement of living conditions. The States Parties will take appropriate steps to ensure the realization of this right, recognizing to this effect the essential importance of international co-operation based on free consent.

2 The States Parties to the present Covenant, recognizing the fundamental right of everyone to be free from hunger, shall take, individually and through international co-operation, the measures, including specific programmes, which are needed:

a To improve methods of production, conservation and distribution of food by making full use of technical and scientific knowledge, by disseminating knowledge of the principles of nutrition and by developing or reforming agrarian systems in such a way as to achieve the most efficient development and utilization of natural resources;

b Taking into account the problems of both food-importing and food-exporting countries, to ensure an equitable distribution of world food supplies in relation to need.

Article 12

1 The States Parties to the present Covenant recognize the right of everyone to the enjoyment of the highest attainable standard of physical and mental health.

2 The steps to be taken by the States Parties to the present Covenant to achieve the full realization of this right shall include those necessary for:

a The provision for the reduction of the stillbirth-rate and of infant mortality and for the healthy development of the child;

b The improvement of all aspects of environmental and industrial hygiene;

c The prevention, treatment and control of epidemic, endemic, occupational and other diseases;

d The creation of conditions which would assure to all medical service and medical attention in the event of sickness.

Article 13

1 The States Parties to the present Covenant recognize the right of everyone to education. They agree that education shall be directed to the full development of the human personality and the sense of its dignity, and shall strengthen the respect for human rights and fundamental freedoms. They further agree that education shall enable all persons to participate effectively in a free society, promote understanding, tolerance and friendship among all nations and all racial, ethnic or religious groups, and further the activities of the United Nations for the maintenance of peace.

2 The States Parties to the present Covenant recognize that, with a view to achieving the full realization of this right:

a Primary education shall be compulsory and available free to all;

b Secondary education in its different forms, including technical and vocational secondary education, shall be made generally available and accessible to all by every appropriate means, and in particular by the progressive introduction of free education;

c Higher education shall be made equally accessible to all, on the basis of capacity, by every appropriate means, and in particular by the progressive introduction of free education;

d Fundamental education shall be encouraged or intensified as far as possible for those persons who have not received or completed the whole period of their primary education;

e The development of a system of schools at all levels shall be actively pursued, an adequate fellowship system shall be established, and the material conditions of teaching staff shall be continuously improved.

3 The States Parties to the present Covenant undertake to have respect for the liberty of parents and, when applicable, legal guardians, to choose for their children schools, other than those established by the public

authorities, which conform to such minimum educational standards as may be laid down or approved by the State and to ensure the religious and moral education of their children in conformity with their own convictions.

4　No part of this article shall be construed so as to interfere with the liberty of individuals and bodies to establish and direct educational institutions, subject always to the observance of the principles set forth in paragraph 1 of this article and to the requirement that the education given in such institutions shall confirm to such minimum standards as may be laid down by the State.

Article 14

Each State Party to the present Covenant which, at the time of becoming a Party, has not been able to secure in its metropolitan territory or other territories under its jurisdiction compulsory primary education, free of charge, undertakes, within two years, to work out and adopt a detailed plan of action for the progressive implementation, within a reasonable number of years, to be fixed in the plan, of the principle of compulsory education free of charge for all.

Article 15

1　The States Parties to the present Covenant recognize the right of everyone:
　　a　To take part in cultural life;
　　b　To enjoy the benefits of scientific progress and its applications;
　　c　To benefit form the protection of the moral and material interests resulting from any scientific, literary or artistic production of which he is the author.

2　The steps to be taken by the States Parties to the present Covenant to achieve the full realization of this right shall include those necessary for the conservation, the development and the diffusion of science and culture.

3　The States Parties to the present Covenant undertake to respect the freedom indispensable for scientific research and creative activity.

4　The States Parties to the present Covenant recognize the benefits to be derived from the encouragement and development of international contacts and co-operation in the scientific and cultural fields.

Part IV

Article 16

1　The States Parties to the present Covenant undertake to submit in conformity with this part of the Covenant reports on the measures which they have adopted and the progress made in achieving the observance of the rights recognized herein.

2　a　All reports shall be submitted to the Secretary-General of the United Nations, who shall transmit copies to the Economic and Social Council for consideration in accordance with the provisions of the present Covenant.

b The Secretary-General of the United Nations shall also transmit to the specialized agencies copies of the reports, or any relevant parts therefrom, from States Parties to the present Covenant which are also members of these specialized agencies in so far as these reports, or parts therefrom, relate to any matters which fall within the responsibilities of the said agencies in accordance with their constitutional instruments.

Article 17

1 The States Parties to the present Covenant shall furnish their reports in stages, in accordance with a programme to be established by the Economic and Social Council within one year of the entry into force of the present Covenant after Consultation with the States Parties and the specialized agencies concerned.

2 Reports may indicate factors and difficulties affecting the degree of fulfilment of obligations under the present Covenant.

3 Where relevant information has previously been furnished to the United Nations or to any specialized agency by any State Party to the present Covenant, it will not be necessary to reproduce that information, but a precise reference to the information so furnished will suffice.

Article 18

Pursuant to its responsibilities under the Charter of the United Nations in the field of human rights and fundamental freedoms, the Economic and Social Council may make arrangements with the specialized agencies in respect of their reporting to it on the progress made in achieving the observance of the provisions of the present Covenant falling within the scope of their activities. These reports may include particulars of decisions and recommendations on such implementation adopted by their competent organs.

Article 19

The Economic and Social Council may transmit to the Commission on Human Rights for study and general recommendation or as appropriate for information the reports concerning human rights submitted by States in accordance with articles 16 and 17, and those concerning human rights submitted by the specialized agencies in accordance with article 18.

Article 20

The States Parties to the present Covenant and the specialized agencies concerned may submit comments to the Economic and Social Council on any general recommendation under article 19 or reference to such general recommendation in any report of the Commission on Human Rights or any documentation referred to therein.

Article 21

The Economic and Social Council may submit from time to time to the General Assembly reports with recommendations of a general nature and a summary of the information received from the States Parties to the present Covenant and the specialized agencies on the measures taken and the progress made in achieving general observance of the rights recognized in the present Covenant.

Article 22

The Economic and Social Council may bring to the attention of other organs of the United Nations, their subsidiary organs and specialized agencies concerned with furnishing technical assistance any matters arising out of the reports referred to in this part of the present Covenant which may assist such bodies in deciding, each within its field of competence, on the advisability of international measures likely to contribute to the effective progressive implementation of the present Covenant.

Article 23

The States Parties to the present Covenant agree that international action for the achievement of the rights recognized in the present Covenant includes such methods as the conclusion of conventions, the adoption of recommendations, the furnishing of technical assistance and the holding of regional meetings and technical meetings for the purpose of consultation and study organized in conjunction with the Governments concerned.

Article 24

Nothing in the present Covenant shall be interpreted as impairing the provision of the Charter of the United Nations and of the constitutions of the specialized agencies which define the respective responsibilities of the various organs of the United Nations and of the specialized agencies in regard to the matters dealt with in the present Covenant.

Article 25

Nothing in the present Covenant shall be interpreted as impairing the inherent right of all peoples to enjoy and utilize fully and freely their natural wealth and resources.

Convention against Torture and Other Cruel, Inhuman or Degrading Treatment or Punishment, 1984

The Preamble and Part I of the Convention against Torture and Other Cruel, Inhuman or Degrading Treatment or Punishment, adopted by the General Assembly of the United Nations on 10 December 1984, appears below; Part II is concerned with institutional and procedural matters.

The States Parties to this Convention,

Considering that, in accordance with the principles proclaimed in the Charter of the United Nations, recognition of the equal and inalienable rights of all members of the human family is the foundation of freedom, justice and peace in the world,

Recognizing that those rights derive from the inherent dignity of the human person,

Considering the obligation of States under the Charter, in particular article 55, to promote universal respect for, and observance of, human rights and fundamental freedoms,

Having regard to article 5 of the Universal Declaration of Human Rights and article 7 of the International Covenant on Civil and Political Rights, both of which provide that no one shall be subjected to torture or to cruel, inhuman or degrading treatment or punishment,

Having regard also to the Declaration on the Protection of All Persons from Being Subjected to Torture and Other Cruel, Inhuman or Degrading Treatment or Punishment, adopted by the General Assembly on 9 December 1975,

Desiring to make more effective the struggle against torture and other cruel, inhuman or degrading treatment or punishment throughout the world,

Have agreed as follows:

Part I

Article 1

1 For the purposes of this Convention, the term 'torture' means any act by which severe pain or suffering, whether physical or mental, is intentionally inflicted on a person for such purposes as obtaining from him or a third person information or a confession, punishing him for an act he or a third person has committed or is suspected of having committed, or intimidating or coercing him or a third person, or for any reason based on discrimination of any kind, when such pain or suffering is inflicted by or at the instigation of or with the consent or acquiescence of a public official or other person acting in an official capacity. It does not include pain or suffering arising only from, inherent in or incidental to lawful sanctions.

2 This article is without prejudice to any international instrument or national legislation which does or may contain provisions of wider application.

Article 2

1 Each State Party shall take effective legislative, administrative, judicial or other measures to prevent acts of torture in any territory under its jurisdiction.

2 No exceptional circumstances whatsoever, whether a state of war or a threat of war, internal political instability or any other public emergency, may be invoked as a justification of torture.

3 An order from a superior officer or a public authority may not be invoked as a justification of torture.

Article 3

1 No State Party shall expel, return ('refouler') or extradite a person to another State where there are substantial grounds for believing that he would be in danger of being subjected to torture.

2 For the purpose of determining whether there are such grounds, the competent authorities shall take into account all relevant considerations including, where applicable, the existence in the State concerned of a consistent pattern of gross, flagrant or mass violations of human rights.

Article 4

1 Each State Party shall ensure that all acts of torture are offences under its criminal law. The same shall apply to an attempt to commit torture and to an act by any person which constitutes complicity or participation in torture.

2 Each State Party shall make these offences punishable by appropriate penalties which take into account their grave nature.

Article 5

1 Each State Party shall take such measures as may be necessary to establish its jurisdiction over the offences referred to in article 4 in the following cases:

   a When the offences are committed in any territory under its jurisdiction or on board a ship or aircraft registered in that State;

   b When the alleged offender is a national of that State;

   c When the victim is a national of that State if that State considers it appropriate.

2 Each State Party shall likewise take such measures as may be necessary to establish its jurisdiction over such offences in cases where the alleged offender is present in any territory under its jurisdiction and it does not extradite him pursuant to article 8 to any of the States mentioned in paragraph 1 of this article.

3 This Convention does not exclude any criminal jurisdiction exercised in accordance with internal law.

Article 6

1 Upon being satisfied, after an examination of information available to it, that the circumstances so warrant, any State Party in whose territory a person alleged to have committed any offence referred to in article 4 is present shall take him into custody or take other legal measures to ensure his presence. The custody and other legal measures shall be as provided

in the law of that State but may be continued only for such time as is necessary to enable any criminal or extradition proceedings to be instituted.

2 Such State shall immediately make a preliminary inquiry into the facts.

3 Any person in custody pursuant to paragraph 1 of this article shall be assisted in communicating immediately with the nearest appropriate representative of the State of which he is a national, or, if he is a stateless person, with the representative of the State where he usually resides.

4 When a State, pursuant to this article, has taken a person into custody, it shall immediately notify the States referred to in article 5, paragraph 1, of the fact that such person is in custody and of the circumstances which warrant his detention. The State which makes the preliminary inquiry contemplated in paragraph 2 of this article shall promptly report its findings to the said States and shall indicate whether it intends to exercise jurisdiction.

Article 7

1 The State Party in the territory under whose jurisdiction a person alleged to have committed any offence referred to in article 4 is found shall in the cases contemplated in article 5, if it does not extradite him, submit the case to its competent authorities for the purpose of prosecution.

2 These authorities shall take their decision in the same manner as in the case of any ordinary offence of a serious nature under the law of that State. In the cases referred to in article 5, paragraph 2, the standards of evidence required for prosecution and conviction shall in no way be less stringent than those which apply in the cases referred to in article 5, paragraph 1.

3 Any person regarding whom proceedings are brought in connection with any of the offences referred to in article 4 shall be guaranteed fair treatment at all stages of the proceedings.

Article 8

1 The offences referred to in article 4 shall be deemed to be included as extraditable offences in any extradition treaty existing between States Parties. States Parties undertake to include such offences as extraditable offences in every extradition treaty to be concluded between them.

2 If a State Party which makes extradition conditional on the existence of a treaty receives a request for extradition from another State Party with which it has no extradition treaty, it may consider this Convention as the legal basis for extradition in respect of such offences. Extradition shall be subject to the other conditions provided by the law of the requested State.

3 States Parties which do not make extradition conditional on the existence of a treaty shall recognize such offences as extraditable offences between

themselves subject to the conditions provided by the law of the requested State.

4 Such offences shall be treated, for the purpose of extradition between States Parties, as if they had been committed not only in the place in which they occurred but also in the territories of the States required to establish their jurisdiction in accordance with article 5, paragraph 1.

Article 9

1 States Parties shall afford one another the greatest measure of assistance in connection with criminal proceedings brought in respect of any of the offences referred to in article 4, including the supply of all evidence at their disposal necessary for the proceedings.

2 States Parties shall carry out their obligations under paragraph 1 of this article in conformity with any treaties or mutual judicial assistance that may exist between them.

Article 10

1 Each State Party shall ensure that education and information regarding the prohibition against torture are fully included in the training of law enforcement personnel, civil or military, medical personnel, public officials and other persons who may be involved in the custody, interrogation or treatment of any individuals subjected to any form of arrest, detention or imprisonment.

2 Each State Party shall include this prohibition in the rules or instructions issued in regard to the duties and functions of any such persons.

Article 11

Each State Party shall keep under systematic review interrogation rules, instructions, methods and practices as well as arrangements for the custody and treatment of persons subjected to any form of arrest, detention or imprisonment in any territory under its jurisdiction, with a view to preventing any cases of torture.

Article 12

Each State Party shall ensure that its competent authorities proceed to a prompt and impartial investigation, wherever there is reasonable ground to believe that an act of torture has been committed in any territory under its jurisdiction.

Article 13

Each State Party shall ensure that any individual who alleges he has been subjected to torture in any territory under its jurisdiction has the right to complain to, and to have his case promptly and impartially examined by, its competent authorities. Steps shall be taken to ensure that the complainant and witnesses are protected against all ill-treatment or intimidation as a consequence of his complaint or any evidence given.

Article 14

1   Each State Party shall ensure in its legal system that the victim of an act of torture obtains redress and has an enforceable right to fair and adequate compensation, including the means for as full rehabilitation as possible. In the event of the death of the victim as a result of an act of torture, his dependants shall be entitled to compensation.

2   Nothing in this article shall affect any right of the victim or other persons to compensation which may exist under national law.

Article 15

Each State Party shall ensure that any statement which is established to have been made as a result of torture shall not be invoked as evidence in any proceedings, except against a person accused of torture as evidence that the statement was made.

Article 16

1   Each State Party shall undertake to prevent in any territory under its jurisdiction other acts of cruel, inhuman or degrading treatment or punishment which do not amount to torture as defined in article 1, when such acts are committed by or at the instigation of or with the consent or acquiescence of a public official or other person acting in an official capacity. In particular, the obligations contained in articles 10, 11, 12 and 13 shall apply with the substitution for references to torture of references to other forms of cruel, inhuman or degrading treatment or punishment.

2   The provisions of this Convention are without prejudice to the provisions of any other international instrument or national law which prohibits cruel, inhuman or degrading treatment or punishment or which relates to extradition or expulsion.

Convention on the Rights of the Child, 1989

The Convention on the Rights of the Child was drafted by the United Nations Commission on Human Rights, and was adopted by the General Assembly on 20 November 1989. The substantive articles of the Convention are those numbered up to 40, and these are reproduced below.

Preamble

The States Parties to the present Convention,

Considering that, in accordance with the principles proclaimed in the Charter of the United Nations, recognition of the inherent dignity and of the equal and inalienable rights of all members of the human family is the foundation of freedom, justice and peace in the world,

Bearing in mind that the peoples of the United Nations have, in the Charter, reaffirmed their faith in fundamental human rights and in the dignity and worth of the human person, and have determined to promote social progress and better standards of life in larger freedom,

Recognizing that the United Nations has, in the Universal Declaration of Human Rights and in the International Covenants on Human Rights, proclaimed and agreed that everyone is entitled to all the rights and freedoms set forth therein, without distinction of any kind, such as race, colour, sex, language, religion, political or other opinion, national or social origin, property, birth or other status,

Recalling that, in the Universal Declaration of Human Rights, the United Nations has proclaimed that childhood is entitled to special care and assistance,

Convinced that the family, as the fundamental group of society and the natural environment for the growth and well-being of all its members and particularly children, should be afforded the necessary protection and assistance so that it can fully assume its responsibilities within the community,

Recognizing that the child, for the full and harmonious development of his or her personality, should grow up in a family environment, in an atmosphere of happiness, love and understanding,

Considering that the child should be fully prepared to live an individual life in society, and brought up in the spirit of the ideals proclaimed in the Charter of the United Nations, and in particular in the spirit of peace, dignity, tolerance, freedom, equality and solidarity,

Bearing in mind that the need to extend particular care to the child has been stated in the Geneva Declaration of the Rights of the Child of 1924 and in the Declaration of the Rights of the Child adopted by the General Assembly on 20 November 1959 and recognized in the Universal Declaration of Human Rights, in the International Covenant on Civil and Political Rights (in particular in articles 23 and 24), in the International Covenant on Economic, Social and Cultural Rights (in particular in article 10) and in the statutes and relevant instruments of specialized agencies and international organizations concerned with the welfare of children,

Bearing in mind that, as indicated in the Declaration of the Rights of the Child, 'the child, by reason of his physical and mental immaturity, needs special safeguards and care, including appropriate legal protection, before as well as after birth',

Recalling the provisions of the Declaration on Social and Legal Principles relating to the Protection and Welfare of Children, with Special Reference to Foster Placement and Adoption Nationally and Internationally; the United Nations Standard Minimum Rules for the Administration of Juvenile Justice (The Beijing Rules); and the Declaration on the Protection of Women and Children in Emergency and Armed Conflict,

Recognizing that, in all countries in the world, there are children living in exceptionally difficult conditions, and that such children need special consideration,

Taking due account of the importance of the traditions and cultural values of each people for the protection and harmonious development of the child,

Recognizing the importance of international co-operation for improving the living conditions of children in every country, in particular in the developing countries,

Have agreed as follows:

Part 1

Article 1

For the purposes of the present Convention, a child means every human being below the age of eighteen years unless under the law applicable to the child, majority is attained earlier.

Article 2

1 States Parties shall respect and ensure the rights set forth in the present Convention to each child within their jurisdiction without discrimination of any kind, irrespective of the child's or his or her parent's or legal guardian's race, colour, sex, language, religion, political or other opinion, national, ethnic or social origin, property, disability, birth or other status.

2 States Parties shall take all appropriate measures to ensure that the child is protected against all forms of discrimination or punishment on the basis of the status, activities, expressed opinions, or beliefs of the child's parents, legal guardians, or family members.

Article 3

1 In all actions concerning children, whether undertaken by public or private social welfare institutions, courts of law, administrative authorities or legislative bodies, the best interests of the child shall be a primary consideration.

2 States Parties undertake to ensure the child such protection and care as is necessary for his or her well-being, taking into account the rights and duties of his or her parents, legal guardians, or other individuals legally responsible for him or her, and, to this end, shall take all appropriate legislative and administrative measures.

3 States Parties shall ensure that the institutions, services and facilities responsible for the care or protection of children shall conform with the standards established by competent authorities, particularly in the areas of safety, health, in the number and suitability of their staff, as well as competent supervision.

Article 4

States Parties shall undertake all appropriate legislative, administrative, and other measures for the implementation of the rights recognized in the present

Convention. With regard to economic, social and cultural rights, States Parties shall undertake such measures to the maximum extent of their available resources and, where needed, within the framework of international co-operation.

Article 5

States Parties shall respect the responsibilities, rights and duties of parents or, where applicable, the members of the extended family or community as provided for by local custom, legal guardians or other persons legally responsible for the child, to provide, in a manner consistent with the evolving capacities of the child, appropriate direction and guidance in the exercise by the child of the rights recognized in the present Convention.

Article 6

1   States Parties recognize that every child has the inherent right to life.

2   States Parties shall ensure to the maximum extent possible the survival and development of the child.

Article 7

1   The child shall be registered immediately after birth and shall have the right from birth to a name, the right to acquire a nationality and, as far as possible, the right to know and be cared for by his or her parents.

2   States Parties shall ensure the implementation of these rights in accordance with their national law and their obligations under the relevant international instruments in this field, in particular where the child would otherwise be stateless.

Article 8

1   States Parties undertake to respect the right of the child to preserve his or her identity, including nationality, name and family relations as recognized by law without unlawful interference.

2   Where a child is illegally deprived of some or all of the elements of his or her identity, States Parties shall provide appropriate assistance and protection, with a view to re-establishing speedily his or her identity.

Article 9

1   States Parties shall ensure that a child shall not be separated from his or her parents against their will, except when competent authorities subject to judicial review determine, in accordance with applicable law and procedures, that such separation is necessary for the best interests of the child. Such determination may be necessary in a particular case such as one involving abuse or neglect of the child by the parents, or one where the parents are living separately and a decision must be made as to the child's place of residence.

2   In any proceedings pursuant to paragraph 1 of the present article, all interested parties shall be given an opportunity to participate in the proceedings and make their views known.

3   States Parties shall respect the right of the child who is separated from one or both parents to maintain personal relations and direct contact with both parents on a regular basis, except if it is contrary to the child's best interests.

4   Where such separation results from any action initiated by a State Party, such as the detention, imprisonment, exile, deportation or death (including death arising from any cause while the person is in the custody of the State) of one or both parents or of the child, that State Party shall, upon request, provide the parents, the child or, if appropriate, another member of the family with the essential information concerning the whereabouts of the absent member(s) of the family unless the provision of the information would be detrimental to the well-being of the child. States Parties shall further ensure that the submission of such a request shall of itself entail no adverse consequences for the person(s) concerned.

Article 10

1   In accordance with the obligation of States Parties under article 9, paragraph 1, applications by a child or his or her parents to enter or leave a State Party for the purpose of family reunification shall be dealt with by States Parties in a positive, humane and expeditious manner. States Parties shall further ensure that the submission of such a request shall entail no adverse consequences for the applicants and for the members of their family.

2   A child whose parents reside in different States shall have the right to maintain on a regular basis, save in exceptional circumstances, personal relations and direct contacts with both parents. Towards that end and in accordance with the obligation of States Parties under article 9, paragraph 1, States Parties shall respect the right of the child and his or her parents to leave any country, including their own, and to enter their own country. The right to leave any country shall be subject only to such restrictions as are prescribed by law and which are necessary to protect the national security, public order (ordre public), public health or morals or the rights and freedoms of others and are consistent with the other rights recognized in the present Convention.

Article 11

1   States Parties shall take measures to combat the illicit transfer and non-return of children abroad.

2   To this end, States Parties shall promote the conclusion of bilateral or multilateral agreements or accession to existing agreements.

Article 12

1 States Parties shall assure to the child who is capable of forming his or her own views the right to express those views freely in all matters affecting the child, the views of the child being given due weight in accordance with the age and maturity of the child.

2 For this purpose, the child shall in particular be provided the opportunity to be heard in any judicial and administrative proceedings affecting the child, either directly, or through a representative or an appropriate body, in a manner consistent with the procedural rules of national law.

Article 13

1 The child shall have the right to freedom of expression; this right shall include freedom to seek, receive and impart information and ideas of all kinds, regardless of frontiers, either orally, in writing or in print, in the form of art, or through any other media of the child's choice.

2 The exercise of this right may be subject to certain restrictions, but these shall only be such as are provided by law and are necessary:

a For respect of the rights or reputations of others; or

b For the protection of national security or of public order (ordre public), or of public health or morals.

Article 14

1 States Parties shall respect the right of the child to freedom of thought, conscience and religion.

2 States Parties shall respect the rights and duties of the parents and, when applicable, legal guardians, to provide direction to the child in the exercise of his or her right in a manner consistent with the evolving capacities of the child.

3 Freedom to manifest one's religion or beliefs may be subject only to such limitations as are prescribed by law and are necessary to protect public safety, order, health or morals, or the fundamental rights and freedoms of others.

Article 15

1 States Parties recognize the rights of the child to freedom of association and to freedom of peaceful assembly.

2 No restrictions may be placed on the exercise of these rights other than those imposed in conformity with the law and which are necessary in a democratic society in the interests of national security or public safety, public order (ordre public), the protection of public health or morals or the protection of the rights and freedoms of others.

Article 16

1 No child shall be subjected to arbitrary or unlawful interference with his or her privacy, family, home or correspondence, nor to unlawful attacks on his or her honour and reputation.

2   The child has the right to the protection of the law against such interference or attacks.

Article 17

States Parties recognize the important function performed by the mass media and shall ensure that the child has access to information and material from a diversity of national and international sources, especially those aimed at the promotion of his or her social, spiritual and moral well-being and physical and mental health. To this end, States Parties shall:

a   Encourage the mass media to disseminate information and material of social and cultural benefit to the child and in accordance with the spirit of article 29;

b   Encourage international co-operation in the production, exchange and dissemination of such information and material from a diversity of cultural, national and international sources;

c   Encourage the production and dissemination of children's books;

d   Encourage the mass media to have particular regard to the linguistic needs of the child who belongs to a minority group or who is indigenous;

e   Encourage the development of appropriate guidelines for the protection of the child from information and material injurious to his or her well-being, bearing in mind the provisions of articles 13 and 18.

Article 18

1   States Parties shall use their best efforts to ensure recognition of the principle that both parents have common responsibilities for the up-bringing and development of the child. Parents or, as the case may be, legal guardians, have the primary responsibility for the upbringing and development of the child. The best interests of the child will be their basic concern.

2   For the purpose of guaranteeing and promoting the rights set forth in the present Convention, States Parties shall render appropriate assistance to parents and legal guardians in the performance of their child-rearing responsibilities and shall ensure the development of institutions, facilities and services for the care of children.

3   States Parties shall take all appropriate measures to ensure that children of working parents have the right to benefit from child-care services and facilities for which they are eligible.

Article 19

1   States Parties shall take all appropriate legislative, administrative, social and educational measures to protect the child from all forms of physical or mental violence, injury or abuse, neglect or negligent treatment, maltreatment or exploitation, including sexual abuse, while in the care

of parent(s), legal guardian(s) or any other person who has the care of the child.

2 Such protective measures should, as appropriate, include effective procedures for the establishment of social programmes to provide necessary support for the child and for those who have the care of the child, as well as for other forms of prevention and for identification, reporting, referral, investigation, treatment and follow-up of instances of child maltreatment described heretofore, and, as appropriate, for judicial involvement.

Article 20

1 A child temporarily or permanently deprived of his or her family environment, or in whose own best interests cannot be allowed to remain in that environment, shall be entitled to special protection and assistance provided by the State.

2 States Parties shall in accordance with their national laws ensure alternative care for such a child.

3 Such care could include, *inter alia*, foster placement, *kafalah* of Islamic law, adoption or if necessary placement in suitable institutions for the care of children. When considering solutions, due regard shall be paid to the desirability of continuity in a child's upbringing and to the child's ethnic, religious, cultural and linguistic background.

Article 21

States Parties that recognize and/or permit the system of adoption shall ensure that the best interests of the child shall be the paramount consideration and they shall:

a Ensure that the adoption of a child is authorized only be competent authorities who determine, in accordance with applicable law and procedures and on the basis of all pertinent and reliable information, that the adoption is permissible in view of the child's status concerning parents, relatives and legal guardians and that, if required, the persons concerned have given their informed consent to the adoption on the basis of such counselling as may be necessary;

b Recognize that inter-country adoption may be considered as an alternative means of child's care, if the child cannot be placed in a foster or an adoptive family or cannot in any suitable manner be cared for in the child's country of origin;

c Ensure that the child concerned by inter-country adoption enjoys safeguards and standards equivalent to those existing in the case of national adoption;

d Take all appropriate measures to ensure that, in inter-country adoption, the placement does not result in improper financial gain for those involved in it;

e   Promote, where appropriate, the objectives of the present article by
    concluding bilateral or multilateral arrangements or agreements, and
    endeavour, within this framework, to ensure that the placement of the
    child in another country is carried out by competent authorities or organs.

Article 22

1   States Parties shall take appropriate measures to ensure that a child who
    is seeking refugee status or who is considered a refugee in accordance with
    applicable international or domestic law and procedures shall, whether
    unaccompanied or accompanied by his or her parents or by any other
    person, receive appropriate protection and humanitarian assistance in the
    enjoyment of applicable rights set forth in the present Convention and
    in other international human rights or humanitarian instruments to which
    the said States are Parties.

2   For the purpose, States Parties shall provide, as they consider appropriate,
    co-operation in any efforts by the United Nations and other competent
    intergovernmental organizations or non-governmental organizations co-
    operating with the United Nations to protect and assist such a child and
    to trace the parents or other members of the family of any refugee child
    in order to obtain information necessary for reunification with his or
    her family. In cases where no parents or other members of the family
    can be found, the child shall be accorded the same protection as any
    other child permanently or temporarily deprived of his or her family
    environment for any reason, as set forth in the present Convention.

Article 23

1   States Parties recognize that a mentally or physically disabled child should
    enjoy a full and decent life, in conditions which ensure dignity, promote
    self-reliance and facilitate the child's active participation in the community.

2   States Parties recognize the right of the disabled child to special care and
    shall encourage and ensure the extension, subject to available resources,
    to the eligible child and those responsible for his or her care, of assistance
    for which application is made and which is appropriate to the child's
    condition and to the circumstances of the parents or others caring for
    the child.

3   Recognizing the special needs of a disabled child, assistance extended in
    accordance with paragraph 2 of the present article shall be provided free
    of charge, whenever possible, taking into account the financial resources
    of the parents or others caring for the child, and shall be designed to
    ensure that the disabled child has effective access to and receives education,
    training, health care services, rehabilitation services, preparation for
    employment and recreation opportunities in a manner conducive to the
    child's achieving the fullest possible social integration and individual
    development, including his or her cultural and spiritual development.

4 States Parties shall promote, in the spirit of international co-operation, the exchange of appropriate information in the field of preventive health care and of medical, psychological and functional treatment of disabled children, including dissemination of and access to information concerning methods of rehabilitation, education and vocational services, with the aim of enabling States Parties to improve their capabilities and skills to widen their experience in these areas. In this regard, particular account shall be taken of the needs of developing countries.

Article 24

1 States Parties recognize the right of the child to the enjoyment of the highest attainable standard of health and to facilities for the treatment of illness and rehabilitation of health. States Parties shall strive to ensure that no child is deprived of his or her right of access to such health care services.

2 States Parties shall pursue full implementation of this right and, in particular, shall take appropriate measures:

a To diminish infant and child mortality;

b To ensure the provision of necessary medical assistance and health care to all children with emphasis on the development of primary health care;

c To combat disease and malnutrition, including within the framework of primary health care, through, inter alia, the application of readily available technology and through the provision of adequate nutritious foods and clean drinking-water, taking into consideration the dangers and risks of environmental pollution;

d To ensure appropriate pre-natal and post-natal health care for mothers;

e To ensure that all segments of society, in particular parents and children, are informed, have access to education and are supported in the use of basic knowledge of child health and nutrition, the advantages of breast-feeding, hygiene and environmental sanitation and the prevention of accidents;

f To develop preventive health care, guidance for parents and family planning education and services.

3 States Parties shall take all effective and appropriate measures with a view to abolishing traditional practices prejudicial to the health of children.

4 States Parties undertake to promote and encourage international co-operation with a view to achieving progressively the full realization of the right recognized in the present article. In this regard, particular account shall be taken of the needs of developing countries.

Article 25

States Parties recognize the right of a child who has been placed by the competent authorities for the purposes of care, protection or treatment of his or her physical or mental health, to a periodic review of the treatment provided to the child and all other circumstances relevant to his or her placement.

Article 26

1 States Parties shall recognize for every child the right to benefit from social security, including social insurance, and shall take the necessary measures to achieve the full realization of this right in accordance with their national law.

2 The benefits should, where appropriate, be granted, taking into account the resources and the circumstances of the child and persons having responsibility for the maintenance of the child, as well as any other consideration relevant to an application for benefits made by or on behalf of the child.

Article 27

1 States Parties recognize the right of every child to a standard of living adequate for the child's physical, mental, spiritual, moral and social development.

2 The parent(s) or others responsible for the child have the primary responsibility to secure, within their abilities and financial capacities, the conditions of living necessary for the child's development.

3 States Parties, in accordance with national conditions and within their means, shall take appropriate measures to assist parents and others responsible for the child to implement this right and shall in case of need provide material assistance and support programmes, particularly with regard to nutrition, clothing and housing.

4 States Parties shall take all appropriate measures to secure the recovery of maintenance for the child from the parents or other persons having financial responsibility for the child, both within the State Party and from abroad. In particular, where the person having financial responsibility for the child lives in a State different from that of the child, States Parties shall promote the accession to international agreements or the conclusion of such agreements, as well as the making of other appropriate arrangements.

Article 28

1 States Parties recognize the right of the child to education, and with a view to achieving this right progressively and on the basis of equal opportunity, they shall, in particular:

a Make primary education compulsory and available free to all;

b Encourage the development of different forms of secondary education, including general and vocational education, make them available and accessible to every child, and take appropriate measures such as the introduction of free education and offering financial assistance in case of need;

   c Make higher education accessible to all on the basis of capacity by every appropriate means;

   d Made educational and vocational information and guidance available and accessible to all children;

   e Take measures to encourage regular attendance at schools and the reduction of drop-out rates.

2 States Parties shall take all appropriate measures to ensure that school discipline is administered in a manner consistent with the child's human dignity and in conformity with the present Convention.

3 States Parties shall promote and encourage international co-operation in matters relating to education, in particular with a view to contributing to the elimination of ignorance and illiteracy throughout the world and facilitating access to scientific and technical knowledge and modern teaching methods. In this regard, particular account shall be taken of the needs of developing countries.

Article 29

1 States Parties agree that the education of the child shall be directed to:

   a The development of the child's personality, talents and mental and physical abilities to their fullest potential;

   b The development of respect for human rights and fundamental freedoms, and for the principles enshrined in the Charter of the United Nations;

   c The development of respect for the child's parents, his or her own cultural identity, language and values, for the national values of the country in which the child is living, the country from which he or she may originate, and for civilizations different from his or her own;

   d The preparation of the child for responsible life in a free society, in the spirit of understanding, peace, tolerance, equality of sexes, and friendship among all peoples, ethnic, national and religious groups and persons of indigenous origin;

   e The development of respect for the natural environment.

2 No part of the present article or article 28 shall be construed so as to interfere with the liberty of individuals and bodies to establish and direct educational institutions, subject always to the observance of the principle set forth in paragraph 1 of the present article and to the requirements that the education given in such institutions shall conform to such minimum standards as may be laid down by the State.

Article 30

In those States in which ethnic, religious or linguistic minorities or persons of indigenous origin exist, a child belonging to such a minority or who is indigenous shall not be denied the right, in community with other members of his or her group, to enjoy his or her own culture, to profess and practise his or her own religion, or to use his or her own language.

Article 31

1 States Parties recognize the right of the child to rest and leisure, to engage in play and recreational activities appropriate to the age of the child and to participate freely in cultural life and the arts.

2 States Parties shall respect and promote the right of the child to participate fully in cultural and artistic life and shall encourage the provision of appropriate and equal opportunities for cultural, artistic, recreational and leisure activity.

Article 32

1 States Parties recognize the right of the child to be protected from economic exploitation and from performing any work that is likely to be hazardous or to interfere with the child's education, or to be harmful to the child's health or physical, mental, spiritual, moral or social development.

2 States Parties shall take legislative, administrative, social and educational measures to ensure the implementation of the present article. To this end, and having regard to the relevant provisions of other international instruments, States Parties shall in particular:

a Provide for a minimum age or minimum ages for admission to employment;

b Provide for appropriate regulation of the hours and conditions of employment;

c Provide for appropriate penalties or other sanctions to ensure the effective enforcement of the present article.

Article 33

States Parties shall take all appropriate measures, including legislative, administrative, social and educational measures, to protect children from the illicit use of narcotic drugs and psychotropic substances as defined in the relevant international treaties, and to prevent the use of children in the illicit production and trafficking of such substances.

Article 34

States Parties undertake to protect the child from all forms of sexual exploitation and sexual abuse. For these purposes, States Parties shall in particular take all appropriate national, bilateral and multilateral measures to prevent:

a The inducement or coercion of a child to engage in any unlawful sexual activity;

b The exploitative use of children in prostitution or other unlawful sexual practices;

c   The exploitative use of children in pornographic performances and materials.

Article 35

States Parties shall take all appropriate national, bilateral and multilateral measures to prevent the abduction of, the sale of or traffic in children for any purpose or in any form.

Article 36

States Parties shall protect the child against all other forms of exploitation prejudicial to any aspects of the child's welfare.

Article 37

States Parties shall ensure that:

a   No child shall be subjected to torture or other cruel, inhuman or degrading treatment or punishment. Neither capital punishment nor life imprisonment without possibility of release shall be imposed for offences committed by persons below eighteen years of age;

b   No child shall be deprived of his or her liberty unlawfully or arbitrarily. The arrest, detention or imprisonment of a child shall be in conformity with the law and shall be used only as a measure of last resort and for the shortest appropriate period of time;

c   Every child deprived of liberty shall be treated with humanity and respect for the inherent dignity of the human person, and in a manner which takes into account the needs of persons of his or her age. In particular, every child deprived of liberty shall be separated from adults unless it is considered in the child's best interest not to do so and shall have the right to maintain contact with his or her family through correspondence and visits, save in exceptional circumstances;

d   Every child deprived of his or her liberty shall have the right to prompt access to legal and other appropriate assistance, as well as the right to challenge the legality of the deprivation of his or her liberty before a court or other competent, independent and impartial authority, and to a prompt decision on any such action.

Article 38

1   States Parties undertake to respect and to ensure respect for rules of international humanitarian law applicable to them in armed conflicts which are relevant to the child.

2   States Parties shall take all feasible measures to ensure that persons who have not attained the age of fifteen years do not take a direct part in hostilities.

3   States Parties shall refrain from recruiting any person who has not attained the age of fifteen years into their armed forces. In recruiting among those persons who have attained the age of fifteen years but who have

not attained the age of eighteen years, States Parties shall endeavour to give priority to those who are oldest.

4   In accordance with their obligations under international humanitarian law to protect the civilian population in armed conflicts, States Parties shall take all feasible measures to ensure protection and care of children who are affected by an armed conflict.

Article 39

States Parties shall take all appropriate measures to promote physical and psychological recovery and social reintegration of a child victim of: any form of neglect, exploitation, or abuse; torture or any other form of cruel, inhuman or degrading treatment or punishment; or armed conflicts. Such recovery and reintegration shall take place in an environment which fosters the health, self-respect and dignity of the child.

Article 40

1   States Parties recognize the right of every child alleged as, accused of, or recognized as having infringed the penal law to be treated in a manner consistent with the promotion of the child's sense of dignity and worth, which reinforces the child's respect for the human rights and fundamental freedoms of others and which takes into account the child's age and the desirability of promoting the child's reintegration and the child's assuming a constructive role in society.

2   To this end, and having regard to the relevant provisions of international instruments, States Parties shall, in particular, ensure that:

a   No child shall be alleged as, be accused of, or recognized as having infringed the penal law by reason of acts or omissions that were not prohibited by national or international law at the time they were committed;

b   Every child alleged as or accused of having infringed the penal law has at least the following guarantees:

i   To be presumed innocent until proven guilty according to law;

ii   To be informed promptly and directly of the charges against him or her, and, if appropriate, through his or her parents or legal guardians, and to have legal or other appropriate assistance in the preparation and presentation of his or her defence;

iii   To have the matter determined without delay by a competent, independent and impartial authority or judicial body in a fair hearing according to law, in the presence of legal or other appropriate assistance and, unless it is considered not to be in the best interest of the child, in particular, taking into account his or her age or situation, his or her parents or legal guardians;

iv   Not to be compelled to give testimony or to confess guilt; to examine or have examined adverse witnesses and to obtain the participation and examination of witnesses on his or her behalf under conditions of equality;

    v If considered to have infringed the penal law, to have this decision and any measures imposed in consequence thereof reviewed by a higher competent, independent and impartial authority or judicial body according to law;

    vi To have the free assistance of an interpreter if the child cannot understand or speak the language used;

    vii To have his or her privacy fully respected at all stages of the proceedings.

3 States Parties shall seek to promote the establishment of laws, procedures, authorities and institutions specifically applicable to children alleged as, accused of, or recognized as having infringed the penal law, and, in particular:

    a The establishment of a minimum age below which children shall be presumed not to have the capacity to infringe the penal law;

    b Whenever appropriate and desirable, measures for dealing with such children without resorting to judicial proceedings, providing that human rights and legal safeguards are fully respected.

4 A variety of dispositions, such as care, guidance and supervision orders; counselling; probation; foster care; education and vocational training programmes and other alternatives to institutional care shall be available to ensure that children are dealt with in a manner appropriate to their well-being and proportionate both to their circumstances and the offence.

European Convention on Human Rights, 1950

It is in the Preamble and Section 1 of the Convention for the Protection of Human Rights and Fundamental Freedoms (which is the full title of the document signed by members of the Council of Europe, and usually referred to as the European Convention on Human Rights) that the substantive rights are to be found, and these are supplemented by parts of the First and Fourth Protocols, which were added in 1952 and 1963, respectively.

Convention for the Protection of Human Rights and Fundamental Freedoms

The governments signatory hereto, being members of the Council of Europe,

Considering the Universal Declaration of Human Rights proclaimed by the General Assembly of the United Nations on 10th December 1948;

Considering that this Declaration aims at securing the universal and effective recognition and observance of the Rights therein declared;

Considering that the aim of the Council of Europe is the achievement of greater unity between its members and that one of the methods by which that aim is to be pursued is the maintenance and further realization of human rights and fundamental freedoms;

Reaffirming their profound belief in those fundamental freedoms which are the foundation of justice and peace in the world and are best maintained on the one hand by an effective political democracy and on the other by a common understanding and observance of the human rights upon which they depend;

Being resolved, as the governments of European countries which are like-minded and have a common heritage of political traditions, ideals, freedom and the rule of law, to take the first steps for the collective enforcement of certain of the rights stated in the Universal Declaration,

Have agreed as follows:

Article I

The High Contracting Parties shall secure to everyone within their jurisdiction the rights and freedoms defined in Section 1 of this Convention.

Section 1

Article 2

1   Everyone's right to life shall be protected by law. No one shall be deprived of his life intentionally save in the execution of a sentence of a court following his conviction of a crime for which this penalty is provided by law.

2   Deprivation of life shall not be regarded as inflicted in contravention of this article when it results from the use of force which is no more than absolutely necessary:

a   in defence of any person from unlawful violence;

b   in order to effect a lawful arrest or to prevent the escape of a person lawfully detained;

c   in action lawfully taken for the purpose of quelling a riot or insurrection.

Article 3

No one shall be subjected to torture or to inhuman or degrading treatment or punishment.

Article 4

1   No one shall be held in slavery or servitude.

2   No one shall be required to perform forced or compulsory labour.

3   For the purpose of this article the term 'forced or compulsory labour' shall not include:

a   any work required to be done in the ordinary course of detention imposed according to the provisions of article 5 of this Convention or during conditional release from such detention;

b any service of a military character or, in case of conscientious objectors in countries where they are recognized, service exacted instead of compulsory military service;

c any service exacted in case of an emergency or calamity threatening the life or well-being of the community;

d any work or service which forms part of normal civic obligations.

Article 5

1 Everyone has the right to liberty and security of person. No one shall be deprived of his liberty save in the following cases and in accordance with a procedure prescribed by law:

a the lawful detention of a person after conviction by a competent court;

b the lawful arrest or detention of a person for non-compliance with the lawful order of a court or in order to secure the fulfilment of any obligation prescribed by law;

c the lawful arrest or detention of a person effected for the purpose of bringing him before the competent legal authority on reasonable suspicion of having committed an offence or when it is reasonably considered necessary to prevent his committing an offence or fleeing after having done so;

d the detention of a minor by lawful order for the purpose of educational supervision or his lawful detention for the purpose of bringing him before the competent legal authority;

e the lawful detention of persons for the prevention of the spreading of infectious diseases, of persons of unsound mind, alcoholics or drug addicts or vagrants;

f the lawful arrest or detention of a person to prevent his effecting an unauthorized entry into the country or of a person against whom action is being taken with a view to deportation or extradition.

2 Everyone who is arrested shall be informed promptly, in a language which he understands, of the reasons for his arrest and of any charge against him.

3 Everyone arrested or detained in accordance with the provisions of paragraph 1c of this article shall be brought promptly before a judge or other officer authorized by law to exercize judicial power and shall be entitled to trial within a reasonable time or to release pending trial. Release may be conditioned by guarantees to appear for trial.

4 Everyone who is deprived of his liberty by arrest or detention shall be entitled to take proceedings by which the lawfulness of his detention shall be decided speedily by a court and his release ordered if the detention is not lawful.

5 Everyone who has been the victim of arrest or detention in contravention of the provisions of this article shall have an enforceable right to compensation.

Article 6

1 In the determination of his civil rights and obligations or of any criminal charge against him, everyone is entitled to a fair and public hearing within a reasonable time by an independent and impartial tribunal established by law. Judgment shall be pronounced publicly but the press and public may be excluded from all or part of the trial in the interests of morals, public order or national security in a democratic society, where the interests of juveniles or the protection of the private life of the parties so require, or to the extent strictly necessary in the opinion of the court in special circumstances where publicity would prejudice the interests of justice.

2 Everyone charged with a criminal offence shall be presumed innocent until proved guilty according to law.

3 Everyone charged with a criminal offence has the following minimum rights;

    a to be informed promptly, in a language which he understands and in detail, of the nature and cause of the accusation against him;

    b to have adequate time and facilities for the preparation of his defence;

    c to defend himself in person or through legal assistance of his own choosing or, if he has not sufficient means to pay for legal assistance, to be given it free when the interests of justice so require;

    d to examine or have examined witnesses against him and to obtain the attendance and examination of witnesses on his behalf under the same conditions as witnesses against him;

    e to have the free assistance of an interpreter if he cannot understand or speak the language used in court.

Article 7

1 No one shall be held guilty of any criminal offence on account of any act or omission which did not constitute a criminal offence under national or international law at the time when it was committed. Nor shall a heavier penalty be imposed than the one that was applicable at the time the criminal offence was committed.

2 This article shall not prejudice the trial and punishment of any person for any act or omission which, at the time when it was committed, was criminal according to the general principles of law recognized by civilized nations.

Article 8

1 Everyone has the right to respect for his private and family life, his home and his correspondence.

2   There shall be no interference by a public authority with the exercise of this right except such as is in accordance with the law and is necessary in a democratic society in the interests of national security, public safety or the economic well-being of the country, for the prevention of disorder or crime, for the protection of health or morals, or for the protection of the rights and freedoms of others.

Article 9

1   Everyone has the right to freedom of thought, conscience and religion; this right includes freedom to change his religion or belief and freedom, either alone or in community with others and in public or private, to manifest his religion or belief, in worship, teaching, practice and observance.

2   Freedom to manifest one's religion or beliefs shall be subject only to such limitations as are prescribed by law and are necessary in a democratic society in the interests of public safety, for the protection of public order, health or morals, or for the protection of the rights and freedoms of others.

Article 10

1   Everyone has the right to freedom of expression. This right shall include freedom to hold opinions and to receive and impart information and ideas without interference by public authority and regardless of frontiers. This article shall not prevent States from requiring the licensing of broadcasting, television or cinema enterprises.

2   The exercise of these freedoms, since it carries with it duties and responsibilities, may be subject to such formalities, conditions, restrictions or penalties as are prescribed by law and are necessary in a democratic society, in the interests of national security, territorial integrity or public safety, for the prevention of disorder or crime, for the protection of health or morals, for the protection of the reputation or rights of others, for preventing the disclosure of information received in confidence, or for maintaining the authority and impartiality of the judiciary.

Article 11

1   Everyone has the right to freedom of peaceful assembly and to freedom of association with others, including the right to form and to join trade unions for the protection of his interests.

2   No restrictions shall be placed on the exercise of these rights other than such as are prescribed by law and are necessary in a democratic society in the interests of national security or public safety, for the prevention of disorder or crime, for the protection of health or morals or for the protection of the rights and freedoms of others. This article shall not prevent the imposition of lawful restrictions on the exercise of these rights by members of the armed forces, of the police or of the administration of the State.

Article 12

Men and women of marriageable age have the right to marry and to found a family, according to the national laws governing the exercise of this right.

Article 13

Everyone whose rights and freedoms as set forth in this Convention are violated shall have an effective remedy before a national authority notwithstanding that the violation has been committed by persons acting in an official capacity.

Article 14

The enjoyment of the rights and freedoms set forth in this Convention shall be secured without discrimination on any ground such as sex, race, colour, language, religion, political or other opinion, national or social origin, association with a national minority, property, birth or other status.

Article 15

1 In time of war or other public emergency threatening the life of the nation any High Contracting Party may take measures derogating from its obligations under this Convention to the extent strictly required by the exigencies of the situation, provided that such measures are not inconsistent with its other obligations under international law.

2 No derogation from article 2, except in respect of deaths resulting from lawful acts of war, or from articles 3, 4 (paragraph 1) and 7 shall be made under this provision.

3 Any High Contracting Party availing itself of this right of derogation shall keep the Secretary-General of the Council of Europe fully informed of the measures which it has taken and the reasons therefor. It shall also inform the Secretary-General of the Council of Europe when such measures have ceased to operate and the provisions of the Convention are again being fully executed.

Article 16

Nothing in articles 10, 11 and 14 shall be regarded as preventing the High Contracting Parties from imposing restrictions on the political activity of aliens.

Article 17

Nothing in this Convention may be interpreted as implying for any State, group or person any right to engage in any activity or perform any act aimed at the destruction of any of the rights and freedoms set forth herein or at their limitation to a greater extent than is provided for in the Convention.

Article 18

The restrictions permitted under this Convention to the said rights and freedoms shall not be applied for any purpose other than those for which they have been prescribed.

First Protocol, 1952

The governments signatory hereto, being members of the Council of Europe,

Being resolved to take steps to ensure the collective enforcement of certain rights and freedoms other than those already included in Section 1 of the Convention for the Protection of Human Rights and Fundamental Freedoms signed at Rome on 4 November 1950 (hereinafter referred to as 'the Convention'),

Have agreed as follows:

Article 1

Every natural or legal person is entitled to the peaceful enjoyment of his possessions. No one shall be deprived of his possessions except in the public interest and subject to the conditions provided for by law and by the general principles of international law.

The preceding provisions shall not, however, in any way impair the right of a State to enforce such laws as it deems necessary to control the use of property in accordance with the general interest or to secure the payment of taxes or other contributions or penalties.

Article 2

No person shall be denied the right to education. In the exercise of any functions which it assumes in relation to education and to teaching, the State shall respect the right of parents to ensure such education and teaching in conformity with their own religious and philosophical convictions.

Protocol No 4: Securing Certain Rights and Freedoms Other Than Those Already Included in the Convention and in the First Protocol Thereto

Article 1

No one shall be deprived of his liberty merely on the ground of inability to fulfil a contractual obligation.

Article 2

1   Everyone lawfully within the territory of a State shall, within that territory, have the right to liberty of movement and freedom to choose his residence.

2   Everyone shall be free to leave any country, including his own.

3   No restrictions shall be placed on the exercise of these rights other than such as are in accordance with law and are necessary in a democratic society in the interests of national security or public safety, for the maintenance of ordre public, for the prevention of crime, for the protection of health or morals, or for the protection of the rights and freedoms of others.

4   The rights set forth in paragraph 1 may also be subject, in particular areas, to restrictions imposed in accordance with law and justified by the public interest in a democratic society.

Article 3

1   No one shall be expelled, by means either of an individual or of a collective measure, from the territory of the State of which he is a national.

2   No one shall be deprived of the right to enter the territory of the State of which he is a national.

Article 4

Collective expulsion of aliens is prohibited.

European Social Charter, 1965

The European Social Charter is the counterpart to the European Convention on Human Rights (see above) in the sphere of economic and social rights; it was opened for signature on 18 October 1961 and entered into force, after ratification by five states, on 26 February 1965. The substantive rights appear in the Preamble and in Part I, which appear below, while Parts II to V are concerned with the procedural methods of ensuring the economic and social rights enumerated in Part I, and with institutional matters.

Preamble

The governments signatory hereto, being members of the Council of Europe,

Considering that the aim of the Council of Europe is the achievement of greater unity between its members for the purpose of safeguarding and realizing the ideals and principles which are their common heritage and of facilitating their economic and social progress, in particular by the maintenance and further realization of human rights and fundamental freedoms;

Considering that in the European Convention for the Protection of Human Rights and Fundamental Freedoms signed at Rome on 4 November 1950, and the Protocol thereto signed at Paris on 20 March 1952, the member States of the Council of Europe agreed to secure to their populations the civil and political rights and freedoms therein specified;

Considering that the enjoyment of social rights should be secured without discrimination on grounds of race, colour, sex, religion, political opinion, national extraction or social origin;

Being resolved to make every effort in common to improve the standard of living and to promote the social well-being of both their urban and rural populations by means of appropriate institutions and action,

Have agreed as follows:

Part I

The Contracting Parties accept as the aim of their policy, to be pursued by all appropriate means, both national and international in character, the attainment of conditions in which the following rights and principles may be effectively realized.

1 Everyone shall have the opportunity to earn his living in an occupation freely entered upon.

2 All workers have the right to just conditions of work.

3 All workers have the right to safe and healthy working conditions.

4 All workers have the right to a fair remuneration sufficient for a decent standard of living for themselves and their families.

5 All workers and employers have the right to freedom of association in national or international organizations for the protection of their economic and social interests.

6 All workers and employers have the right to bargain collectively.

7 Children and young persons have the right to a special protection against the physical and moral hazards to which they are exposed.

8 Employed women, in case of maternity, and other employed women as appropriate, have the right to a special protection in their work.

9 Everyone has the right to appropriate facilities for vocational guidance with a view to helping him choose an occupation suited to his personal aptitude and interests.

10 Everyone has the right to appropriate facilities for vocational training.

11 Everyone has the right to benefit from any measures enabling him to enjoy the highest possible standard of health attainable.

12 All workers and their dependants have the right to social security.

13 Anyone without adequate resources has the right to social and medical assistance.

14 Everyone has the right to benefit from social welfare services.

15 Disabled persons have the right to vocational training, rehabilitation and resettlement, whatever the origin and nature of their disability.

16 The family as a fundamental unit of society has the right to appropriate social, legal and economic protection to ensure its full development.

17 Mothers and children, irrespective of marital status and family relations, have the right to appropriate social and economic protection.

18 The nationals of any one of the Contracting Parties have the right to engage in any gainful occupation in the territory of any one of the others on a footing of equality with the nationals of the latter, subject to restrictions based on cogent economic or social reasons.

19 Migrant workers who are nationals of a Contracting Party and their families have the right to protection and assistance in the territory of any other Contracting Party.